THE LANCE OF JUSTICE

LONDON : HUMPHREY MILFORD
OXFORD UNIVERSITY PRESS

Arthur v. Briesen

THE LANCE OF JUSTICE

A SEMI-CENTENNIAL HISTORY OF

THE LEGAL AID SOCIETY

1876-1926

By JOHN MacARTHUR MAGUIRE

I thank God that such a society exists in New York as a witness of the chivalry of the nineteenth century.

Bishop Henry Codman Potter in 1898

Cambridge

HARVARD UNIVERSITY PRESS

1928

PRINTED AT THE HARVARD UNIVERSITY PRESS
CAMBRIDGE, MASS., U. S. A.

Die Gerechtigkeit ist die Liebe der Weisen
GOTTFRIED WILHELM v. LEIBNITZ

To the Memory of

ARTHUR v. BRIESEN

WHO

LOVED HIS FELLOW MEN

AND

BEING WISE

STROVE TO GIVE THEM JUSTICE

FOREWORD

In this book Professor Maguire has written a very interesting and comprehensive history of the organization and development of The Legal Aid Society of the City of New York. His narrative of the fifty-two years of the existence of this noteworthy institution strikingly recalls many of the grave economic and social problems that have arisen during that period by reason of immigration and the concentration of population in our cities; it depicts the hardship, suffering, and ruthlessness of conditions which seem to be, or at least so far in modern life have been, inseparable from highly industrialized and congested communities, and it records noble services on behalf of the unfortunate poor. The author is not exaggerating when he asserts that legal aid has been the greatest movement of all English and American legal history for bringing justice to the poor, and there can be no doubt that it has furnished, as this book now shows, the greatest object lesson in modern judicial administration of both civil and criminal justice. It has been a philanthropic labor of the highest value, and the growth of this field of patriotic service and the widespread interest in the subject are most encouraging. The story, as the author tells it, is verily a romance of life in a great modern city, and it is illustrated by him with all the power and aid of a lucid and attractive style. It shows hundreds of thousands of cases where deserving poor have been afforded, under legal aid, the blessing of impartial and equal justice, and protected against those who would make a prey of their necessities, misfortunes, and tragedies. The men who have rendered this fine service and who, for more than half a century, have thus labored, indefatigably and self-sacrificingly, year in and year out to serve, protect, and shield the poor and otherwise helpless, merit the deep gratitude of all classes.

Legal aid of the character furnished by the New York Society and other similar societies directly tends to promote, among the unfortunate poor, ignorant, and helpless, respect for the law, belief in the impartiality of the administration of justice by our courts, confidence in the fairness and honesty of our institutions, and loyalty to a government that affords to all classes the equal protection of the laws. These are the sentiments that create contented and good citizenship; and without them a drift toward communism, revolution, and anarchy would have been inevitable. It must always be borne in mind that our system of democracy could not long endure if the poor in our populous and congested cities became convinced that they were being denied redress, protection, and equality before the law because of inability to pay for legal services, and were in consequence being oppressed and placed at an unfair disadvantage before our courts of justice in securing their legal rights. Such a conviction would inevitably generate a bitter feeling of intense resentment and disloyalty, and the existence of this feeling would be a constant and terrible menace to society. In a word, failure of the legal aid movement might have spelled ultimate national disaster.

The task of the author has been excellently done. The suffering, misery, and tragedy among the poor of the great American metropolis have been told with full sympathy and understanding and with much eloquence. The reader will find himself carried on from chapter to chapter until the end, with ever-increasing interest and thankfulness, and few will fail to be deeply stirred with gratitude and admiration for the high public spirit and devotion of those who directed and guided the movement he records, and who from time to time endowed it and thus rendered possible its continuance and expansion. In no other field of patriotic and humanitarian service has finer or more praiseworthy work been done during the past fifty years; and it is probable, as the author prophesies, that its greatest day and its largest problems are yet to come. Legal aid is no longer an experiment: it is an established and permanent institution.

Professor Maguire's book supplements the admirable and instructive essay entitled "Justice and the Poor," written by Reginald Heber Smith and first published in 1919 by the Carnegie Foundation for the Advancement of Teaching, and also the recent comprehensive review made by the Joint Committee for the study of Legal Aid of the Association of the Bar of the City of New York and the Welfare Council of New York City, which was prepared under the auspices of the Russell Sage Foundation. From these three works an adequate idea can be obtained of the services that have been rendered by The Legal Aid Society of the City of New York and its predecessor, the Deutscher Rechts-Schutz Verein, in laying the foundation of an institution that must be recognized as having become indispensable and which it is now the imperative duty of all populous communities permanently and generously to maintain.

The New York Society has always, and too long, been hampered and compelled to curtail its usefulness for want of adequate financial resources, notwithstanding the crying need of additional funds in order to prevent cruel injustice to the poor in criminal as well as civil cases. This is to be greatly deplored and ought to be remedied as soon as possible. There is no field of public service in which more practical and fruitful good can be done. The defence in criminal cases of those unable to pay for competent advice and protection ought especially to have adequate support, as will be readily appreciated by reference to the account of the organization and fine services of the Voluntary Defenders Committee, which the author well declares to be the flower and crown of New York legal aid development.

As has been very truly said, and cannot be too often emphasized, the first duty of society to the poor is not to give them charity but to secure them justice — not, as should likewise be emphasized, to offer them alms, which generally in such cases they do not ask, but the means of securing fair play and justice. This end cannot be more effectively realized under modern conditions, and especially in congested industrial communities, than through adequately equipped legal aid organizations.

Many will regret that the limited scope of the present book necessarily excluded any detailed account of the growth and development of legal aid throughout the United States and Canada and the extent of the services which are now being rendered by other legal aid societies. But the experiences and problems of the New York Society, which the author so graphically recounts, are undoubtedly typical of most, if not all, of these other societies, each in its own field of operation and service, and hence the book should be of widespread interest.

It was singularly right and just that the author should pay a tribute of praise to the founders and managers of the New York Society. Those who know personally of the immense labor and the self-sacrificing devotion of these men to the cause of legal aid in the City of New York, under adverse circumstances and lack of adequate support and funds, and preëminently the services of Edward Salomon, Arthur v. Briesen, and J. Augustus Johnson, will be immensely gratified at the due recognition of their several contributions throughout this valuable work. They all merit the praise that is given them. The Bar of the City of New York should be particularly grateful for the high estimate of the nobility, the lofty character, the passion for justice, the resolute constancy, and the self-sacrificing enthusiasm and devotion of Arthur v. Briesen. In a very literal sense, he devoted thirty-two years of his life to the cause of legal aid and the conduct of a great law office with millions of clients among the poor. Mr. Chief Justice Taft once said that Mr. v. Briesen was the philanthropic leader of the Bar, and the author of the present book fittingly and justly ends his narrative by acclaiming him to be one of mankind's great benefactors. Surely, so long as self-sacrificing devotion to the highest ideals of civic duty commends itself to the hearts and sympathies of men and women, so long should be honored the memory of the founders and builders of an institution that has rendered and is continuing to render immeasurably beneficent service.

WILLIAM D. GUTHRIE
Ex-President of the Association of the Bar of the City of New York and of the New York State Bar Association

NEW YORK
August, 1928

CONTENTS

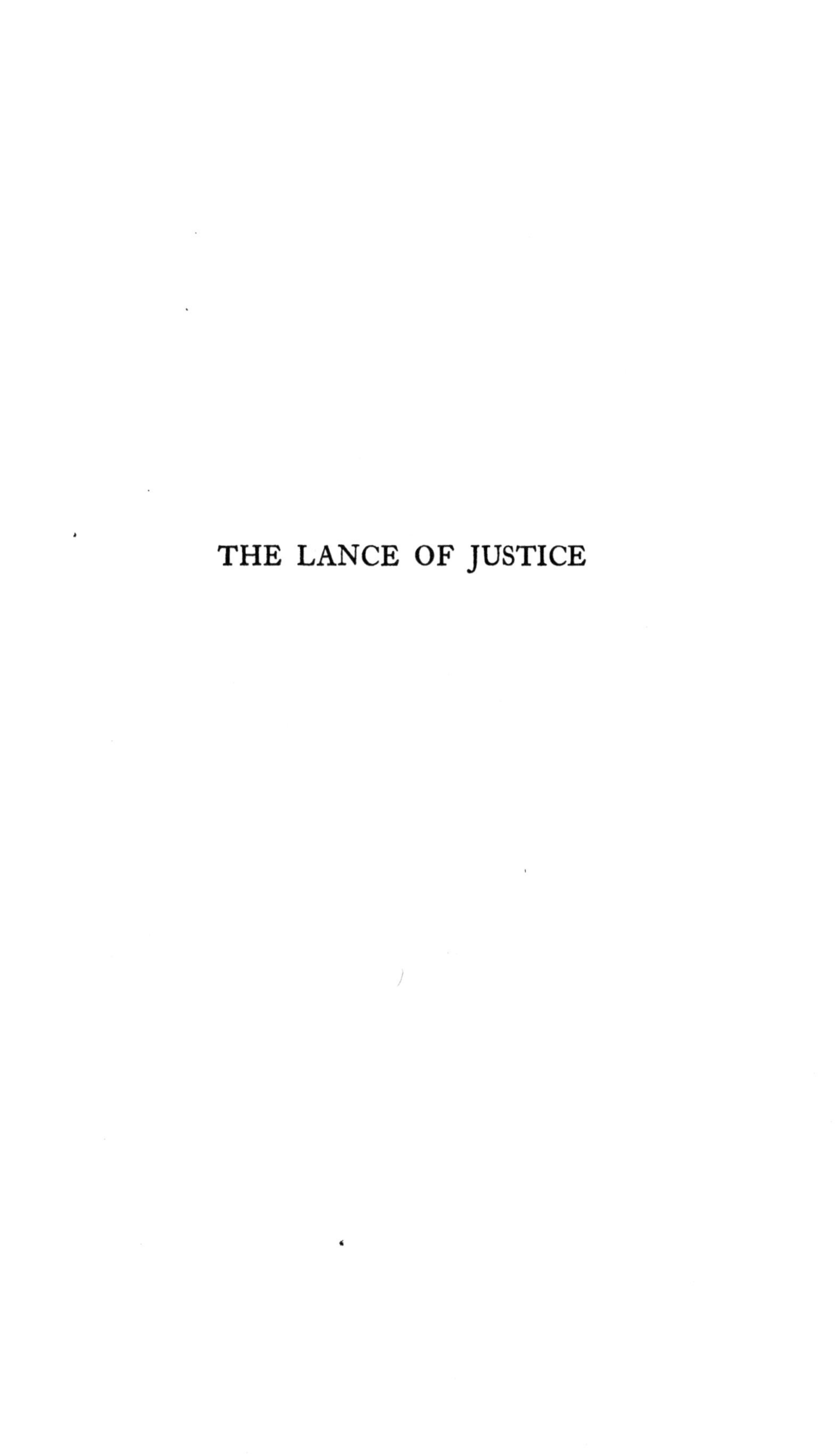

THE LANCE OF JUSTICE

Plate sin with gold,
And the strong lance of justice hurtless breaks;
Arm it in rags, a pigmy's straw doth pierce it.

—SHAKESPEARE: *King Lear*, Act IV, Scene 6

Nulli vendemus, nulli negabimus, aut differemus, rectum aut justiciam.

—MAGNA CARTA

Neither justice nor right should be sold to any person, nor denied, nor deferred; and writs and process ought to be granted freely, and without delay, to all persons requiring the same, on payment of the fees established by law.

—NEW YORK BILL OF RIGHTS

The purposes of the Society shall be: to render legal aid, gratuitously, if necessary, to all who appear to be in need of such aid and deserving thereof and unable to procure it elsewhere, including gratuitous legal aid to any poor person accused of crime; and to promote measures for the protection of poor persons with respect to their legal rights.

—CONSTITUTION OF THE LEGAL AID SOCIETY

I

1876

ON April 20, 1896, an application for change of corporate name was presented to Justice Abraham R. Lawrence of the New York Supreme Court. The learned judge saw that the corporation's original name was Deutscher Rechts-Schutz Verein. His eye stumbled over the unfamiliar German words, and momentarily came to a dead stop at the seven successive consonants packed away amidships. But as he looked farther his brow cleared and he said in a relieved tone: "It wants to be called The Legal Aid Society — why, by all means!" And the motion was granted. Superficially viewed, this was only a mildly amusing court-room incident. In fact, it had profound symbolic significance. It was the final outward and visible sign that citizens of New York City had fairly launched the greatest movement of all English and American legal history for bringing justice to the poor.

Of course the lawyer representing the petitioner made no such dramatic statement. He did not need to. Had the judge demanded specifications, however, he could have been told that the Verein was more than twenty years old; that, as its existing name implied, it had at first operated for the benefit of Germans exclusively; but that within the four years from 1892 to 1895 it had rendered legal assistance to 27,288 persons, of whom 13,685, or more than half, were not from Germany at all, being natives of thirty-two other countries, including the

United States. And had the judge further demanded proof that the petitioner was performing services of unique character and value, the mere statement of three cases which it had conducted or was conducting would fully have met his demand. First: two lads named Williamson and Donovan, having been convicted of robbery, were sent to the Elmira Reformatory. Williamson's mother ascertained that the principal witness for the prosecution, a twelve-year-old boy, had testified falsely. She had no money to buy a lawyer's advice or assistance. In agonizing distress she went to the Charity Organization Society, which referred her to the legal aid organization. This body procured voluminous affidavits by the perjured witness and others, obtained a new trial for the convicted youngsters, and won them an honorable discharge from the coils of the criminal law. Second: Joseph Arnold worked twelve days for Floyd Bailey. Then he was discharged as incompetent. Penniless and desperate, he came to the legal aid office. An attorney investigated the case, finding that Arnold was probably legally in the wrong and Bailey legally in the right. He then persuaded Bailey that, as he had the benefit of the man's work, he ought to pay something and not insist upon the harsh letter of the law. Bailey made a compromise offer and Arnold accepted it. They left the office at peace with one another. Third: a poor man was confined for several years in a lunatic asylum on Ward's Island. Actually, his commitment had been mistaken — he was not insane. But his case seemed hopeless because he had no means of bringing it to a lawyer's attention. Somehow, though, one of the legal aid attorneys discovered the situation. He investigated fully, became convinced of the man's sanity, and by legal process restored him to the working world. It is no exaggeration to say that this poor victim of circumstances was saved from a living burial.

There are the three cases: one utterly commonplace and deeply pitiful; two with distinctly dramatic elements, but equally pitiful; all three involving the most obviously fair and rudimental legal adjustments. It is astonishing that in the year of our Lord 1876 the poor of the English-speaking nations were not anywhere assured of getting such adjustments as a matter of right. It is humiliating to our general civilization that as late as 1896 they had still no such assurance except in New York City and Chicago. A swift historical survey will best indicate the causes for this glaring social deficiency.

The survey must begin far back in history. Our law from its earliest days contains expressions of desire to make justice universal, and serious attempts to translate that desire into fact. By the most often-quoted words of Magna Charta the English king undertook neither to sell, deny, nor delay right or justice. This clause, in the words of Maitland, was "full of future law."[5] But it was vaguely phrased, premature in spirit, and certainly not self-enforcing. Standing alone, it was at best the expression of a pious wish. The efforts of kings, legislatures, and courts to enforce its terms form a record of trial and error, with emphasis rather strongly on the errors. Very shortly after the original execution of Magna Charta by King John, free judicial writs were given to the poor, so that they might commence their suits without expense. This was a step in the right direction. The king's itinerant justices, who periodically patrolled the country for his interests, went further by developing a special procedure under which poor folk directly presented their claims without the interposition of lawyers. Unfortunately these justices made their rounds quite rarely. They visited a given locality rather less often than once in seven years. To a needy man, delayed justice is no justice at all. And, during the fourteenth century, these judicial visits were abandoned. The chancellor — the "Keeper of the King's Conscience" — sometimes took jurisdiction "in consideration of the fact that the suppliants because of poverty cannot have recovery by the common law." This quotation is painfully pointed. It is an open admission that the ordinary legal system was not giving justice to all. The chancellor's aid did not fully meet the situation. Procedure before him was dilatory and complex. He was far away from many who suffered wrong. He was more likely to be concerned with matters of magnitude than with the small affairs of poor men. But some time in the fifteenth century a special Court of Poor Men's Causes, later known as the Court of Requests, was established. Here we find a really intelligent and distinctly successful endeavor to carry legal justice into the lower strata of society. The court's procedure was equitable, its judges honest. There was an arrangement for local trials, although the tribunal's headquarters were at Westminster. Unluckily the Court of Requests became involved in the political upheaval of the early seventeenth century and went out of existence about 1642. Its success, however, was not forgotten. Other courts later bore its name and carried out its general purposes until they were succeeded about eighty years ago by the English County Courts, which now serve the poor admirably in lesser litigation. The United States is following out the same idea with the establishment of small-claims courts and other tribunals where minor disputes are handled swiftly, simply, and cheaply. But this form of relief is not, and probably never will be, completely adequate. Neither England nor this country has succeeded in such a comprehensive simplification of legal procedure that poor suitors are beyond the need of trained assistance.

Briefly, all the foregoing partial solutions hit the problem only around the edges. A more central attack was made at an early date. In 1495, under Henry VII, Parliament passed an act providing that poor plaintiffs should have their writs without expense and should also have gratuitous assistance in litigation from lawyers designated by the courts. This was followed by legislation exempting such plaintiffs from costs when their suits failed, but subjecting them in this event to "other punysshment as . . . shall be thought reasonable." There is a persistent legal tradition, somewhat lacking precise proof, that this "punysshment" was by whipping. These laws read well. But practically they failed. Desire greatly outran performance, and good intentions vapored mistily away. The reasons are complex and rather obscure. Apparently great trouble and confusion arose from lack of designated procedure for discriminating between honest and dishonest plaintiffs, and good and bad causes of action. The courts tried to fill the gap with a system of rules and practices which in the end became so rigid as to make it difficult for *any* plaintiff to get relief. It seems likely that there was a deficiency of free legal service. Lawyers, like anybody else, must earn money in order to live. And any layman can see the ridiculous lopsidedness of a system which helps plaintiffs but does nothing whatever for defendants who are dragged into lawsuits willy-nilly. One of the early recorded cases in the New York Society involved a poor woman who had hired a room for six months, and whom the landlady was attempting to evict because another person offered her more rent. The Legal Aid Society successfully defended the tenant's possession. According to the English plan, no help would have been given. But under this plan of legal poor-relief England limped along for more than four centuries. A slight modification in 1883 accomplished little or nothing. Real reform did not begin until 1914. Fairness calls for one modifying statement. Obstinately ineffective as the official plan remained, from 1891 to the present English charitable agencies have endeavored with some success to give the poor gratuitous legal advice. This will be spoken of again.

We now turn to America. During our early colonial days it was seriously contended that society would be better off without the lawyer. In Pennsylvania the Quakers bitterly opposed lawsuits in every form, and lawyers and physicians were spoken of as "equally destructive of men's estates and lives." Maryland displayed similar distaste for the legal profession. Virginia legislated against the practice of law. A writer in North Carolina said that the persons there holding themselves out as attorneys were scandalous to their profession. Presumably the people of these localities had some happy idea of administering justice according to the dictates of conscience and common sense, without the accustomed weary formalism of English law. As late as 1786, at the time of Shays' Rebellion, staid old Massachusetts echoed with appeals to crush or at least check the lawyers, and it was urged that the court of common pleas and general sessions of the peace "be removed in perpetuam rei Memoriam." The Massachusetts memory was somewhat short. The Salem witch trials of 1692 were held before judges none of whom was a lawyer or had ever studied law. Their results scarcely vindicated the idea of ruling by conscience and common sense, and left Massachusetts some hundreds of pounds the poorer by reason of the damages appropriated in 1711 for the heirs of the "witches" who were executed.

On the abandonment of this radical scheme for simplifying the administration of justice, there was a natural swing toward the existing English law. New York at least as early as 1801 adopted the 1495 act, lock, stock, and barrel, bad points as well as good ones; and not much later the New York legislature expanded the law by inserting a paraphrase of the principal English restrictive court rules. As has been said, this system lamentably failed in its country of origin. Its American history has been less disappointing only where legal aid agencies of a newer type have guided or supplemented its operation. These agencies, usually voluntary and private rather than official and public, owe their existence to the imperative pressure of necessity caused by peculiar American conditions. Of these conditions, by all odds the most important during the nineteenth century was immigration on an unprecedented scale. Since New York has been the great gateway to the new continent, it is natural that the first clean-cut legal aid development occurred in this city.

The immigrant's comparative helplessness is proverbial and easily accounted for. Rooted out of his native environment and brought overseas, he is dropped in a country not only strange but also inconsiderate of him and more hostile to him than he easily realizes. He is the easiest prey of cheats and sharpers. Long before the middle of the nineteenth century, " . . . New York . . . swarmed with a host of runners, agents, and solicitors of every kind, who fleeced the newcomers without remorse or pity. These runners were themselves mostly earlier immigrants, who could more readily gain the confidence of the aliens." The source of the disease suggested an antidote. In 1804 the German Society in the City of New-York, which had already existed for twenty years as a voluntary body, was incorporated to assist ". . . German emigrants and to afford relief to other poor distressed Germans, and their descendants." Forty years later the Irish Emigrant Society of New-York was incorporated "to afford advice, information, aid and protection, to emigrants from Ireland, and generally to promote their welfare." There were other organizations of similar character, such as the United States Immigrant Society for the protection of English and Scotch immigrants, but the German and Irish societies were particularly marked for prominence because of the tremendous number of aliens coming to the port of New York from their two countries.

Certainly there was a vast work to be done. The transatlantic voyage of the early days was almost inconceivably horrible for poor travellers. As late as 1867 the ship *Lord Brougham* from Hamburg lost 75 of 383 passengers before she reached New York. Toward the end of the same year the *Leibnitz* left Hamburg with 544 passengers. Of these passengers 108 died at sea or in port. These two instances were particularly shocking, but there were others like them, and the mortality was terribly high under the best conditions so long as immigrants were brought in sailing ships. With the installation of steerage quarters on steamers and the consequent shortening of the voyage, matters took a distinct turn for the better. Still, immigrants were always arriving in need of medical attention, and this need might continue for a long time after their landing. Poverty was constantly a serious factor from the earliest days. Towns and boroughs in Germany, like similar governmental units of other countries, had a cheerful practice of shipping off to the United States their paupers and criminals. The heavy influx of German paupers led the Corporation of the City of New York in 1847 to memorialize Congress. Next year the German Society memorialized the New York legislature, presenting figures which tended to show that the head taxes which the state collected from German immigrants greatly exceeded the sums expended by the public authorities on their charitable relief. This was due partly to the fact that these immigrants arrived in better condition than the great mass of those from other countries, but also partly to the fact that the Germans regarded public poor relief with horror and applied instead to the Society for work, funds, and medical service. Therefore the Society asked as a subsidy a modest share of the head taxes. Almost immediately after this incident a most valuable body of German immigrants began to arrive. Cast forth by political upheaval, Carl Schurz and many another of "those who dreamed high in 1848" reached our shores. This stream of middle-class liberalists, persons of good character and independent spirit, came with an increasing flood. In 1854 the enormous number of 215,009 Germans crossed to America. Many went farther west. But the body of Germans in New York City was constantly and greatly augmented. Nor were the additions always of the highest and most serviceable type. Weaklings are much more likely to stay where they land than to push on. The plan of exporting paupers and disabled persons to the United States had not been dropped. In 1855 Wurtemberg, which followed this practice, had the effrontery to complain to the German Society because the latter had assisted in shipping back individuals "who desired to return home on account of sickness, or incapacity to labor"!

Immigration declined during the Civil War, only to increase after the fighting was over. The swift revival of American prosperity, with its ambitious projects for material development of the country and the great internal migration westward, acted on Europe like a social suction pump. During 1870 Germany sent 91,779 immigrants. Long after, Arthur v. Briesen [1] thus described this post-war influx: "We probably have all seen them as they traveled along the streets of New York — great big men and their modest-looking wives and numerous children, with the big bundles and big boots and the home-spun clothes, and the visor caps, and the anxious and hopeful faces — great expectations, mostly realized. But, as the hawk hovers over the brood of little chicks, so the robbers and plunderers watched their opportunity to see how they could take from these strangers, men who did not know the language of the country, men who did not know the habits of the country, men who were perfectly devoted to the idea that they came amongst *friends* — how they could rob them of their belongings!"

It must not be supposed that such obvious rascality as was practised upon the immigrants escaped official notice, or that the governmental authorities failed to act. While the United States for various reasons passed no general law to regulate immigration until 1882 and

[1] Since this name will appear again and again, it may not be amiss to note that abbreviation of "von" to "v." shows the word to be used as a title or indication of social rank, rather than as a mere individual designation.

did not firmly take hold of the problem until 1891 and 1893, the state legislatures did what they could for the local situations. This was notably true in New York, where a series of statutes beginning in 1820 and continuing for about sixty years was enacted, not so much to restrict immigration as to protect the aliens and furnish the government either with guarantees that the newcomers would not become public charges or with a fund for their care if they did. A detailed law of 1847 established the Commissioners of Immigration. The presidents of the German Society and the Irish Emigrant Society were *ex-officio* members of this board. A law of the next year regulated immigrant boarding-houses, runners, transportation agents, and others who had been preying upon the strangers from abroad. The Commissioners decided to fit up a single landing-place for all immigrants, who might thus be inspected and at least temporarily guarded from the attacks of the "hawks" whom Mr. v. Briesen has described. They encountered obstinate opposition. Having leased a pier at the foot of Hubert Street in 1848, they were promptly enjoined on application by neighboring property owners from using this location. It is fair to say that an immigrant landing-place was then dreaded as a source of disorder and disease, but one cannot help suspecting that ulterior motives played some part in the controversy. Not until 1855 were the Commissioners able to obtain additional legislation which enabled them to carry out their plan. On May 5, 1855, they leased for landing purposes the old fort at the foot of Manhattan Island known as Castle Garden. This building, as many New Yorkers know, has a varied and interesting history. Here in the early fifties of the last century Jenny Lind sang; here in 1880 was held the first American meeting of the Salvation Army; and here the sightseer now finds the Battery Park aquarium. The Commissioners successfully repelled fresh legal attacks and by the first of August had their quarters ready for use. At this time Castle Garden rose out of the water at a distance from the shore, with which a bridge connected it. Thus the immigrants obtained a protected spot where they made their landing safely, speedily, and cheaply.

But the interests opposed to the Commissioners' operations were not so easily balked. They carried on for years, with fairly consistent success, an onslaught upon the constitutionality of the New York immigration statutes. What might be described as a duel between the legislature at Albany and the Supreme Court at Washington brought the former off decidedly second-best. This aspect of the situation alone was calculated to take much of the spirit out of the Commissioners' administration. No doubt they were hampered by underhand methods of interference. And fundamentally the problem of immigration was too great for any state to solve while playing a lone hand. So it is not surprising to find indications of irregularity in the public safeguarding of aliens. To judge from the account by Jacob A. Riis of his arrival in 1870, immigration inspection did not amount to much. Never a word does he say about it. Some four years later, though, Michael Pupin received a vigorous quizzing. He passed the inspectors with the impression that he entered the country through special favor, and only because he had enlisted the sympathies of one of the officials, a one-legged Swiss veteran of our Civil War. Now of course young Riis was in a passionate hurry to get ashore and comply with the imagined custom of the country by purchasing the huge navy revolver with which he swaggered up Broadway. His concentration upon this may have led him to overlook the landing formalities. Moreover, as compared with Pupin, he was a plutocrat. Yet it is quite significant that in 1873 the Commissioners had been stimulated by the passage of a revised New York immigration act, which the United States Supreme Court did not overthrow until 1875. Even under these circumstances, Pupin was not thoroughly safeguarded. He slept and had breakfast in Castle Garden at the public expense; but no sooner did he issue from the haven of refuge than an old woman cheated him out of five cents — all the money he had — by selling him a purported prune pie filled with prune pits!

At best, then, during the seventies an immigrant's financial interests were constantly imperilled. And much worse conditions soon appeared. The sudden prosperity which lured so many hundreds of thousands from European countries had a train of political and economic calamities. Mere mention of a few of these in rough chronological order will suggest the whole picture. First comes the Tweed Ring, which in its nefarious operations augmented the debt of New York City by about seventy million dollars and left a deposit of political slime not soon cleaned away. Then there were the audacious and devastating financial operations of Fisk and Gould. Next may be noted the scandalous matter of the Credit Mobilier, which smirched so many important politicians. Next, and with particular emphasis, the failure of Jay Cooke & Company on September 18, 1873, and the terrible subsequent panic and business depression. Men still alive can recollect how along Broadway scores of business houses were closed, with receivers' notices on the doors and windows. The depression lasted for years. Bankruptcies, for example, did not reach their maximum until 1878. The filthy police lodging-rooms of New York were crowded with honest men out of work, as well as with the habitual vagrants who always infested them until Police Commissioner Roosevelt finally shut them down in 1896. Soon after the panic came the disclosure of the prodigious whiskey tax frauds on the Federal government. In this matter President Grant's own private secretary was deeply involved. As a fitting climax to this sorry tale of public and private disaster and corruption, the Secretary of War was accused of jobbery and graft. He resigned hastily, with impeachment proceedings actually pending. This was in the early months of 1876. In November the city of New York had a sharp reminder of its particular and none-too-remote scandal: Tweed, who had made a spectacular escape to Florida, Cuba, and Spain, was brought back on the U. S. S. *Franklin* to spend his remaining days in jail. A responsible historian has described this period as "the nadir of national disgrace." Incidentally, by a bitter irony, 1876 was the Centennial Year of American Independence.

At this time, and against this sombre background, came the first establishment of legal aid as a specialized social activity. The word "specialized" is inserted with a purpose. Legal aid as an adjunct to other social activities was no stranger. For proof of this we need not look beyond New York City itself, where the Working Women's Protective Union — a corporation which still exists and carries on its beneficent activities — was established in 1868 "to promote the interests of women who obtain a livelihood by employments other than household service, *and especially to provide them with legal protection from the frauds and impositions of un-*

scrupulous employers, to assist them in procuring employment, and to open to them such suitable departments of labor as are not occupied by them." Truth to tell, independent legal aid grew out of the incidental rendering of legal assistance by the German Society. The third annual report of the Deutscher Rechts-Schutz Verein for the year 1878 points out that in 1876 poor or unemployed Germans could apply to the German Society, while the sick and injured found free treatment in the German hospital and dispensary. "Only for those impecunious Germans who had fallen into the hands of the police through ignorance of the laws here, through recklessness or misguidance, or for those who by cunning or deception had been robbed of their property, or from whom their hard-earned wages were withheld, was there no place where they could seek counsel or aid. Many poor innocent Germans were kept for weeks and months in prison or detained as witnesses because they were unfamiliar with ways and means for their release. Servants and workmen had their promised wages withheld by dishonest employers on some pretext or other, because their poverty and ignorance of the language and conditions here prevented their seeking judicial protection and aid. Frequently such cases were brought to the knowledge of the German Society and disposed of or adjusted without charge by members belonging to the legal profession. The more frequently and successfully this occurred, the greater became the number of applicants, so that at last it proved impossible for these members to meet the demands made, and the only choice left was to desert these petitioners to their fate or to establish an independent society for their protection. This latter was done under the auspices of the directors of the German Society. . . ."

This independent society was, of course, the Deutscher Rechts-Schutz Verein.[1] Not many details of its formation have been recorded. The original suggestion came from Sigismund Kaufmann and Charles Hauselt. According to its first annual report: "In view of a long-felt urgent need, a number of gentlemen met in March of last year [1876], after thorough preliminary discussion, and established this society as a legal corporation. . . ." The exact date of incorporation was March 8, 1876. The incorporation meeting is supposed to have been held in the office of Edward Salomon, a lawyer who had come to New York after having been governor of Wisconsin from 1862 to 1864. The remaining charter members were Edward Lauterbach, Bernard Roelker, James Eschwege, John J. Freedman, Jacob A. Grass, Frederick K. Schack, Philip Bissinger, Willy Wallach, and Charles L. F. Rose. One of these gentlemen, Mr. Roelker, was an importer, and at least three — Messrs. Hauselt, Wallach, and Rose — were merchants. The infusion of non-legal incorporators and members was most fortunate. It would have been fatal for such a society, formed to meet a perfectly untechnical social emergency, to become over-legalistic. The lawyers left to administer legal aid in England made a pretty botch of it. At the end of the first year the Society had fifty-eight members, each paying annual dues of twenty dollars — no inconsiderable sum during the mid-seventies. These men were solid, thoughtful, courageous, public-spirited citizens. Three of them had been members of, or connected with, the famous Committee of Seventy which hastened the fall of the Tweed gang. Others had "done the state some service" and were to do more.

[1] The name is thus given in the printed constitution and by-laws. In the certificate of incorporation it appears as "Der Deutsche Rechts Schutz-Verein."

Simplicity and brevity marked the Society's constitution and by-laws. The object was "to render legal aid and assistance, gratuitously, to those of German birth, who may appear worthy thereof, but who from poverty are unable to procure it."[1] These early draftsmen should be given credit for language so precise and comprehensive that similar societies all over the United States have copied it verbatim. In the whole development of legal aid work, occasion has arisen for only two or three important amendments of this purpose clause. These amendments are referred to at appropriate points later in the book. On the side of administration, the president was to make annual reports of the organization's activities. Current supervision of these activities was entrusted to a committee of three directors, called the Law Committee. The actual legal work was to be done by an Attorney, designated by the directors from among the members. The Attorney alone was to be paid for his services.

Governor Salomon became the first president. Because of his important services in the achievement of equal justice a brief sketch of his previous career is desirable. He was born near Halberstadt, Prussia, on August 11, 1828, his father being Christopher Salomon, who had fought in the Napoleonic Wars and been severely wounded at the Battle of Waterloo. Edward Salomon received a careful general education, completed in the University of Berlin. One of his brothers fled to the United States as a political refugee because of participation in the Revolution of 1848. Edward Salomon followed in 1849. He settled at Manitowoc, Wis-

[1] The certificate of incorporation runs thus: ". . . to render gratuitously legal aid and assistance to such persons of German birth in the City of New York as may appear to be worthy thereof, but from poverty are unable to employ legal assistance . . ."

consin, where he taught school and for a time held a deputy county clerkship. In 1852 he entered the law office of Judge E. G. Ryan at Milwaukee, and after three years' study was admitted to the bar, forming a partnership with Winfield Smith. Mr. Salomon soon obtained distinction as a lawyer, carrying many important cases to the Supreme Court of Wisconsin.

He ought, indeed, to be remembered as a careful, painstaking, and successful practitioner rather than as a politician. Politics would scarcely have claimed his energies had it not been for the extraordinary conditions then leading up to the Civil War. Originally a Democrat, Mr. Salomon was moved by the events of 1854 and the subsequent doings in Kansas to sympathize with the Republicans. Even so, until 1861 he took no very prominent part. In that year, however, he was nominated for lieutenant-governor on the ticket with L. P. Harvey. This ticket carried the election, and when the governor met a tragic accidental death in April, 1862, Edward Salomon succeeded to the office at a most critical stage of the war. The event is notable because he was the first citizen of foreign derivation to hold Wisconsin's highest executive position. It now appears that he devoted to the task his very best energies and that, considering the grave difficulties encountered, his administration was a genuine success. But, being defeated when he ran for election in 1863, he abandoned the political arena and resumed the practice of his profession. Several years later the ex-governor moved to New York City, where he became councillor for the Prussian government and established a reputation for solid, if not spectacular, merit.

Perhaps the most delicate problem in launching practical legal aid work was that of obtaining an Attorney able to cope with the somewhat unusual features of poor men's litigation. Now it happened that most of the cases reaching the German Society had been turned over to Sigismund Kaufmann's office. Mr. Kaufmann in turn had delegated them to an alert, vigorous, and ambitious young man in his employ. This young man was Charles K. Lexow, who later held several responsible public offices, and who at the time of writing is the New York City Commissioner of Records. An ideal candidate for the position of Attorney, he accepted the place at a salary of $1000 per year.

Having in mind depressed financial conditions, some people no doubt considered the organization of the Society an ill-timed floating of a new charity. But the quotations already given show how pressing was the need for legal aid. Hard times make harsh creditors and elusive debtors. More than mere materialism demanded the step. The brazen corruption of the day offered at once a temptation to the thoughtless and an affront to the thoughtful. When Tweed was finally arrested, Jay Gould was the most prominent signer of his bail bond for one million dollars. Legislators, administrative officers, and even judges were being found at the receiving ends of improper financial schemes. If, coincidentally with all this, a poor man or most particularly a poor immigrant found that his poverty disabled him to enforce his rights or to protect himself against unfair legal aggression, what was he to conclude except that the vaunted equality and fairness of America were mere empty words? What choice had he but to join the ranks of the spoilers or, bitter and disillusioned, to get out of the community as best he might? Again and again in its American history, legal aid has answered the call of civic duty. Never was the call clearer or the answer truer than in 1876.

One more thing should be said emphatically. Legal aid workers have always bristled at the suggestion that their organizations should be classed with charities or philanthropies — that is, with bodies which give help from mercy or favor. Joseph H. Choate, with his happy judgment for the apt word, called legal aid a humane movement. Such indeed it was, but it occupied a delicate position which no single word can adequately describe. Governor Salomon, in his report for 1880, put the point clearly and succinctly: "Our Society procures [for its clients] not alms, which these applicants do not ask and would not accept, but justice." No human power can promise a man happiness, physical well-being, material success, or intellectual ability. These matters are beyond our certain control. But organized society which prescribes the rules of social conduct can promise, and with us does promise, justice according to law. The New York Bill of Rights in 1876 made this pledge, and has ever since continued to make it, practically by repetition of Magna Charta: "Neither justice nor right should be sold to any person, nor denied, nor deferred. . . ." The Deutscher Rechts-Schutz Verein deliberately set itself up to redeem the pledge in part at least. So doing, it entered upon no charitable course of action. It did not propose to *give* anybody anything. It undertook simply to procure for its clients the money, the goods, or the protection which the law explicitly said those clients were entitled to have. In order fully to discharge its chosen duty, it had to become and be recognized as an unofficial cog of the machine of justice — a voluntary partner to the sheriffs, the judges, and the other public servants required for the proper operation of our legal system. This recognition could not be hoped for without the complete confidence and approval of at least the leading public officials working for the same end. The first step toward confidence is full understanding, and here an immediate difficulty arose. The Society was a curious bilingual mixture. Its name was German, its constitution and by-laws English, but its annual reports, again, German. These reports were never translated into English until about December, 1926. Probably they were unread by the judges of the inferior courts before which the Attorney had most of his early cases. Yet only from them could a clear idea be gleaned of the object of legal aid. The language difficulty was the symptom of a more fundamental weakness. Judges could scarcely believe that the Society was entirely disinterested and without bias. Had it purported to act for *all* poor men with just claims or defences, impartiality might have been convincingly asserted. But when the Attorney acted only for poor clients of German birth, there was probably a tinge of suspicion that he must unduly favor the chosen racial group in opposition to other racial groups. And of course the Germans' opponents in litigation were often or usually non-Germans. This situation was unavoidable at the beginning, because of the Society's origin. It cramped the development of the legal aid idea. Happily, as we shall see, the unfortunate restriction was overridden within less than fifteen years.

In other respects, however, the organization began promptly to operate along the soundest lines. Says the first report, speaking of the collection of wage claims: "It is a well-known fact that in such cases really practical results are rarely secured except through *threat* of action; if the debtor lets matters go to the filing of a suit, he is either really in the right or he knows that nothing can be got from him in the way of execution.

Nevertheless, such suits have to be filed, or otherwise even the threats soon cease to have effect." The Attorney knew when he began, or very soon learned, that the quickest, cleanest, and happiest collection of all is the one accomplished without court action. He realized that, to get its clients their rights extrajudicially, the organization must make itself known as a fair foe but a fierce one. So, at apparently disproportionate outlay, he resolutely pushed matters to the end against a few "hardshell" debtors—*pour encourager les autres*. The Society has reaped a rich harvest from the reputation thus early established.

Again, the organization offered its clients an Attorney who gave them all his energies and who conducted a well-rounded practice for their assistance. On the first of these points, Governor Salomon is explicit in his initial report: "He [the Attorney] has devoted his entire time and attention to the affairs of the Society. . . ." Men cannot serve two masters, and legal aid lawyers with private professional interests have rarely been satisfactory. That is one reason for the comparative failure of the volunteer English legal aid already briefly referred to in this chapter. In England since 1891 kindly practitioners have, as "Poor Man's Lawyers," held consulting sessions under the auspices of religious denominations, charitable institutions, and law societies. They do so at night, after their day's work. It takes gallant enthusiasm for a weary man to face such evening tasks, and all too often this enthusiasm has waned and the conferences have been abandoned. By speaking further of English legal aid, the second point of this paragraph may be most easily developed. The statute of 1495 providing relief for poor litigants has already been dubbed a lopsided enactment because it helped plaintiffs only and left defendants to their fate. Truth to tell, the whole English conception of legal aid was lopsided for centuries and is none too symmetrical now. The original conception may fairly be described as pugnacious. There was a wealth of legal provisions for aiding litigants in waging court battles, and an utter lack of any for giving general advice or patching up or warding off trouble. By the English, the conciliatory procedure which so happily adjusted Arnold's wage claim against Bailey would have been officially cold-shouldered. Yet every lawyer knows that much of his work never leads anywhere near a court. His clients' affairs are largely non-contentious, and they are often wise enough to use the law office as a service station instead of a repair shop. In England, the poor have never had a real law office. Even the Poor Man's Lawyers, whose function it is to advise, have to work under such conditions of personal weariness and hurry, crowding, lack of privacy, absence of clerical facilities, and general inconvenience that their assistance has been quite inadequate, and not at all comparable with what the paying client gets from a good solicitor. As to this matter, nothing explicit is said by the earliest reports of the Deutscher Rechts-Schutz Verein. These rather feature the litigation which the Attorney conducted. But from the first they carry a column headed "Other Violations of Law." And, says the report for 1889, "Under this heading belong, *e. g.*, the numerous inheritance matters in which the Society is always active as well as the drawing of wills, contracts, powers of attorney and other documents." So it would seem that our legal aid organization promptly upon its opening supplied to the poor Germans of New York a complete legal service not obtainable by the needy elsewhere in either England or America. With this statement, the introductory matter appropriately ends. The next chapter describes the nature, and traces the chronological development, of the Society's work.

II

THE DEUTSCHER RECHTS-SCHUTZ VEREIN

ON March 30, 1876, the Society opened its office in an upper room of 39 Nassau Street. The proper introduction to this chapter would be a picture of the office's first client, and a description of his claim. Unfortunately, existing records do not make possible that dramatic touch. The first client has long vanished into the dusky past. But from the tabulation of cases we may make a shrewd guess that he was a working-man with wages overdue and unpaid. Of 212 complaints laid before the Society's Attorney during his first year of activity 113 were wage claims. We may imagine the client, then, as a very puzzled and probably very indignant German, not long in this country. Quite possibly he was cold and hungry, and therefore in a great hurry for his money. His English was guttural, confused, and fragmentary. At an ordinary New York law office he could hardly have made himself understood. Still less could such an office have made him understand why he should not have "the prompt, summary, and rather patriarchal justice exercised in Germany in trifling matters by the lower court judge or the police judge. Convinced of the justice of [his] own demands [he would] consider the necessary obstacles of the rules for summons, the producing of evidence, and especially the delay in execution to be exceedingly unjust and burdensome." Thus the Society's fourteenth annual report spells out for us the mental attitude of the original client. Add the fact that his claim, if of typical size, was for ten or twelve dollars only, and it becomes apparent that this man would fare ill at the hands of the average lawyer. Even if his case were understood, taken up, and forced to a successful outcome, charges for legal service would leave him only a pitiful core of the recovery. The inexorable expense account would have eaten the apple.

But direct our perplexed working-man to the German Legal Aid Society, and see what happens. He finds a lawyer who understands the German tongue, and who in that tongue can sympathetically explain the differences between the legal procedures of the fatherland and of America. The lawyer makes no bones about the small size of the claim — rather welcomes it all the more heartily because it *is* small and could not be collected elsewhere. If collection is made, nothing, or at most only a small percentage, will be deducted for services. The case may have a truly satisfying outcome for the client.

And by shifting our attention from the first to the hundredth wage-claimant of 1876, we shall discover additional merits in the legal aid office. The Attorney has through hard experience become a past master of wage collection. He will get the money in many an instance where an ordinary lawyer would be put off with excuses, beaten at trial, or left stranded with a barren judgment. Not only will he collect more surely, but he will collect more quickly. Wage debtors know his understanding of their ways and wiles. Many surrender without fighting. Says the report for 1876: "A letter from the attorney as a rule brought the desired result." These letters came to be known as "demand notes" and have an honorable record of just efficiency. The element of justice — fairness to the debtor as well as to the creditor — was vital. The demand notes would lose effect if based upon exaggerated or fraudulent claims. And here again the legal aid Attorney's constant experience stood him in good stead. He could swiftly detect either the impostor or the innocently mistaken claimant, send the former packing, and straighten out the latter's confused ideas of his rights.

It is also socially advantageous to concentrate many poor men's claims in a single hand, because wholesale dishonest practices and defects in the laws intended to curb them are vividly exposed. That, year in and year out, half or thereabouts of the cases brought to the legal aid office involved wage collections gave very sound basis for a belief that something was wrong with the New York method of making employers pay their employes. Likewise the discovery by the German Legal Aid Society that judgments for small sums could rarely be satisfied showed that the theory or the practice of execution in civil cases must be defective. The Society was to make an important contribution to social welfare not merely by discovering these bad conditions, but by exposing and helping to remove their causes.

While the early reports are tactfully silent upon the point, it seems that the success of the Society in wage collections and its comparatively frequent appearance at court for enforcing such claims roused some judicial distrust. The report for 1894 frankly confesses the old difficulty: "For a long time the Courts were of the opinion that we were but a collection agency, and only in the law business for the purpose of making money. . . ." Fortunately, one of the Society's directors, Charles J. Nehrbas, was elected to the bench in 1880. Undoubtedly in his new position he was able to make clear to his fellow judges the truly disinterested aims of the organization which he had helped to administer.

Other beneficent agencies such as the various charitable bureaus, the Immigration Commissioners, and the Commissioners of Charities and Correction more easily and promptly realized the Society's pure intentions. Successful clients spread the news that a new legal force had come into being to help the poor man. The influence and success of the Society increased with startling rapidity.

In attempting to measure this success statistically we might count the dollars collected for clients. Of course, it was important that poor people should recover the largest amount of money possible. And on that score, the record was always excellent. The period now under consideration runs from 1876 through 1889. Even during the first tentative year, returns to clients balanced expenses. The comparison swiftly became much more favorable. The year 1878 saw over $8000 collected at a total expense of $1700; 1883, $17,000 at an expense of less than $3400; 1889, $20,000 at an expense of $4000. A good showing from a so-called "charity," particularly in view of the fact that the applicants for aid themselves paid a substantial portion of the expenses!

But this has been far from the primary object or the most important achievement of legal aid in New York. It is, for example, no reflection upon the Working Women's Protective Union that at about this time it expended in one year more than $1700 to bring in about the same amount for its beneficiaries. The value of such an organization is rather to be measured by the feeling of happiness and security which the individual applicant derives from its operations. He may be a defendant, not seeking money but striving to repel an unjust claim. His case may involve domestic infelicity only, and have no monetary aspect. He may be merely an inquirer for legal advice. Yet in each instance the poor man's law-office stands ready to help. It is therefore fair to say that we get a much better indication of the German Legal Aid Society's success from watching the numerical growth of its clientele. As already stated, 212 cases were submitted during the first year. During the next year 750 cases reached the office. The figures then jump to 856, to 1923, and to 2122 in the three years succeeding. By 1882 the number of cases was 3413. In 1886 President Salomon made a curiously accurate prediction "that apparently we may now assume that in the future we shall have annually an average of 3500 applicants." Of course, at the present day The Legal Aid Society has yearly applications vastly exceeding this figure. But it must not be forgotten that the original purpose was to care only for the legal difficulties of Germans and persons of German extraction. If throughout the Society's history the number of cases received during any year from individuals fitting this description is examined, it will be found that only seldom has the first president's estimate been exceeded.

The prompt demonstration that the poor Germans of New York emphatically needed services such as the Society could render proved almost fatal. Legal aid nearly smothered in its own success. With respect to the year 1882, President Salomon wrote as follows: "The more good we do and the greater the demands become upon the Society, the more poor needy Germans threatened in their rights who call upon our assistance, the more we fulfill the purpose of our organization, the higher the expenses mount. If we are unable to increase considerably the number of our members and thus [to increase] our income . . . we shall be compelled to suspend an activity which, by its results, should indeed be justified in appealing to the support of the Germans of our great and wealthy metropolis."

It may be well to elaborate this statement by speaking of the elements of expense. As appeared in the last chapter, the salary paid the Attorney was extremely small. At the start this salary was the principal, indeed almost the only, cash expenditure required. For the first year an office was given rent-free. But in short order it became apparent that one man could not handle the Society's business. Little argument is needed to prove that a one-man lawyer's office is an inefficient office. Every time the lawyer goes to court he has to lock his door and the reception of clients is suspended. Every time he writes a letter his mind and energies are distracted from true legal work and wasted upon mechanical detail. Hence the directors early came to the conclusion that the Attorney must have a messenger and an assistant. The first assistant attorney, Alois Faller, began to serve gratuitously in October, 1879. He continued his work as a labor of love for about sixteen months. In 1881 the directors voted that from the first of February in that year he should receive a salary of $50 a month. By this time the office staff had considerably increased. There were at least two clerks. Also rent was paid beginning with the second year. In addition, there were disbursements for janitor services, stationery, stamps, and the like. One very important element of outgo was money paid for court costs and fees. In 1881 the amount expended for this purpose was about $200. Next year it jumped to more than $500 because of "the increased cost of lawsuits." New York, as has already been said, had adopted the English system supposed to exempt poor litigants from the payment of costs and fees. The fact that the Society in its early struggling years was compelled to expend substantial sums for such charges is a stinging commentary upon the workability of the English system in its New York application. These particular expenditures put the Society in a most difficult and embarrassing situation. They were a serious drain upon its slender resources. But the alternative was painful in the extreme. President Salomon puts it as follows: "When one considers that in the past year [1886] the Society brought suit in District Courts alone in four hundred and twenty-four cases [where the plaintiffs were financially unable to contribute to the expenses], so that the Society is compelled either itself to advance the money *or to turn away unaided the man entirely without funds*, then one will understand the increased outlay."

With all these separate items of expense added together the Society's annual outgo, beginning at $1000 in 1876, doubled by 1880, tripled by 1887, and quadrupled by 1889, if in the year last named we include the discharge of a deficit. Nowadays these expenses seem ridiculously small for the excellent results obtained. But at the moment they were staggering and almost drove the officers and directors to despair. Constant urgent appeals were made for more adequate support. To a large extent the annual reports contained these appeals and consequently they had only a limited circulation. The German newspapers, however, did what they could to help. In February, 1879, the *Staats-Zeitung* published a long statement about the work and needs of the Society, beginning with the sentence: "A helper in distress needs help." The report for 1879 hopes "that the wealthy Germans of New York will not fail to join the Society which so extensively secures to their less fortunately situated countrymen, not charity and support, but justice and the securing of their just claims. It would indeed be a certificate of moral poverty for the Germans of New York if they were unable to maintain such a society whose activity directly and indirectly helps thousands of their poor countrymen to secure their rights which would otherwise be unobtainable for them and which lends them and others the important moral support of feeling that they are not without [legal] recourse." Four years later: "If one remembers that in the course of the year 1883 day after day an average of eleven poor Germans, for the most part unacquainted with the language of the country, came to us with their complaints; that all these thirty-four hundred cases were investigated by a competent attorney and were settled in one way or another so that justice was secured through our legal assistance, provided it *could* be secured; that aside from the numerous cases involving non-payment of money we helped these poor plaintiffs to the payment of their claims to a total amount of over $17,000, most of the claims being for less than $10; that but for the existence of such a Society as ours most of these people would probably have remained without redress; that the fact of the existence and operation of our Society and the threat of claiming its aid is in many cases alone sufficient to prevent acts of injustice; that the sums annually contributed by us and expended for the legal defense of our poor German countrymen certainly do far more good than if we distributed the same amount among poor beggars; then one may indeed assert that this German Legal Aid Society deserves the fullest support of the wealthy."

At the time, of course, the Germans formed a very substantial fraction of New York's population. But the appeal to them was not and could not be so wide or so convincing as an appeal to the whole community for a beneficent society ready to serve *any* poor person in legal difficulties. Throughout this first period the appearance on the lists of officers or members of a name not obviously German is strikingly rare. When Judge Nehrbas resigned from the Law Committee in 1881, Edward Robinson was elected to fill his place. But this name may well have been of German derivation; and it disappears from the membership list in 1883. Henry Villard, the well-known journalist and financier, supported the Society generously. He, however, was German by birth, his baptismal name having been Ferdinand Heinrich Gustav Hilgard.

President Salomon believed that the back log of the Society's financial scheme should be a body of at least 100 members paying annual dues of $20 each. He felt, and to a large extent the figures of the early years bear out his feeling, that with this sum of $2000 assured the remaining expenses could be defrayed by contributions reasonably sure to come from other quarters. Hence the president and the directors struggled constantly to bring their membership to the desired goal of 100. It proved an impossible task. Twenty dollars was a good deal of money in the seventies and eighties of the last century. Moreover, the hand of financial panic had not yet been lifted. Times were bad, and men who in more happy years of prosperity could easily have produced the double-eagle for their annual dues found difficulty in doing so. The number of members shifted with an undulating movement, now up, now down. It sank sometimes below 50 and never during President Salomon's administration passed above 90, let alone attaining the 100 mark. In 1881, under stress of extreme financial need, the Society tried a distinctly doubtful experiment.

It was voted "to elect to life-long membership persons contributing $250 to the Legal Aid Society." This would have been bad financing. Under existing conditions it was morally certain that any life-membership fee would be used for current expenses. Yet after receiving such a fee the Society would be in no position to approach the donor for further periodical contributions. As a matter of fact, not one life-member was admitted until 1900.

Another perfectly obvious source of income lay in those cases successfully prosecuted for clients. At an early date this was tapped. The report for 1877 states that where the Society secured payment of "considerable amounts" suitable compensation for services was deducted. Two years after, we find the scheme to be that the Society retains 10 per cent on paying over all sums amounting to more than $20. In the next year this rule is changed so that the 10 per cent is deducted from all sums of more than $10. Pitched at this scale the percentage deduction system was carried on for many years. In 1889 the additional provision was made that where clients possessed the means to pay an attorney they should be called upon for an appropriate fee. The aggregate amount thus received was very substantial. In fact, President Salomon said about 1885 that without this contribution "the Society would long ago have had to discontinue its activity." But unfortunately the source of revenue was not reliable. The amounts realized either on the percentage basis or by way of reasonable compensation had striking and unpredictable variations from year to year. The item was not one upon which an intelligent budget could be based.

It has already been explained that the German Society was the mother of the German Legal Aid Society. The parent had a strong feeling of responsibility toward her offspring. From 1877 on, almost without interruption, the German Society made substantial annual contributions to legal aid expenses. But this again was a precarious income. The main reason for making the German Legal Aid Society a separate organization was to disjoin its work from that of the older body and to have it stand independently upon its own legs. While kindly assistance during the earlier years might be justly asked and generously given, it was painfully manifest to the men fighting to establish effective New York legal aid that the German Society was likely to cut off its contributions if experience showed that the younger organization, instead of becoming self-sufficing, bade fair to be a sort of parasite. So these reports refer to the German Society's contributions in a tone of grateful hope rather than of confident assurance. President Salomon and his brother officers and directors realized clearly enough that each might be the last.

As a result of its appeals the Society received substantial occasional donations from public-spirited citizens of German extraction. Gifts of this sort in 1880 amounted to over $800 and cleared away a large deficit. Again in 1885 comes an anonymous gift of $200. Once more in 1887 donations were received from a dozen different sources aggregating considerably over $400. One particular present of this era deserves a special word. Years later, when the organization was prosperous and soundly established, it was frequently stated that early in 1888 no less a person than Emperor Wilhelm I had given money to the German Legal Aid Society. Mr. v. Briesen himself makes this statement in the report for

1907: "One of the last acts of . . . Emperor Wilhelm the Great, was to transmit, early in 1888, the sum of $250 to our Society, an action which showed the warm heart and the kindly encouragement which he ever held out to those who represented an important principle." When, in 1912, Mr. J. P. Schmitt prepared his well-known history of the Legal Aid Society of New York, the story of the imperial gift acquired another circumstantial detail. The money had come out of the Emperor's "privy purse." Now the historian's critical pen must puncture many a pleasant legend. President Salomon's report for 1888 says not a word of any royal patronage. As the Society was in hard straits at the moment, it is difficult to believe that such interesting and appealing news would have been omitted. Moreover, the statement of receipts contains the following item:

Gift of the Committee of the Memorial Exercises for Emperor William $250

Nevertheless, we cannot utterly abandon the idea of an imperial present. For Mr. Lexow recollects that in some form money *did* come from the old Kaiser. But $250, whether from Emperor or from Memorial Committee, is still only a quarter of $1000. It is not a contribution regularly to be repeated. The president and the directors of the Society were under no illusions as to the possibility of maintaining their beneficent activity on the basis of casual gifts. They solicited these only to meet unusual financial emergencies.

In the same way they arranged for entertainments, the proceeds of which were to further legal aid operations. This idea is first mentioned in 1881, when a committee was appointed "to get in touch with Messrs.

Karl Schurz, Judge Brady, Henry Ward Beecher, and others for the purpose of inducing these gentlemen to deliver one or more lectures for the benefit of the Legal Aid Society." Simultaneously a second committee was appointed "to appeal to Mmes. Geistinger and Sontag, who are giving guest performances here at present, and request them to take part in a performance to be arranged for the benefit of the Society." Nothing further is said about the activities of the first committee. We may therefore assume that for one reason or another they were unsuccessful. But the next annual report states that the Society had received the goodly sum of $504 from a benefit performance arranged at the Germania Theatre by Adolf Neuendorff. In 1884 preparations were made for a benefit concert on Washington's Birthday of 1885. William Steinway put Steinway Hall at the disposal of the Society without charge and otherwise energetically assisted. He obtained the coöperation of the Liederkranz Male Chorus. This concert was notably successful, the Society realizing more than $1150 from it. Here again, however, the officers must have felt that they were dealing with a sporadic income only.

Such were the revenues of the period. Throughout their enumeration, a question must have been growing in the reader's mind: Where was the Bar? Why was it not at once the foremost and the adequate supporter of a struggling legal reform with such great potential value? Nothing could have been more desirable, and in a way nothing would now appear more natural. For the Association of the Bar of the City of New York was already active. Legal aid work seems exactly calculated to appeal to that progressive, vigorous, and soundly idealistic organization. The Society and the Association might have joined hands forthwith to their mutual benefit. But hindsight is a deceptive guide. We can fairly judge the inadvertent failures of the nineteenth century only by throwing ourselves back into its atmosphere. Democracy, speaking broadly, was well enough known. All men had seen in Lincoln a glorious personification of idealism drawn from poor and humble sources. Possibilities of human self-improvement were not only recognized but frankly relied upon. Yet when it came to shaping economic and legal institutions so that those possibilities might be given full play, nineteenth-century American society was not to any great degree realistic or practical. The necessity of acting to democratize our administration of justice passed almost unperceived. Neither the Bar collectively, nor many of its members individually, could see what legal aid might mean to them and to the whole community in which they lived. Indeed, it is obvious that the nascent phenomenon quite escaped their notice. Little wonder! For legal aid workers themselves, modestly limited of vision, had clapped over their small light a bushel, and a Teutonic bushel at that. Only Germans were to be helped; all accounts of their Society's activities were to be couched in the German language, and to have a restricted circulation among Germans. Prior to 1890 there is very little indication that these earnest, self-sacrificing gentlemen realized that they were cherishing the germ of a conception which ought to enlist the Bar and every one of its members. So, naturally enough, at this time New York legal aid was receiving but the most scanty, hit-or-miss support from New York lawyers.

Of the revenue sources above described, only the first — membership dues — held out any promise of permanency and reliability. And even the membership dues fluctuated so that they never maintained an adequate level. The persons controlling the destinies of legal aid in New York were involved in a constant struggle to keep the wolf outside the office door. Financial events moved through repeated cycles. Starting at the end of 1876 with a slight surplus, the Society promptly rolled down grade into a heavy deficit not finally cleared up until 1882, when a tiny credit balance appeared. In the very next year there was again a deficit of $440. By hard work this was cleared away in 1885, at the end of which year there was a substantial surplus. Next year came a bigger deficit than ever, and not until 1889 did this vanish and a small surplus replace it.

Money uncertainties, besides constantly worrying the officers and making precarious the continuance of legal aid, had at least one definitely hampering effect. The report for 1883 indicates this by saying: "The Attorney of the Society is Mr. Charles K. Lexow, *whose office hours are 9–10 A.M. and 3–5 P.M.*" Suspicion of a divided allegiance receives full confirmation within two years: "In reference to Mr. Lexow's position . . . the Directors have found themselves compelled to make him certain concessions to retain . . . his excellent services, now all the more valuable because of ten years' experience; this was necessary since our financial situation did not permit a direct increase of his salary, which is certainly very modest. The principal points are that he is allowed to devote to his private practice a portion of his time, especially the morning hours, and retain from the suits won in the higher courts half of any costs allowed . . . and paid." So, for the moment and for some years to come, fell the standard of the single allegiance. Most emphatically no criticism can justly be levelled at Mr.

Lexow. He had sacrificed himself from the first by working at a sub-starvation wage, and the sacrifice had increased with the passage of time. But from now on until the system again changed, he and his successors were to be subjected to painful counter-hauling of their private interests on one side and the Society's interests on the other, a tension made all the more painful by their great general devotion to the poor legal aid clients.

Two incidents of the period call for special comment. The first was closely connected with the financial problem. It can best be told by quotation from President Salomon's report for 1886: "A man living in very humble circumstances and apparently poor, by the name of Wilhelm Eger, who as our books show had sought and found opportunity to ask the services of the Society for himself, died suddenly in the attic room occupied by him. At the coroner's inquest there were found in the trunk of the deceased securities to the value of something like $4000 together with a last will drawn by himself and dated 8 July 1883, in which he bequeathed his property to our Society. The man had no near relatives here, he lived in a quarter of the city from which come a great part of our clients seeking aid, had himself found help with us, and wished to make the Society his heir. Unfortunately the will was invalid since it was not executed in the presence of witnesses, and the good intentions of this grateful client are going to be thwarted." Subsequent investigation shows that the estate of Mr. Eger passed through the hands of a public administrator to the comptroller's office to await problematical next of kin. Whether they appeared and made successful claim, or whether the fund ultimately escheated to the state, the German Legal Aid Society never saw a dollar of it.

Of course this incident inflicted no actual loss upon the Society. None of its members had ever dreamed that a legacy might come from the poor client. But to have had so fair a chance and then to have failed was extremely discouraging. The incident clearly made President Salomon feel that the fates were against his enterprise. Incidentally it seems to be a piece of tantalizing injustice that an organization whose great aim was to give sound legal advice to poor persons should find itself worse off because a would-be donor lacked such advice. Possibly Mr. Eger fell into error by taking counsel of some dog-eared "Everyman's Lawyer." But without too deeply infringing the maxim, *de mortuis nil nisi bonum*, we may hazard another explanation. It has perhaps occurred to the reader that a man worth $4000 is no proper client for a poor person's lawyer. Very possibly a similar reflection entered Mr. Eger's mind. Hence he dared not ask advice upon the subject of making a will. And thus because a client was imposing upon it the German Legal Aid Society failed to receive in one lump enough money to carry on its work for an entire year or to insure it against deficits for many years to come.

The same twelvemonth signalized by this disappointment contained another even more important and vastly more encouraging incident. About 1885 suspicious advertisements of a society calling itself "New York Legal Aid Society" (New Yorker Rechtsschutzverein) began to appear in the German newspapers. These advertisements offered services free to poor persons in need, and especially declared readiness to conduct the collection of inheritances. The officers of the German Legal Aid Society investigated and found "that the affair was not in very clean hands; and although the society was regularly incorporated . . . nevertheless succeeded by suit brought against it by [their own] Society in stopping its activity since [they] proved that it had adopted its name, so similar to [that of the German Legal Aid Society], for improper purposes." The court appealed to permanently enjoined the promoters of the New York Legal Aid Society from using the name which they had adopted. That decree should be printed in letters of gold and hung on the Society's wall. It marks the earliest known case in which a genuine legal aid organization suppressed what Mr. v. Briesen aptly terms "a wolf in sheep's clothing." We shall see that similar cases arose again and again. Establishment of the original precedent was of the highest moment to legal aid in the United States. Had not the president and directors taken prompt action, had not the New York courts wisely made their action effective, the term "legal aid" would unquestionably have become infected in this country with the same taint of suspicion and bad odor which now infects it in England.

At the beginning of 1889 an important change occurred. Mr. Lexow, who had for thirteen years conducted the legal activities of the Society with such skill and ability that the directors found constant reason to praise him, felt compelled to resign. His salary was ridiculously meagre. He could not continue indefinitely his personal financial sacrifice. Hence his resignation was accepted as of January 17, 1889, and Herman C. Kudlich was appointed to his place. When closing their contract with Mr. Kudlich, the officers and directors entered upon a new policy. They undertook to pay the incoming Attorney a lump sum of $250 per month, in exchange for which the Attorney was to pay the rent, all expenses of the office including the salary of his assistants, and his own salary. This, of course, relieved the directors of considerable detail. But it required a high spirit of self-sacrifice on the part of the Attorney. He needed ample office facilities and working force to serve his clients adequately. He would be tempted to skimp on expenses in order to make his own compensation — small enough at best — as large as might be. It is a pleasure to say that there is no evidence that any Attorney yielded to the temptation.

Coming thus to the end of the first period of the Society's existence, we may appropriately close by speaking in some detail of the report for 1889. Its most striking feature, tucked away toward the end, consists of a tabulation of the nationality of the Society's clients. This tabulation shows that during the year 1889 only 2438 clients were of German nationality or extraction. The remainder, nearly 1100, came from a score of other countries including the United States itself. Interestingly enough, two clients are noted as from Jerusalem. Perhaps we are discovering the record of a changed policy at its very inception. Mr. Lexow is clear and positive that during his incumbency no non-German cases had been taken. Now according to its constitution the Society was confined to the relief of those of German birth. Consequently the employment of its funds for the sake of Americans, Austrians, Serbians, Englishmen and Frenchmen, Dutch, Russians, Peruvians, and all the others in the long list, constituted what lawyers term an *ultra vires* act of the deepest dye. But we suspect that the recording angel who keeps the celestial account books for corporations with souls has somehow twisted his statements here, and put this *ultra vires* act into the credit column! It manifested an attitude that was to have profoundly beneficial results.

Otherwise this report for 1889 is not cheering. To be sure, its words and tone are far from downhearted. The writer speaks enthusiastically of the benefits brought about by the Society's work: "We may . . . assert definitely that no other institution . . . accomplishes more and better results with such slender resources. With double its present membership this Society could exist independently, and we hope to reach this goal in not too distant time." Whether President Salomon in view of his repeated disappointments could have penned the last sentence is doubtful. When this report was prepared, however, the president was in Europe on an extended absence and the writing was done for him by F. W. Holls, president *pro tempore*. It is to be feared that Mr. Holls sounded optimistic largely because he had less often experienced the causes for pessimism.

His report shows that even from its clients the Society did not receive undiluted praise or gratitude. "In spite of all the sacrificing effort of the Attorney he is . . . blamed for any lack of success and must often put up with hints of 'selling out' and other injustice. However, we are concerned to bring our aid to precisely these poor and ignorant and ungrateful folk and to help them to secure their rights wherever possible, and for that reason the demands we have to make upon our officers are so heavy. All complaints presented on the part of our clients have been carefully examined by the undersigned and the directors, and up to the present all of them could justly be refuted as unfounded." This is a difficulty which has been constantly experienced and steadfastly faced throughout legal aid history. The pathetic gratitude of most clients has an unpleasant counterpoise in the even more pathetic suspicion of others.

The year closed with a small surplus. But this was obtained only because the German Society contributed no less than $1968.96, a much larger amount than it had ever given in any single preceding year. Moreover, as has already been pointed out, the Society had for fourteen years been swinging through an uncomfortable series of debt cycles. First a small surplus, then almost at once a heavy deficit followed by a long slow pull to solvency, and then again a sudden heavy deficit. Hence, on the basis of the past, another sinking spell might be expected for 1890.

More serious still, the body of men who had worked so hard to wipe out deficits and build credit balances was now greatly depleted. In 1882 Mr. Faller, the generous and competent assistant attorney, had died. President Salomon, whose resolute constancy had been of great value, never again actively took the lead. He remained for several years as a vice-president, but his interest, although continued until his death at an advanced age, became a long-range matter after his removal to Germany in 1894 because of his wife's ill health. Willy Wallach, a founder of the Society, who for years rendered active and effective service as vice-president, had died in 1882. Another founder and the original vice-president, Sigismund Kaufmann, died on August 17, 1889. He was a man of eminent generosity and his loss was a heavy one. Charles Hauselt died February 7, 1890, just before the report for 1889 went to press. He had been a director of the German Legal Aid Society and also president of the German Society. In the latter capacity he was ever ready to urge the interests of the younger, more struggling organization. The large and constant aid which the German Society had granted was for the most part due to his advocacy. Thus the old personnel was breaking down. With the passing of the few whose individual efforts had kept the enterprise afloat for fourteen years there seemed real danger that the whole organization might founder in the collective indifference of the community.

III

THE NEW LEADER

BUT how different was the fact from the foreboding! The opening sentences of the report for 1890 come like a clean sea-breeze, freshening the air and dispersing lowering thunder-clouds at the end of a dark sultry day. A ringing quotation from Emerson leads the way: "The demon of reform has a secret door into the heart of every lawmaker, of every inhabitant of every city. The fact that a new thought and hope have dawned in your breast should apprise you that in the same hour a new life broke in upon a thousand private hearts." Then the Society's new president speaks for himself — and speaks no longer in German alone, but also in English: "The progress made by our Society during the past year is unprecedented. From an organization but charily supported, unable to maintain itself without assistance from other charitable institutions, and ever struggling to do justice to its aims, it has, during the past twelve months, grown into stout and healthy proportions. Its membership was increased from eighty-one to one hundred and seventy. The income which resulted from this increase in membership enabled us to pay all needful expenses, still leaving a substantial surplus in our treasury." Plainly the Society had experienced a dramatic rebirth. No more was it to fight for life with its back to the wall. During its long history it has suffered many disappointments. But since 1890 these have been always the disappointments of impeded progress. Practically never is there any retrogression, and certainly never even a thought of giving up the work. This vigorous rebirth was to affect the social conditions not only of New York City, but also of the whole United States and, in a measurable degree, of the civilized world.

To a most extraordinary extent the striking change resulted from the personality of a single man — Arthur v. Briesen. Mr. v. Briesen came of an honored German family which can trace its pedigree back into the ninth century. He was born at Borckendorf, in northern Posen, on July 11, 1843, and obtained his early education in the gymnasia (high schools) of the towns of Hohenstein and Braunsberg. His father, Richard v. Briesen, a retired officer of the Prussian army, realizing the great opportunities offered by America, sold his landed estates in Prussia and came to New York in 1856. Soon he appears as representing the German Association of the State of Missouri (Deutsche Gesellschaft des Staates Missouri), and so helping to place German immigrants in the West. His son Arthur reached New York during the summer of 1858. A few months later the elder v. Briesen returned temporarily to Germany, leaving Arthur behind. The boy lived partly with his older brother, and for some time was a housemate of Franz Sigel. In after years Arthur v. Briesen told of having undergone extreme poverty. He had existed on one dollar a week, short commons even in the mid-nineteenth century. Very likely this experience fell at the time of his father's absence. Thus he gained an insight into, and a lifelong sympathy for, the hardships of the poor.

Richard v. Briesen came back to America, bringing the rest of his immediate family, about the beginning of 1861. They arrived, the v. Briesens used to say, just in time to fall into the Civil War. The youth Arthur had meanwhile gone through a miscellaneous industrial training. He worked in a cigar-maker's establishment; learned the cabinet-making trade at his father's desire; worked for William Gibson, a manufacturer of stained-glass windows; and later entered the office of Olmstead & Vaux, the landscape architects who collaborated with General Veilé in laying out Central Park. Then came the war and Lincoln's first call for troops. Now Arthur v. Briesen was only eighteen. Also he was slightly lame. But he responded unhesitatingly to the call, passed the sketchy medical examination, and went off with the First New York Volunteer Engineers. He participated in the capture of Beaufort, Fort Pulaski, and other Confederate strongholds, and as a sergeant served before Forts Wagner and Beauregard.

Richard v. Briesen remained at New York, having invested his capital in a chemist's or drug concern. He financed experiments intended to produce compressed household yeast such as is commonly used to-day. He had at one time several business establishments, but by 1863 had concentrated his plant in a single building at the corner of Thirty-fourth Street and Second Avenue. His eyesight was failing, and in the summer of this year Arthur v. Briesen came north on furlough to learn about the situation at first hand. He had reached New York when the draft riots terrorized the city on Monday, July 13, 1863, and the days following. These riots incidentally brought business disaster to the v. Briesen family.

Colonel H. F. O'Brien, having been put in command of troops against the mobs, acted with severity which the rioters regarded as brutality. At or near Richard v. Briesen's place of business, the Colonel recklessly separated himself from his soldiers, tried to brave a mob single-handed, and was attacked. Accounts of what followed are naturally somewhat confused and inconsistent. The New York *Tribune* paraphrases a detailed description by an eye-witness, the Reverend Father Clowry. From this it appears that O'Brien was at once overpowered, and slowly battered to death with a measured ferocity almost inconceivable. The wretched man did not die until after hours of this torture; his murderers grimly prevented outside interference, and "when a humane druggist went to him and gave him a drink of water, the mob entered [the druggist's] store and gutted it from end to end." The druggist, of course, was Richard v. Briesen. In addition to demolishing the contents of his shop, the mob inflicted severe personal injuries upon him. Arthur v. Briesen reached the scene just as the work of destruction was at its height, and aided his father to escape. For Richard v. Briesen this was the final blow. He retired from commercial activity. In the next year he went blind.

It became necessary for one of the sons to look after the family home. The elder was at this time in the navy, and wished to remain. As Arthur's term of enlistment was about to expire, the choice fell upon him. He took over responsibility for the family, joined the staff of the *Scientific American*, and worked for the next eight years on draftsmanship and the preparation of patent specifications. He was notably competent and ingenious. For example, he devised a peculiar method of mechanical drawing which enabled him greatly to increase his output. He also had remarkable powers of concentration. Thus, simultaneously with his regular work, he studied law at New York University, prepared for and passed his examinations in a phenomenally short time, and was admitted to the Bar in 1868. This rounded out his first ten years of life since immigration.

Certainly the period had been packed to bursting with experience and progress.

His employers, Messrs. Munn & Company, realized Mr. v. Briesen's unusual ability and generously did everything they could to help him. They made his work more and more responsible, and, after his admission to practice, permitted him to attend to some of their clients' patent litigation. In 1874 Mr. v. Briesen launched out independently as a lawyer, specializing from the beginning in patent work. Later, partners joined him and he became the senior member of three successive law firms. He gained distinguished success. A German of the best type, he was thorough, honest, and kindly; a trained handicraftsman, he was practical; a volunteer soldier for liberty and union, he was courageous, enterprising, and a lover of freedom. Moreover, all his qualities were shaped and directed by a veritable passion for justice. This happily led him to his greatest and most enduring achievement in securing equality before the law for the poor.

Mr. v. Briesen was not, as is generally supposed, a charter member of the German Legal Aid Society. He joined in 1884 or early 1885; became a director in 1889, being then or shortly thereafter placed upon the Law Committee; and in 1890, when Governor Salomon could no longer lead the organization, was elected president. He later jocosely explained the election by saying that "there was no other fool upon whose hands to let the Society die." But his acts thoroughly belie this little pleasantry. He galvanized the failing invalid into astounding activity.

Mr. v. Briesen had the straightforward power of expression which goes with earnestness and clear thinking — a very genuine, effective type of eloquence. His annual reports for the next ten years contain the classic justifications of legal aid. Thus: "I believe in the support of hospitals, in diet-kitchens, dispensaries and all those things which are calculated to bring the animal in man into a normal and satisfactory condition; but after the animal has been satisfied there is in the human existence that which longs for a higher grade of gratification and satisfaction, and that which in the absence of the highest principle of liberty leaves the well-fed and otherwise healthy man nevertheless perfectly unhappy. To bring happiness into the households of the poor, to restore it where it has been unjustly marred, to withdraw from the suffering heart the sting which the tyranny of the individual is liable to leave, is the principal object of [this] institution. . . . It is strange that the human mind more readily appreciates the suffering of the body than that of the soul. We are always ready to come to the assistance of those who are afflicted in the body; we generously support hospitals innumerable in which that phase of suffering seeks and finds relief; but though we all know what it is to suffer from tyrannical or unjust treatment, and have undergone and tested the agony of soul which follows the unsuccessful effort to right our wrongs, still we do not readily appear to sympathize with these sufferings in others. By the efforts of the German Legal Aid Society great and harrowing sorrow has frequently been made to vanish, and many thousands have through its work been sent to their homes satisfied that even the poorest has the opportunity for the enforcement of his rights. No one will dare withhold wages from one entitled to receive them, so long as the German Legal Aid Society stands on guard; no one will dare to trample the rights of the poor and helpless under foot, as long as the appearance of the Society's attorney in court demands respect and a careful consideration of the rights of its clients."

"Whosoever reads this report with care, if able to come to our assistance, yet [failing] so to do, should assign good and sufficient reason for staying away. The work done by us comes home to every citizen; it keeps the poor satisfied, because it establishes and protects their rights; it produces better workingmen and better workingwomen, better house servants; it antagonizes the tendency towards communism; it is the best argument against the socialist who cries that the poor have no rights which the rich are bound to respect. Communism and socialism have, it seems, lost their grip upon our New York population since our Society has done its effective work in behalf of the poor, *whose wrongs it righted.* The more than fifty thousand clients who have been served by our Attorneys are the best preachers for the fairness of our institutions that can be sent amongst the masses. . . . For what we do is not only to help the individual. We are satisfied that we help preserve within a large city, which is peopled by incongruous elements drawn from all the nooks and corners of the universe, a moral equilibrium. We teach those who try to wrong others that they can no longer do so with impunity, and, therefore, better them. We teach those who have been wronged against that their suffering is our matter, and that the injustice done them must be undone, and we undo it, thereby turning dissatisfaction into delight and happiness."

Mr. v. Briesen's enthusiasm roused a kindred flame in others. "One of the associate counsel, Mr. Sanders . . . abandoned his office to come to us, and has worked for . . . $4 per week." For this kind of pittance members of the Attorney's force labored from seven A.M. to nine

P.M. The rush of applicants was tremendous, toward the end of the century rarely under fifty a day. The work was so heavy, the pay so small, that no room existed for sloth or selfishness. "Under the circumstances," wrote Mr. v. Briesen, "these attorneys are really entitled to at least three times the amount now received by them. We are too poor to do [pay?] this and are, therefore, forced to draw on their generosity. *It is like a charity concert. The performers give their time and effort — the public enjoy the performance and receive an equivalent for their expenditure, but think that THEY are doing the charitable work.*" Nothing, perhaps, has more touchingly retained the spirit of the office than an obituary published in 1893. Its author was Robert Goeller, the Society's third Attorney, who succeeded Mr. Kudlich on October 1, 1892. "This Report would be incomplete if it did not chronicle the death of Clemens H. Harder. For fourteen years he was the book-keeper and head of the Information Bureau in the office of the Attorney. One administration of attorneys succeeded another, but the same old familiar figure sat year after year in the same position. Most of the clients believed that he was the head of the office, and that the Attorney was only his clerk or assistant. He had a loving, tender way and soft speech which gave hope to the hopeless and cheer to the cheerless. There were none so old whom he could not call child, and toward whom he did not act as a father. He died in harness. On the 28th day of November, 1892, he complained of pain and left the office at three o'clock in the afternoon. He grew worse on his way home to Paterson, and had to be carried from the station to his house. He never left his bed, and died of typhoid fever on the 9th day of December, 1892. The gap he leaves in the Attorney's office is large, and his successor must be a man of generous and sympathetic heart and great tact, to begin to fill the vacancy."

Nor will another quotation from Mr. Goeller be amiss: "As we look back over the old year, the amount of money collected for our clients seems hardly commensurate with the amount of time, energy, worry and money expended, but after all, the principal good done is that which does not appear in a report, and does not even come to our knowledge. Many a man and woman has been given courage to keep up the battle of life by a kind word of sympathy and advice, and many reconciliations have been effected. The spirit of equality before the law, which teaches that the poor man has equal rights with the rich, has been instilled into the minds of our clients. On the other hand, the litigious spirit has been suppressed as far as possible. Anarchy and socialism have been combatted, and the whole trend of the work of the Society has been toward the uplifting and encouragement of our fellow-men who have been less fortunate than ourselves, by giving them a glimpse of a higher culture and of a higher life, and implanting in them a sincere belief, founded on acts, in the universal brotherhood of man and the fatherhood of God."

Thus the men, young and old, working out the Society's destiny were dreaming dreams and seeing visions. As early as 1898 they began to receive requests from persons in other states for suggestions as to organizing legal aid societies. Their horizon broadened swiftly. They believed that to their hands had been entrusted an instrument for social well-being which would override city, state, and even national boundaries. They felt the inspiration of a great future.

Had this been all a matter of fine words and exalted sentiment, nothing lasting would have come of it. But the new president at once proved his practical wisdom. Boldly and soundly he broadened the base of activities. In October, 1890, the purpose clause was revised to read thus: "[The Society's] object and purpose shall be, to render legal aid and assistance, *gratuitously if necessary*, to *all* who may appear worthy thereof and who, from poverty, are unable to procure it." The italics show the changes. The first change regularized a well-established practice of charging what clients could afford. Rarely was this the full cost of service. Even the smallest normal lawyer's bill would utterly unsettle the finances of a man supporting his family on ten, fifteen, or twenty dollars each week. But this man is no pauper; he usually has a fine disdain for pure charity, and genuine dignity in paying to the limit of his means for service received. The second constitutional change made New York legal aid a universal matter, unbounded by racial lines. This involved serious considerations. It meant foregoing the support of the German Society, which could not properly donate funds for cosmopolitan purposes. Hence there was hesitation and doubt. Mr. v. Briesen, however, stood to his guns and put through the alteration. Having done so, he gave it the greatest possible public emphasis. "When we say," asserts the report for 1891, "'to *all* who may be worthy thereof' we mean '*all*.' No distinction is made because of nationality or color." While the rich, who might become the patrons and supporters of the organization, did not too quickly catch the significance of this, the poor, who were to be the clients, took the point instantly. Without tracing the shifting figures in detail, it suffices to say that by 1900 only about one fifth of the current clients were Germans, and nearly one quarter were natives of the United States. The other clients originated in about seventy different countries, spread over the globe from Iceland to Australia.

Curiously enough, and yet quite naturally, it proved harder to broaden the Society's name than to broaden its purposes. Old names enshrine much sentiment, and we cling to them. The president felt that the title "Deutscher Rechts-Schutz Verein" definitely handicapped the institution's progress outside German circles. He hammered the point both orally and in his reports, finally obtaining the alteration to "The Legal Aid Society" in 1896. Here again was real and enduring doubt. Even Mr. Goeller, not an inch behind his chief in desire to help every proper applicant, saw merit to the old name; the word "German," he said, had "a ring of sincerity, pertinacity and justice." Well along in the twentieth century one of the local German language newspapers, after recounting the Legal Aid Society's achievements, closed the item with a gently plaintive "Pity it is no more the German Legal Aid Society" ("Schade, dass sie nicht mehr der 'Deutsche Rechtsschutzverein' ist"). Yet there is no possibility of doubt that Mr. v. Briesen was right, and the sentimentalists wrong, about the change to an accurately descriptive English name.

The new president appreciated the desirability of drawing men of the highest standing to the Society as officers and directors. Evidently with this purpose he caused the constitutional provision for "*a* Vice-President" to become a provision for "*one or more* Vice-Presidents." Carl Schurz, whom Mr. v. Briesen numbered among his friends, came to the Society as a member and a director in 1890. In 1896 he became one of six vice-presidents. Next year there were ten vice-presidents, including James C. Carter, Joseph H. Choate, Robert

W. DeForest, Elihu Root, and Theodore Roosevelt. Also Jacob A. Riis appears among the directors. The fourteen vice-presidents for 1898 include Jacob H. Schiff. Many more names known and respected far beyond New York City might be noted. Nor were these men mere figureheads. The directors and officers of The Legal Aid Society have always generously devoted their time to the furtherance and careful supervision of its work.

On the growth of this work, a brief statistical statement may be tolerated. When Mr. v. Briesen paused for breath and to take stock of the situation in 1896, he wrote that "during the first year of our existence, to wit, in the year 1876, the number of our clients was 212, and the amount they recovered was $1000. In the twenty-first year of our existence we had 35 times as many clients and recovered 71 times as much money. During the first year the Society's expenses were $1000; during the last year a little less than $7000. Every dollar expended by the Society, therefore, during the first year only brought $1 to the clients in return; while at the present time every dollar spent by us brings $10 to our clients. Altogether, The Legal Aid Society gave its services during the twenty-one years of its existence to 80,872 clients, and recovered in their behalf the sum of $581,146.55." And once more he emphasized the non-financial side: "In addition to the actual work connected with claims for compensation, the Society's attorneys give a large part of their time to what may be called educational work. Tens of thousands of the inhabitants of this city are foreigners, totally ignorant of our laws, incapable of appreciating the prevailing ideas of right and wrong. Many of them are permeated with distorted and absurd notions in that regard. It frequently happens, therefore — and this applies to thousands of cases in the Attorney's office — that persons deem themselves wronged who, as a matter of fact, are either not wronged at all or have themselves transgressed the boundaries of propriety. To these the attorneys act as guides and as instructors, thereby tending to make them more enlightened and better citizens." The climax comes in 1900, when the Society handled the prodigious number of 14,365 cases. The increase over 1899 was 5000, and over 1898 about 9000. During the single year 1900 the organization recovered for its clients $96,704.45. In its twenty-five years of existence it had served 115,661 individuals and recovered for them $869,970.74. The cases had been handled at a total cost of $112,764.79, or under ninety-eight cents apiece. In 1894, a star year for economy, the average cost per case was seventy-six cents! This was no visionary philanthropy, but perhaps the largest and certainly the most money-saving law-office ever conducted in the United States.

Inevitably the question arises whether this huge, swift expansion caused the quality of service to decline. The managers of the Society were keenly awake to the danger. It was possible, to begin with, that inadequacy of mere physical accommodations would fatally hamper the Attorney's force. This was guarded against. During the first quarter-century of its existence the Society moved half-a-dozen times. On the whole, each move brought it into better-placed and more adequate quarters. In 1895 it left Nassau Street entirely because the building housing its office was to be torn down. This change carried the office to 233 Broadway, an excellent location. After some shifts and rearrangements at this address, the Society in February, 1897, moved to

239 Broadway. Here adequate quarters were available and here the main office stayed for over thirty years.

We have already observed the unfortunate division of the Attorney's time necessitated by his inadequate salary from the Society. Mr. v. Briesen fully appreciated the hardships and dangers of a divided loyalty. It seems that almost immediately after his election as president the Attorney's contract was altered so that he might no longer devote any part of his time to private business. In connection with this change it should be stated that from time to time during the period now being discussed the salaries of the Attorney and his assistants were increased to the very limit of the Society's means. Attention has been called to the fact that the contract with Mr. Kudlich made the Attorney a sort of independent contractor with the Society. In return for a lump-sum payment he was to provide a complete working office, including assistants and the necessary clerical staff. The contract for the exclusive services of the Attorney did not extend to his assistants. Thus arose the anomalous situation of a chief Attorney bound to devote his entire time to the Society, but with subordinates who might take such private business as they could sandwich in. In 1897 Mr. Goeller resigned, being succeeded by Carl Lincoln Schurz, son of the elder Carl Schurz. This occasion was seized upon to correct the anomaly just described. The contract of Mr. Schurz provided that the Society should furnish the Attorney with an office to be used exclusively for the Society's business; also that all persons there employed by the Attorney should be engaged with the approval of the directors and subject to discharge if the directors so determined. Obviously this accomplished a much closer articulation of operating and supervising activities.

In dealing with the great mass of cases now presented, the Society took special care to make adequate preliminary investigations of the applicants' claims. This was perhaps the most important part of Mr. Harder's work. After his death the system of preliminary investigation was steadily carried on and developed. Ultimately this work grew into what is now termed the "front desk" department of the main office. It was and is the normal practice to take no legal action against a defendant without giving him full opportunity to explain his side of the case. Thus the Society could fairly say, as it did in its reports, that it had protected the prosperous from the poor, as well as the poor from the prosperous. Every vicious or clearly erroneous demand was rejected. No "applicant" became a "client" until shown to have a righteous cause. Naturally enough, too, the investigative procedure tended to make the registrar or "front desk" man a very effective arbitrator. Thousands of disputes were settled by mutual agreement of the contending parties under his advice. Often, perhaps usually, it was not merely expedient but just to meet a settlement offer by knocking off a few dollars. The calm, disinterested, experienced front-desk man had the best chance in the world to smooth down an angry claimant and make him see reason. Very frequently, too, he could persuade claimants theoretically entitled to money that the sums sought were too small to justify the wasting of their time on legal proceedings, or the chances of satisfying judgments too visionary to be worth pursuing. Every sort of baseless or useless litigation met firm discouragement.

In its anxiety to weed out futile claims and those stained with bad faith, the Society temporarily adopted a provision that, where investigation showed court action to be the only practicable method of enforcing a demand, the client should pay a litigation fee of one dollar before the case was started. This sum rarely sufficed to cover the bare cash expenses of commencing suit. Moreover, the money was never required of clients genuinely without means, "but in a great many cases, persons perfectly able to pay were restrained from pressing unimportant or imaginary claims by the fact that it would have cost them one dollar to set the machinery of the Society in motion." At a later time this requirement of a litigation fee was revoked, more satisfactory methods of winnowing out bad cases having been devised. Still, as a rough and ready test it worked well for several years. Incidentally, though for a somewhat different purpose, the practice of taking a ten-cent retainer fee was introduced. Here the thought was to remove the sting of charity and make the client feel that he received assistance as a regular business matter, and not by favor. Also the percentage charge on recoveries of ten dollars or more was continued. To place its stand still higher above reproach the Society began definitely refusing certain classes of claims. For instance, it would not lend aid to the adjustment of tenement-house quarrels, appear in cases of barroom brawls, or intervene where both parties were about equally at fault. We shall have occasion to trace further the development of this practice.

The natural consequence of such careful sifting was a notably high degree of success in those cases actually accepted and prosecuted. Moreover, the very fact of painstaking selection gave opportunity for tendering valuable advice to many who did not understand the customs and habits of the country. On the whole, they gratefully received and faithfully followed this counsel.

Many a poor man called at the office saying: "I do not come here to sue, but want your advice. What shall I do under such and such circumstances?" Thus the Society entered the field of preventive law. Looking over its work as a whole it could truthfully state: "We are loved by the poor, feared by the unjust, and respected by those whose tendencies and instincts are noble."

Certain particular matters may be referred to as indicating growing energy and power. It will be recollected that the panic of 1873 for years hampered free development of legal aid work. In 1893 came another extremely severe financial disturbance. But the Society's balance-sheet shows at the end of 1893 more cash on hand than had been available at the end of 1892. While the sum shrank somewhat before the end of 1894, the next year closed with a substantial credit balance. There are constant indications of a valuable and growing good-will. Practically all the other beneficent organizations in New York coöperated freely and enthusiastically. On January 22, 1898, the officers of the Society gave a dinner at Delmonico's. Among the speakers were Rabbi Gustav Gottheil, Bishop Henry C. Potter, Honorable Seth Low, and Father Ducey. This list of names vividly indicates the universal appeal of legal aid work. It is significant that during this period and throughout its later history the Society has had a "good press," ever ready with favorable publicity for its efforts and accomplishments. Even before 1900 the informal partnership between legal aid and the official machinery of justice began to function. Through the nineties many cases were sent in, and many clients helped, by policemen, court officials, and judges. Foremost among its public allies the Society counted City

Marshal Morris Einstein. From the date of his appointment under Mayor Strong, this official did practically all the Legal Aid's city-marshal work, serving process upon slippery defendants and levying execution against elusive property with ingenuity, energy, and persistence which brought tears of gratitude to the Attorney's eyes.

But one difficulty in collecting under small executions would have balked even this doughty marshal had not good friends of justice cleared it away. A marshal or sheriff levying execution must carefully confine his efforts to property of the particular individual against whom judgment has been rendered. If he sells or seizes the goods of another person, he may properly enough be sued for damages. Hence in case of doubtful ownership the officer quite justly calls upon the plaintiff for indemnity against painful consequences. Now, the typical legal aid client is in no position to indemnify anybody. Here, then, was a condition made to order for exploitation by the shifty, unconscionable debtors whom the Society so often pursues. The marshal preparing to levy upon articles apparently belonging to the judgment debtor would be faced with an affidavit, bill of sale, chattel mortgage, or other document indicating ownership or some claim by a third person, and would be told that he proceeded at his peril. To be sure, the third-party claimant was often the wife or a near relative of the defendant. Appearances indicated a fraudulent scheme to hinder the creditor. Yet the marshal feared putting it to the test. The consequence was no light one. A poor man, seeing his judgment thus rendered futile, would gain a low idea of the law's practical efficiency.

This was bad enough, but only the beginning of the story. Let an incident still vividly remembered by the first Attorney suggest further details. Late in the afternoon preceding a Memorial Day holiday, some time between 1880 and 1889, a distressed German mechanic waited upon Mr. Lexow. A creditor had seized the applicant's necessary working-tools. These being exempt from execution, the seizure was quite unlawful. The man urgently desired the immediate return of his tools so that he might continue earning his livelihood. With great patience and difficulty Mr. Lexow explained that the only summary method of getting back the property was to give a bond with sureties or security of some sort. Of course the poor workman had no security and those members of the Society who might have met the emergency by pledging their personal credit had already left town. The case must wait until the business houses reopened and business men came back. Having heard this explanation, the applicant went dejectedly away. Mr. Lexow spent his holiday in the country. When he returned, the newspaper headlines fairly leaped to his eye. The workman, despairing of justice, had committed suicide by throwing himself off Brooklyn Bridge. Oddly enough, and most unjustly, this tragedy brought down upon the Society much resentful criticism. No wonder that the second president bent his energies toward solving the whole indemnity problem!

After long consideration of ways and means, it was decided that the best remedy would be an indemnity fund from which could be produced security whenever reasonably demanded by marshals or sheriffs. To Mr. v. Briesen's delight Mrs. Lucy L. Schroeder in 1897 offered to deposit $2500 for the purpose, provided that another person could be found to contribute a similar amount. Within twenty-four hours after Mrs. Schroeder's offer, William G. Low notified Mr. v. Briesen that he stood ready to produce the other half of the fund.

The collateral was deposited with the Lawyers' Surety Company as security for bonds.

Good results followed immediately. It rarely proved necessary actually to pledge any part of the fund. The levying officers now had backbone and confidence; the rascally defendants were, after all, mere bluffers. Usually the judgments were paid to avoid seizures of property. But in less contentious matters the fund saw active service. A woman, lately widowed, sought administration of her husband's estate. She must give a bond and, being penniless, could not do so herself. The fund bonded her. Minor children were entitled to money in the hands of the City Chamberlain or Comptroller, which money could be paid only to a duly appointed guardian. The fund bonded the guardian. These cases are but illustrations of dozens in which this deposit of security enabled the Society to obtain swiftly for its needy clients assets which otherwise might have been frozen for months or even years. By careful selection of the cases to be taken up and the persons to be bonded, the Attorney maintained the Schroeder–Low fund intact without loss.

Once more, as might have been expected, came on the battle with the "wolves in sheep's clothing" — the false legal aid societies. This developed into a fairly continuous fight. The courts were evidently ready to give all help within their power, and several injunction suits went through successfully. To obtain an injunction, however, it was necessary to prove that a money-making concern had by false use of a name containing the magic words "legal aid" actually deceived specified persons. Such proof could not always be had. Besides, the injunction carried little sting for the immediate defendant's past actions and no sting at all for future "wolves" who must be suppressed by fresh proceedings. Plainly, penal legislation was the proper remedy, and it is a wise departure from strict chronological presentation to cover the entire matter by stating that in 1908 an adequate bill was drafted under the supervision of the Legal Aid Society, duly introduced in the New York legislature, and finally enacted into law. Its terms were broad, and it now protects many worthy institutions from a very vicious form of unfair competition. This law forbids anybody, under criminal penalty, to use for gainful purposes the name, or a deceptive variant of the name, of a New York benevolent, humane, or charitable corporation. Also there is a provision for injunctive relief against actual or threatened violation of the act, without the necessity of proving that any person has in fact been misled or deceived. Since this legislation the Society has been forced to protect its good name only against the guerilla activities of false subscription agents and similar minor social vermin.

We have already seen how greatly the membership increased immediately after Mr. v. Briesen's election. The preceding administration, in order to raise more money from dues, had unsuccessfully tried the experiment of instituting expensive life memberships. The new administration felt that a given money contribution counted more heavily if it came from many small donors rather than from a single great philanthropist. So it began on precisely the opposite tack. In 1890 the constitution was amended to provide for a class of members to be called "associate members," whose annual dues should be one half the annual dues of the regular members. This was an extremely successful move. A great many people genuinely interested in the Society and desiring to help it could not afford to pay $20 a year but could and would pay $10. In 1900, 278 out of a total of 510 members were of the "associate" class. Having accomplished this development in the low-priced direction, the Society again turned its attention to more costly memberships for wealthier supporters. By a constitutional amendment adopted during December, 1900, it was provided that persons paying $1000 or more in a lump sum might be admitted as life members, while those members paying $100 annually should be designated as patrons. This change also was well timed, since no fewer than nine patrons are immediately disclosed on the list of members, the leading name of the group being Andrew Carnegie.

Mr. v. Briesen had always a pleasing courtly turn of thought and speech toward the other sex. He refers to the Working Women's Protective Union as the Society's "one lovely sister." So he rejoiced greatly when in 1891 Mrs. Anna Woerishoeffer appeared upon the membership records. Had he been able to look a decade ahead and see a woman as chief attorney, his pleasure would have doubled. Additional women members enrolled themselves, and by 1899 a strong Women's Committee was coöperating with the officers and directors. The first group of patrons included Mrs. Woerishoeffer. The first and only life member admitted before the Society's twenty-fifth birthday was Mrs. Schroeder. Her selection was a graceful and well-deserved recognition of the fact that, after lending her share of the security fund for some years, she gave it to the Society. Here we see the proper method of dealing with life-membership payments. The fund was carefully held in its integrity and not dissipated upon current expenses.

But the Society still had to strike a balance between limited resources and growing ambition for service.

There were disappointing indications that the community as a whole did not appreciate what was being done through legal aid work. In 1894, Mr. Goeller quoted a popular recent novel by Frank R. Stockton in which a leading character proposed "to found a law hospital, where those persons who were unable to pay for legal protection should receive it as freely as the ailing poor receive medicine and treatment in hospitals of the other kind." Plainly it did not occur to the author, and apparently not to his readers, that such a law hospital was already busily operating in New York City. In 1897 on the average but one out of every seventy-five hundred inhabitants of Greater New York was a member of the Society. In 1898 one of the leading members of an important local educational institution was found to know nothing whatever about legal aid. In the same year, when Mr. v. Briesen lectured to the League for Political Education, the presiding officer took occasion to say that any information concerning the Legal Aid Society would be of value because so little was known of it.

It was particularly regrettable that the Society did not receive organized support from the Bar. Of course many lawyers were members, and some very important lawyers were on the board of directors or held office. But not until many years later did the Society succeed in obtaining really effective coöperation with the lawyers' organizations of New York City. It may be suggested that the lawyers hung back because they found in legal aid a dangerous competitor working at cut-throat prices. That, however, was never the truth. The Society's Attorney did not take claims merely because they were small. He must in addition be convinced that the claimants lacked means to employ regular practitioners at regular prices. By way of example, collections even of the smallest sums were not normally undertaken for shopkeepers. Nor, indeed, were *all* claims accepted from poor people. When a would-be client arrived with a personal-injury case he was usually told that he must go to some lawyer who would take up his claim on a contingent basis. Hence the New York Bar has never had reasonable occasion to fear the Society as an unfair competitor. On the contrary, the Bar should have been intensely grateful for relief from the moral duty of rendering services in poor men's cases where there is no possible hope of adequate recompense. We have seen one explanation of the lack of coöperation by bar associations in the fact that until 1890 or even 1896 the breadth of legal aid work was hidden behind a German appellation and German management. By the time these disguises were shaken off, the bar associations had already cut for themselves definite channels of activity and it was hard to divert a share of their energies to new channels.

We find, then, between 1890 and 1900 much annual scrambling by the Society for donations from people and institutions interested in its work yet not numbered among its regular members. The sums thus realized were substantial but fluctuating, and the whole procedure of soliciting casual donations was highly distasteful to Mr. v. Briesen. The organization giving justice to the poor as a matter of right should neither be forced to exist upon an unstable basis nor be reduced to the embarrassing position of a perennial mendicant.

Financial stringency kept the Attorney's force so small that the office had to work at a furious pace in order to keep even. Not uncommonly the Society was called on to appear in five district courts at the same time, or to conduct the trials of twenty or thirty cases in a single day. For a force of between three and five lawyers this necessitated an impossible degree of ubiquity. Yet with the legal aid attorneys it was a sound point of pride never to seek postponement. Speed was their clients' crying need. Mr. Goeller devised sundry plans for lessening the pressure. One of these was to bring as many cases as possible in the shape of criminal proceedings before the police magistrates. This could be done with numerous domestic difficulties, as, for instance, where it was desired to compel an errant husband to pay his deserted wife a weekly stipend. A police-court case required no preparation of pleadings, obviated almost all delay, and avoided money disbursements. Mr. Goeller said: "The application . . . is disposed of in a swift, sure, and inexpensive manner. The justice is at times poetic, but always satisfactory." Along a similar line, it became the practice to make some clients try their own cases. The prodigious and perhaps unavoidable elaboration of court procedure prevented this from becoming in any sense a universal usage. But often where a claim involved no point of law it was possible and practicable to prepare the client's papers, give him careful instructions about where to go and what to do, and then let him fend for himself. He was reasonably sure to get a kindly reception and adequate assistance from the court officers and the judge. Mr. Goeller and his successors were also able to use their professional friends for the purpose of filling in gaps. This, however, was a precarious resource.

Even if the personnel had been adequate, it could not have coped with the whole difficulty from the Society's single office. New York always covered a wide area. The Greater New York Charter made it wider. Poor clients and courts open for their use were spread everywhere. Brooklyn had long needed a local legal aid establishment. Here again the charitably minded professional friend was pressed into the breach. Beginning with 1895 Henry C. Underhill, a Brooklyn lawyer, conducted hundreds of cases referred to him by the New York office. Later, George P. Beebe continued the generous work. But there was more trouble nearer headquarters. In the magistrates' courts helpless people suffered much injustice because of confusion, haste, language difficulties, and sometimes, it is to be feared, police persecution or the tricks of shyster lawyers. The situation could have been greatly cleared by the presence of legal aid representatives, constantly on duty during court sessions. To the name of the so-called "pauper summons," granted without charge to poor people in civil cases, Mr. v. Briesen heartily objected. The Society's clients were not paupers and did not deserve to be so badged. But more than the name of the free summons was objectionable. It could issue only from the District Court for the district of the applicant's residence. Thus the Society had to choose between conducting widespread trial work with comparative freedom from expense and concentrating its court activities at an increased cost. Most important of all, no single office, however centrally located, was likely to become universally known among the poor or to be practically accessible to those who lived and worked in distant quarters. Branch offices, as well as an enlarged working force, were imperatively needed.

And in 1899 the branch offices began their career. This expansion was admirably conceived and executed. The Society exercised caution as far as caution was a virtue. No branch was opened until it had definite sponsors and definite promises of support. The Women's Committee assumed responsibility for a Woman's Branch in the United Charities Building at Twenty-second Street and Fourth Avenue. Appropriately, women lawyers staffed this office. The University Settlement Society gave a room rent-free at 57 Rivington Street for what was to become famous as the East Side Branch, and individuals connected with this society pledged financial support. The American Seamen's Friend Society, the Seamen's Church Institute, then called the Protestant Episcopal Church Missionary Society for Seamen, and other allied organizations and individuals undertook to contribute to a Seamen's Branch, which has done notably picturesque and valuable work. In no case was there confident assurance that all the expenses of any branch office would be met by the sponsors. But so far as energy and persuasion could go, good foundations had been laid. Beyond that point, Mr. v. Briesen and his associates decided, caution degenerated into unworthy timidity. They opened the three branches, furnished each with an office force and a supervisory committee from the directors, took the risk of using for current expenses a timely $3000 legacy just received from the estate of John Hein, and drove boldly ahead. Thus New York legal aid sent out the first missionaries to spread its gospel.

IV

APPLICANTS AND CLIENTS

ASIDE from the mention of a very few particular cases, the practical functioning of legal aid has so far been described in quite general terms. To the reader it must have seemed that the Society's multitudinous clients were marching past as a shadowy background, imagined rather than seen, the individual figures anonymous, inchoate, lacking bulk and substance. Hence a deliberate pause is now made to sketch by specific illustrations a cross-section of the work. Because poor men's troubles before the law are so obstinately recurrent in fundamental nature, the order of time has here little significance. Therefore the cases come from all stages of the Society's history. But they are arranged to illustrate, first, the scrutiny to which the attorneys subject every claim; second, the invariable attempts to make peaceful settlements; and third, the fighting out of claims neither rejected nor settled without litigation.

Some time in 1909 the Seamen's Branch heard that a sailor was being held for stealing a blanket from the ship which had just paid him off. The case against the man seemed ironclad. A blanket found in his possession had been positively identified by the ship's officers as part of her equipment. But the sailor firmly maintained his innocence. The legal aid workers racked their brains for an explanation. At last, partly by questioning their client, partly by independent investigation, they discovered the truth. For some reason the sailor had been in a great hurry to leave the vessel after she docked. So he asked a shipmate to bundle up his clothing and other effects in his blanket, leaving the bundle on the dock to be picked up later. This shipmate by mistake selected the wrong blanket, and the accusation of theft followed naturally enough. A Seamen's Branch lawyer found his client's blanket still aboard, hunted up the erring shipmate, and obtained an acquittal. Investigation, although consuming much time, prevented an utterly unjust conviction.

So much for the honest applicant who needs help to overcome unfair appearances. A dozen more instances might be added, but the single case is sufficiently illuminating. Turn now to the protection which preliminary inquiry gives the public against fraudulent or mistaken claims. Here several illustrations are necessary, not because false claims arise more commonly than true ones, but because misrepresentation or inaccuracy has so many varying antecedents. One Tuesday morning a garment worker appeared at the East Side Branch. His story was that on the preceding day his boss had picked a quarrel with him, struck him, and thrown him out of the shop. A fresh bruise on the applicant's face to some extent substantiated this story. The man was not so depressed by the assault and battery as by the withholding of his wages. He asserted that he had been employed on a weekly basis and was therefore entitled to a week's pay in lieu of notice. A letter went out to the employer, who appeared next morning with quite a different tale. According to him the applicant was a pieceworker and therefore subject to discharge at any time. Accounting records sustained this claim, and showed that on the preceding Saturday the man had been paid up to date. On Monday the employer discovered that the applicant had stolen goods intrusted to him. Therefore the discharge and a refusal to pay any additional sum except for Monday's work. The applicant thereupon lost his temper and struck the employer. Consequently he was violently ejected. Faced with these charges, the applicant denied the theft. But to the practised eye and ear of the attorney he seemed to protest too much. The employer was straightforward and had certainly proved the workman's story false as to the terms of employment. The attorney refused the case except to superintend the exchange of one day's pay for a proper receipt. The workman blustered, left the office in high dudgeon, then came back and took the money.

The foregoing incident is chosen because it is thoroughly typical and perfectly commonplace. But the same principle operates under more highly colored circumstances. A man in the Tombs prison lays claim to a starving family outside and insists that the only cause for his incarceration was the cashing, in good faith, of a money order payable to him and apparently sent by a beneficent relative abroad. Discreet preliminary investigation reveals that the prisoner had insinuated himself into the financial affairs of a helpless old German woman entitled to pension money and small monthly insurance payments from Germany. The plausible rascal arranged to have the remittances made to his order, calmly pocketed them for several months, and was laid by the heels only when the old lady, nearly penniless, wrote a letter of inquiry to Germany. The sharper stays in the Tombs. Perhaps all honest men are poor, as some story-books hint, but certainly not all poor men are honest! On another occasion a demand letter for unpaid wages brought from the employer a prompt remittance plus the startling information that the applicant might have had his money long before if only he had not run away after killing a fellow employee with a pair of ice-tongs. The Society afforded the grateful police force an opportunity to collect the slayer when he came to collect his money.

In lighter vein we may view a woman claiming damages for the tearing, staining, and spotting of a dress in course of dry cleaning. She had refused to accept the dress or pay the cleaner's charges. The cleaner unwisely ignored the Society's request for an explanation. Action was brought, and at the trial the dress appeared as an exhibit. To the apparent consternation of the applicant and the very real consternation of the attorney, the garment seemed perfectly whole and unspotted. Some careful mending and re-cleaning had been crowned with success, and no lawsuit need have been brought if only the cleaner had disclosed the truth. The case was settled by surrender of the dress without payment for the work. Another humorous case involved an irate tailor who had rented a front basement tenement as a shop, only to have the landlord tear down his sign when he displayed it. This landlord, wiser than the dry cleaner, blandly suggested a view of the premises. The surprised attorney found *five* signs, one in each of the tenant's four street windows and one on his door. He was not likely to blush unseen even though the landlord *had* removed a sixth sign extending directly across the sidewalk!

One class of clients calling for very special scrutiny and treatment is composed of those colloquially described as "cranks." Probably few people other than physicians, social workers, and lawyers understand how many somewhat demented people can be found moving freely about New York or any other large modern city. Every legal aid organization receives a very full share of attention from these unfortunates. Frequently their condition involves no danger whatever to society, and only comparatively slight distress to themselves. An assistant attorney of the Society found little difficulty in giving kindly, ingenious, and comforting advice to a poor man who believed that white rats constantly destroyed his clothing. Another applicant, a Russian, also had the white-rat delusion, but in his case the rats were camouflaged by gray paint! In addition, this applicant's feet were scorched by the heat of bake-shop ovens beneath the sidewalks, and he underwent mental distress because mounted policemen of prodigious girth rode about the streets on scrawny horses whose backs bowed beneath their ponderous riders. The attorney consulted promptly advised a rat trap and thicker boot-soles, and promised to take up the equestrian question with the Police Commissioner. Truly, not all legal aid work is legal. It might indeed have become political had one of the attorneys felt able to accept the Russian premiership when offered by Alexander Nikolai Michaelovich Romanoff, surviving brother to the late Czar. There was, alas, a string to this offer — as a condition precedent the attorney must raise an army of fifty million men and rout the Bolsheviks.

But these matters take a more serious turn when mentally affected individuals suffer from delusions of specific persecution or legal wrong. Mrs. O'Hare reached the Society in 1897 with a staggering tale of plague at sea which left her husband the sole survivor of a large ship's company; of the lone man's successfully bringing the vessel to a Brazilian port, where he received a huge sum for salvage; of the husband's death; and of a forty-year search by Brazilian authorities for his widow. Finally she was found at an obscure Bowery address, and thirty million dollars was expressed to her in a black tin box. A mysterious priest living one floor below Mrs. O'Hare intercepted the delivery man and made off with the precious shipment. Asked how she knew what the box contained, the lady glanced cautiously about and whispered that her fortune-teller had answered that problem. Even with this culminating touch of the improbable, Mrs. O'Hare's claim might have made much trouble for the priest if she had been able to designate him. Annoyance could more justly have sprung from a refined, pathetic little old lady who hovered about the office during the early nineties. Her son had squandered her fortune in stock-market speculation, and died leaving his mother only the illusion of mysterious voices repeating that a Wall Street vault held twenty-five thousand dollars in gold belonging to her. No doubt "Count Metternich" gave the Bleecker Street Bank some angry if not really uneasy minutes with his claim for a million dollars against it. Had the amount been more within reason, had he lodged his case with a shady or gullible lawyer, or had he succeeded, as many litigious lunatics do, in enlisting the press, the lot of the bank might have become really unhappy. But he went to The Legal Aid Society, where the claim was justly appraised and dealt with. Here we see a public protective function of the "poor man's lawyer" which has its obvious counterpart when a person either demented or of inferior intelligence has been imposed upon by an unscrupulous employer or some other trickster. There the Society strikes hard for the wronged individual, and usually with success. More often than not the exploited victim will tell a clear story on direct examination, and the court or jury will shrewdly discount vagaries which cross-examination lays bare. The judgments recovered in such cases are usually paid with a promptness betokening that wise selection has eliminated the merely delusive claims.

The preceding chapter indicates that certain whole categories of litigation have been rejected for one reason or another. Personal-injury cases, for instance, the Society has never felt generally free to handle. It wishes to avoid entirely the suspicion of commercial taint and also to assure the lawyer dependent on professional earnings that it is not snatching the bread from his mouth. These reasons suggest that certain personal-injury claims ought to be and will be accepted. Where probable money recoveries are so small as not to promise fair contingent fees, some legal aid office must take a hand, and unhesitatingly does so. Also many personal injuries, while giving rise to no legal liabilities, do create moral claims of more or less force. These the Society's lawyers may take up, and they often obtain by persuasion much-desired compensation which could never have been recovered in a lawsuit. Their reputation for fair dealing gives them an uncommonly advantageous position. In the ordinary personal-injury case, too, the organization has made one particularly helpful arrangement. Beginning in 1921 it compiled, with the help of local bar associations, lists of lawyers willing to handle these cases and other poor clients' litigation which the Society felt itself unable to accept. The method is not to recommend any particular lawyer to an applicant but to show the names of all practitioners who have volunteered for the kind of work he desires and permit him to make his own choice from the group. This arrangement gives some assurance that meritorious clients will come in contact with honest and competent legal representatives.

Another problem causing vast difficulty has been that of divorce. From the very beginning of the Society's history a "hands off" attitude was manifest with respect to this kind of litigation. There always existed genuine doubt as to the proper social policy. Only where the conditions of a particular divorce case made it clear beyond cavil that the Society would do good by acting for an applicant was the matter undertaken. Naturally the result has been that the attorneys of the Society appear rarely for a husband either seeking a divorce or defending against a claim for one, but fairly frequently for wives wronged by their husbands. With the growing modern instability of marriage, the divorce question, for poor folk as well as rich, has become more and more pressing. Further consideration of it as affecting the Society's activities is postponed until the next chapter.

The reader will remember that the founders of legal aid plainly intended relief in criminal as well as civil proceedings. But by the early twentieth century it had become a settled rule of the New York organization never to appear in any criminal case without special authorization from the Law Committee, president, or vice-president, unless the defendant was a seaman. This rule emphatically did not arise because gratuitous legal service was needless in criminal prosecutions or because the peculiar conditions of such litigation made intervention unwise. The sole and simple reason for keeping out was lack of personnel and money. A later chapter will show how far this condition has been remedied.

One of the Society's long-standing rules is that an applicant to have his case accepted must present a claim sound not merely in the technical sense but also in the moral sense. Many miscellaneous illustrations of this doctrine might be adduced, but its largest and most striking application provides the very best example. It is law, at least in New York, that a person employed for an indefinite period is subject to discharge without notice and, correspondingly, may throw over his position without notice and without forfeiting his right to unpaid compensation for time actually worked. In the field of domestic service this principle may originally have operated favorably for employers, but of late years, with an increasing demand for and a decreasing supply of competent servants, it has had quite the reverse effect. The New York cook not infrequently walked out at six P.M. with a dinner party coming on, the New York coachman or chauffeur sometimes abandoned his box or steering-wheel in the very midst of a shopping trip. And on top of such annoying action the departed servant could and would make a legally enforceable demand for back pay. At worst, this sort of thing verged on swindling, for there was reason to suspect that certain employment agencies furnished servants who stayed just long enough to entitle the agencies to retain their placement fees. At best, the practice indicated and encouraged irresponsibility, suspicion, and general bad feeling. The Legal Aid Society was much criticized for assisting the decamping "help" to collect their money claims. In 1910 Leonard McGee, then and now Attorney-in-Chief, decided that the criticism was just. The word went forth that, where a domestic servant abandoned his or her employment without reasonable notice, the Society would refuse to further recovery of back wages. New York gasped. Mere man had dared to tackle the servant problem! A roar of mingled praise and blame arose by word of mouth, by letter, and in the press. But Mr. McGee had fought his way up through the rough school of the Seamen's Branch, and neither soft words nor harsh ones deflected his gaze from actual results. What he saw was that after thousands of servants' cases had been refused, employers were far less often left in the lurch; and when the World War brought enormous pressure to bear upon the labor market, he had sound reason to conclude that the restrictive rule kept domestic service from cataclysmic disturbance.

Having indicated the operation of the rule that clients must come clean-handed, we should also note its limitation. When a criminal serving time at Sing Sing asked the Society to collect wages which he had earned before his imprisonment, the retainer was accepted and a somewhat difficult collection made, to the convict's great satisfaction. There was no connection between the crime and the wage debt. In respect of the latter the man was as much entitled to equal protection of the law and unfaltering legal aid service as though he had never seen or deserved to see the inside of a prison.

Quite enough has been said to show the importance and difficulty of sifting cases presented for legal aid treatment. Next comes the practice of settling out of court as many claims as possible. The Society has always been a strong believer in Abraham Lincoln's motto that a good settlement is better than a doubtful lawsuit. Its obvious advantages are speed and cheapness. Five irate tinsmiths appeared one day at a branch office. It seemed that these men had worked a whole week for a firm which then went out of business and discharged them unpaid. The applicants were angry to the core. They desired the issuance of attachments, orders for arrest, and every other legal process against the defendants. The attorney in charge of the branch did not share this vindictive excitement and succeeded in calming four of the five applicants. He arranged a meeting between these four and a member of the defunct partnership. The meeting began with storm signals flying, but became more peaceful after all the participants had blown off steam. An adjustment was reached which resulted in prompt payment of practically the full amounts demanded. Meanwhile the fifth applicant, still breathing fire and slaughter, had rushed to court. Here his ardor gradually congealed. His case did not even come on for hearing until eleven days after all the others were settled. Very likely he suffered further postponements. He may have lost at the trial, or recovered a judgment of unsatisfactory amount. Even by victory he obtained only an execution far from easy to translate into coin of the realm. Of the five applicants, he came off last best.

As another instance of speed by settlement we have the case of an applicant who had paid a tailor eight dollars as a deposit for making a suit "to be ready in a week." After four weeks, during which nothing save excuses had emanated from the tailor's shop, the applicant decided to cry off the bargain and appeared with his tale of woe one day at noon. The Attorney immediately telephoned the tailor and argued him into agreeing to return the deposit money. A messenger went forthwith to the shop. At fifteen minutes past twelve the relieved applicant left the office, money in pocket, his legal troubles completely behind him.

A third instance is too amusing and too unusual to be omitted. The attorney in charge of a Legal Aid branch one afternoon saw a parade of lads and lassies moving toward his office. The marchers bore large placards reading thus:

BLANK SCHOOL
STUDENTS ON STRIKE
JOIN US

The entire procession came crowding through the office door, chattering like a flock of magpies. It seemed that these earnest young seekers after knowledge had enrolled as students for the purpose of taking a course including chemistry, physics, and biology. The instructor was to teach these subjects by lectures supplemented with experiments performed before the class. Ere the course was completed the school installed laboratories and levied a fee to cover the cost of experimental materials and breakage. The students came from families of very limited means and could not easily obtain the laboratory charge. When it was insisted upon, they struck and paraded in front of the school until dispersed by the police. Then they came to the Legal Aid. Instead of giving advice on the right to "picket," the lawyer called up the principal and brought him to the office, where his first utterances were of a highly violent nature. The mildest epithet was "Bolsheviks." After considerable discussion, however, the attorney persuaded him to meet the difficulty by having two kinds of classes — lecture classes without laboratory fees for old students, and laboratory classes with fees for new students. Thereupon the strikers and the principal returned to the class-rooms. The placards were left behind in the office. The attorney examined one of them. He found the ink still wet — and the strike already settled.

When to the benefit of speed and cheapness can be added the still greater benefit of mutual good feeling, peaceful settlement has certainly reached its highest value. Here again the Society's experience is rich in examples. Three Italian laborers who had worked on a truck garden owned by a wealthy New Yorker of their own nationality were — so they said — discharged without payment after three months. The defendant replied to the letter of inquiry by asserting breach of contract, part-payment, and various counter-claims. He argued that, as the men had been employed for the whole season and had left five days before its close, they were not entitled to any wages. He offered evidence of small payments made from time to time, and credit given for a considerable quantity of merchandise. Even in view of this communication the Society's Attorney felt confident that some money was due to his clients. But this sort of case when tried in court will use up hours and days. After much long-distance wrangling with the defendant and his lawyer, a conference at the Society's office was arranged. In about fifteen minutes the whole matter was thrashed out and settled to everybody's satisfaction. The clients received a substantial sum in cash and were offered the same jobs for next season, which offer they accepted. Employer and employed left in perfect amity.

Another applicant, a woman with several small children, rented some rooms and made an advance deposit to apply against rent. A few days after this transaction she went to prepare the rooms for occupancy. To her horror she saw on the building a board-of-health notice bearing the dire words "Infantile Paralysis." Return of the deposit being refused, the applicant sought the Society's help. The landlord came to the office in great indignation. His house had been fumigated; he had a board-of-health certificate that the rooms were fit for use. The attorney looked him in the eye and asked just one question: "Granting all you say is true — would you as the father of a family move into those rooms?" The landlord gulped and answered: "Well, you've got me there—no." Then he returned the money. Perhaps the most perfect evidence of good feeling imaginable is embodied in the following card from a city marshal:

> I have just been notified by plaintiff and defendant in the case of Braunschweig *v.* Davidokowitz that they are married and I am requested to return the execution "unsatisfied."

It may be suggested that the parties here accomplished their own reconciliation. But the case does not stand alone. On numerous other occasions "settlements" of the same type have occurred. The lawyer's influence must not be ignored. He can do much either to reconcile or to estrange adverse parties. The Legal Aid attorneys have always striven to remove causes of friction and break down hostility.

In seeking to accomplish settlements the Society must act with great care. It would not do to give an impression of weakness and encourage potential defendants to believe that by offering half or three fourths of the face amount of a claim they can escape responsibility for the remainder. Consequently compromise is neither urged nor accepted unless the offer bears a fair relation to the sum honestly due. It must also be confessed that settlement attempts sometimes lead to disaster. A negro reached the office in a badly battered condition. Being questioned he spoke as follows:

> Boss, yo' honah, Ah was heah once befo' this aftehnoon 'bout some money owin' to me by a frien' o' mine, an' while Ah was settin' heah waitin' Ah read dat momentum in de frame on de wall deah 'bout what ole Abe Linkum said 'bout 'voidin' litigation an' compromisin' wid folks. Boss, Ah always had a heap o' respeck for ole Abe, an' Ah jest went right out again an' went roun' to see mah frien' 'bout c'llectin' dat money peac'ble like widout goin' to no

Co't 'bout it, an' das how dis face ob mine happen. Dat ad-vice o' Abe's did'n seem to wuk no good a-tall.

It is pleasant to balance this disaster with the tale of another negro. Although too poor to pay the ten-cent retainer fee, he of course received a retainer card. Instead of waiting for the "lawyer's letter" from the Society to have its effect, he personally renewed his demand for the money due, flashing the precious card before the debtor's vision. The effect was noteworthy, for payment was made then and there. Whereupon the client, as honest as he was resourceful, returned to the office, reported the collection, and paid his ten-cent fee.

In 1917 the Society received a convincing tribute to its honesty as an informal court of conciliation and arbitration. A painter applied for assistance in collecting more than $100 due on a completed contract. The debtor's attorney, when he heard who had taken the claimant's case, promptly sent his client to talk the matter over, advising him that he needed no lawyer of his own to be sure of fair treatment. The parties conferred, adjusted some differences of opinion about the quantity and quality of the work, and wound up the whole controversy on the spot, including the passing of a check in full payment. The two men went away asserting that they would likewise settle their future legal difficulties. Another defendant's lawyer, at first most indignant with The Legal Aid Society for attempting to enforce what he considered an unjustified claim, became so fully converted that he paid the applicant from his own pocket.

Extreme ingenuity and flexibility have marked the adjustment of some difficult cases. A New York Jewish paper charged a "shochet" [1] or official Hebrew slaugh-

[1] A roughly accurate phonetic spelling, often rendered "schochet."

terer with being unfit for his position. This was a serious assertion, likely to ruin the shochet both in reputation and financially. After correspondence with the accusing editor it was agreed to leave the question to the arbitration of five East Side rabbis. As the client's rights depended upon matters understood only by those learned in Hebrew law, this was an eminently wise way to dispose of the controversy. The resulting decision satisfied both sides. A shirtwaist presser made claim for wages due. Her employer asserted that she had not been sufficiently skilled to earn the compensation claimed. Questions of comparative ability are hard to settle if tried according to ordinary court procedure. Hence an arrangement not unworthy of King Solomon. The applicant went to her employer's place of business and there pressed several waists while a regular employee of average skill pressed an equal number. The demonstration showed the applicant's inaptitude. Her claim was cut down and the whole matter closed without litigation. A simpler test sufficed where the uncle of a young Irish immigrant girl asserted that another relative was victimizing the girl. During a conference at the office the uncle insisted that the young lady was too green to distinguish the denominations of paper money. The Attorney promptly produced two bank bills, one for five dollars and the other for one dollar, and in the presence of all parties asked the girl which she would prefer to have. Without hesitation she indicated the five-dollar bill. This spiked the uncle's guns and led him to stop further proceedings.

Turning to cases which have had to be fought out, any reader of the Society's records will find a multitude of striking examples fairly clamoring for recognition. Only a few can be presented here, even in the briefest form. Fortunately the bare facts are vivid enough in themselves and will suggest many unexpressed details. One of the omnipresent wage claims provides the opening illustration.

About 1911, two boiler-makers named Croughwell and Wylie accepted an offer from the Guayaquil & Quito Railway Company to work in Ecuador, South America, under specified terms as to pay, hours, living conditions, and so forth, and with all expenses of transportation out and back to be paid by the company. Once in Ecuador, the men found themselves worked overtime, grossly underpaid, and subjected to great risks of disease. Protesting, they were told to grin and bear it — the United States was a long way off, and they could not walk or swim home. The boiler-makers were determined fellows, however. Scraping together enough to get to Panama, they worked there for the United States government, and finally earned their way back to New York. The railway company had offices on Wall Street and a legal day of reckoning followed, Croughwell emerging with $300 and Wylie with $250.

Harshly as these two mechanics were used, they can never have felt such black depression as did two other clients whose troubles arose in or near New York City itself. Although this pair of cases occurred perhaps ten years apart, their facts run closely parallel. The first client was a Russian immigrant who used his little all to buy a push-cart and a tiny stock of goods. The second was Arthur Brown, a harbor junk-dealer plying his trade in an eighteen-foot rowboat. Scarcely had the Russian set out to look for customers when a truck capsized his cart and hurled the entire stock-in-trade higgledy-piggledy into a muddy street. The junkman met even more complete disaster. The steamship *Albion* backed out of a slip at the Communipaw coal docks in Jersey City, crashed against his boat, and sank it so quickly that Brown himself barely escaped by diving overboard. These petty merchants by land and by water shared a feeling of utter desperation. Each had lost his means of livelihood in the twinkling of an eye. The Legal Aid Society saved them both. The push-cart man had a clear case for damages, and was soon re-equipped. He prospered, shifted to the painting trade, and was last heard of as a successful contractor in that line. But he always remembered what retrieved his first crushing business misfortune. Brown's mishap presented more difficulties. To his assertion that the ship had backed into the stream without a warning whistle the owners of the *Albion* replied that the junk-man had negligently tied his boat to their vessel's rail. Luckily for Brown, the yacht *Teresa* had been lying near the coal docks, and two of her sailors — with the oddly overlapping names of Thomas Edward and Edward Thompson — were able to testify in his favor. The Society had to bring a libel and attach the *Albion*, but in the end her owners paid for the junk-boat and its cargo.

Such desperate cases might be described by the dozen. A starving boy from Kansas, alone and friendless in New York City, wounded when he attempted suicide and then cast into the Tombs on the charge of having a concealed weapon; a pathetic little up-state seamstress whose sewing-machine was in the clutches of a crafty city employer; a wretched Italian marionette operator, his puppets withheld by a theatre proprietor; a sweat-shop worker between the Scylla of a landlord preparing to evict him and the Charybdis of a chattel-mortgage concern threatening criminal prosecution if the man moved his cheap furniture; a deserted wife, all bent and twisted with rheumatism, unable to get money from her husband's savings bank for lack of $50 to meet preliminary expenses in a separation action; a cripple, misled by an advertisement into buying with all his ready money a grotesque article quite useless to him, coming to New York for recompense and sleeping at night in City Hall Park in his hand-propelled chair; an unpaid dishwasher shivering in raw December weather without overcoat or underwear — all these and thousands more like them The Legal Aid Society has comforted and helped. Some applicants have discovered the Society only by a lucky chance, like the unjustly discharged young actress who happened to pick up a copy of the *Ladies' Home Journal* containing an article on legal aid; or at the latest possible moment, like the Spanish maid who wandered half-starving for weeks after her mistress turned her out of doors with a flat refusal to pay the wages due. How many of the poor, in deep legal difficulties, have never even heard that there was a legal helper?

But the picture is not all dark. Consider Tony, the small boy who managed for his great-grandmother a boat-house on the Harlem River. At the opening of the boating season Tony's father, a peripatetic person of doubtful habits and resources, suddenly brought habeas corpus to get custody of his son. The old lady and the youngster resisted. "Ask the judge," suggested Tony, "whether he ever heard of a great-grandmother running a boat-house." Perhaps it was this novel consideration; or perhaps the woman's helplessness; or possibly a vision of June when sun and wind and waves and little boys play together, which influenced His Honor. At any rate, the Harlem boating season was saved. Then there was the perky little Broadway variety actress who gave a persuasive "angel" fifty dollars to write her a song. The words turned out to be scarcely angelic — in fact, they invited police interference. So the Legal Aid intervened. Whereat the angel changed his tune if not his words, and proclaimed himself execution-proof. But lo and behold, an inquiring attorney found that the fellow actually had produced one song then paying royalties, and by appropriate legal process diverted the golden stream to the actress's reticule. Still considering problems of professional advancement, we come to the student at a police-force school who was two inches under minimum height but could, the school's proprietor averred, be "stretched" to the necessary elevation. Stretching involved neck- and leg-pulling, both figurative and literal, brought on a sore jaw, and finally brought up against a curt rejection by the medical examiner. But at least the Society got back the disappointed candidate's tuition fee. Not even the acutest Legal Aid attorney, however, could manage any recovery for the pie baker who dozed off in a barber's chair and awoke to find his mustache shorn away; yet the poor fellow suffered so from this injury to his appearance that he could not bake pies for a week!

The pursuit of pleasure oft leads to sorrow. So found two gaily inebriated French sailors who pelted pebbles at a lineman of the city electrical department, while they roared with glee over the consequent antics of this human monkey on a stick. Thanks to the Society's explanations, a diverted police magistrate released the chastened mariners with a reprimand and paroled them in the custody of their skipper. More lugubrious was the fate meted out to a defaulting guardian who retreated to the Jersey side and then dared the Legal Aid lawyers to do their worst. One Saturday night the lure of the great city drew him to a ball. Alas for Terpsichore, three deputies lurked without the dance-hall door, gathered up the faithless guardian as he stepped from the street-car, and hastened him away to a week-end in durance vile. On Monday he very promptly paid over the funds he had detained. Long-distance travel, too, has its peculiar difficulties. Witness the three Russian immigrant women who arrived with nine great bales of feathers wherein they had cunningly packed sundry other personal possessions. Were those feathers household furniture or merchandise? Surely the latter, decided a custom-house appraiser, who clapped on $170 tax. And to alter this decision The Legal Aid Society had to work all the way up to the Collector of the Port with a learned disquisition upon the Russian practice of collecting feathers early and often so that each child of the family may take a proper bed for a wedding outfit. Note also a traveller from Indiana, an old Scotchman returning to the land of his birth. He carried all his money, and a revolver to repel the brigands of New York. The ship's doctor found the old man's eyes so badly affected by cataracts that immediate treatment must be given. Off went the patient to Bellevue Hospital, where the revolver came to light and the bewildered Scotchman landed in the prison ward for violation of the Sullivan Law. The attorney from the Society hastened the trial, had his client plead guilty, and obtained a suspended sentence from an understanding judge. Away sailed the old fellow for bonnie Scotland without loss of an hour more than was actually necessary.

Now come the rogues and swindlers who constantly rub shoulders with the poor, and craftily exploit their natural human desires. Have you saved a little money which you wish to multiply in sporting fashion? A clairvoyant will for a modest but perceptible portion of your hoard put you up to quite a sure thing in the way of a lottery. If something goes awry the first time — try, try again. It is hard to believe, yet true nevertheless, that one simple soul was fleeced for a year and a half in this fashion, paying out by instalments of fifteen, twenty, and twenty-five dollars his entire life-savings. If you are touched by the tender passion and a bit superstitious, you can buy love powders — which do not work. Or a girl with some savings may acquire a handsome lover; he does not work, either, but is most effective as a borrower until the girl's money is gone; then he goes also. Those yearning for bargains in furniture may choose from the contents of a doctor's office, put up at forced sale. Oddly enough, the office connects with the rear of a furniture shop and seems to keep as full as Utgard-Loki's horn which Thor vainly strove to drain. Moreover, the purchases when divested of their bargain glamor are very cheap-Jack stuff indeed. Another dodge used commonly to be worked with phonographs; nowadays radio sets probably furnish the subject-matter. Certainly the instruments displayed were good ones and far below standard price. But if you were wise, you covertly scratched a distinguishing mark on the machine selected, for the dealer would under no circumstances let you break your back by carrying it away, and the one he delivered was a very different article. Since 1920 The Legal Aid Society has fought scheme after scheme to trick the age-old yearning for a foothold in the soil. A delightfully surprised victim is told that he has "won a building lot." But he must pay expenses of transfer, say $50; or else no single lots are conveyed, so he has to buy one or two more to accompany his prize; and probably there lurks unseen an octopus of a mortgage tightly clutching the whole tract and reducing purchasers' equities to the vanishing-point.

Fine print and much of it enters into the machinery of many a fraud. Fine print was disastrous to the Russians and Poles who thought they were buying bargain tickets for a return trip to the old countries, and later found themselves laboring on seabound liners as stokers or coal-passers. Fine print enabled the "business exchange" proprietor to extract fat commissions from owners of little shops and industries and pieces of real estate. Each owner supposed that his money would be given back if no sale or exchange were accomplished. But the small type in the contract allowed the business exchange to keep the commission practically without turning a finger and certainly without effectuating any transfer. Fine print in prodigious quantities made the trick "accident insurance policy" no protection whatever against any accident at all likely to occur. Less lavishly employed, fine print made receipts in full out of documents which the signers supposed to be only acknowledgments of partial satisfaction. But fine print, particularly when garnished with contradictory oral statements, gives a pretty civil action for fraud; and sometimes it leads to the District Attorney's office, the criminal courts, and jail. Largely because of constant efforts by The Legal Aid Society, small type no longer forms a safe shield and buckler for New York sharpers.

Against many types of swindling, however, constant vigilance and unwearying willingness to enter fresh fights are the only successful weapons. The school for movie actors which teaches nothing of any value may fade out, but a correspondence airplane or radio school will fill its place. "Trade schools," likewise teaching nothing and calculated merely to make would-be learners pay for the privilege of working hard in little manufacturing plants, shade into schemes of "trial employment," whereby more expert handicraftsmen are deluded into giving away a week's labor for a song. Employers who have exacted deposits for security will refuse to return them when the depositors leave their employ. The execution-proof restaurant proprietor will put off his dishwashers' demands for wages until it is too late to obtain judgments permitting arrest for non-payment. "Sleeping partners," persuaded to put capital into "well-established businesses," will be kept slumbering while their "active" associates make away with the money. Contracting dentists will extract and drill and fill and bridge on the instalment payment plan, trusting that agonized patients will never get proper expert witnesses to prove how unnecessary the work was and how badly it has been done. Landlords will still quietly attach their hall lights to the tenants' meters. Oldest of all, yet seemingly quite immortal, the Spanish prisoner will walk again at appropriate intervals. Perhaps now he is a Russian prisoner. But the Society knows him well in any guise and of late years has completely thwarted his designs.

Many poor men's cases which could not possibly yield just compensation to an ordinary practitioner necessitate a prodigious expenditure of time, energy, and ingenuity. The resolute conduct of these matters by The Legal Aid Society justifies the suggestion that a bulldog should be added to the allegorical figures on its corporate seal. About 1910 a woman quite without means came to the office, saying that she was still entitled to $83 from the estate of her Uncle James, who had died before she came of age. With this, and no more, to start upon the

Society began an investigation. Sure enough, the administration of the estate had come to an end some ten years before, and there *was* an order to pay $83 apiece to the applicant and certain other nephews and nieces of the dead man. But where was the money? The administratrix had died, her lawyer's mind was a blank on this point. The City Chamberlain had no record of the matter. No general guardian had ever been appointed for the minor beneficiaries. The Legal Aid lawyers burrowed and grubbed for a clue; they found other surviving beneficiaries — four of them, at least two being in as great need as the original applicant; and then they found a forgotten bank account of Uncle James's. The remaining steps were routine: appointment of an administrator "de bonis non" and a fresh order of distribution. The pot of gold had been dug up at the rainbow's end; a small pot, to be sure, but full of value and happiness for the recipients.

Very similar cases have concerned life-insurance policies. In December, 1903, the parents of a missing boy sought information about their son. They understood he had shipped on a Chesapeake Bay oyster dredge and been drowned. With the help of the Federal authorities in Maryland and of a Maryland newspaper the sad news was verified. To escape hardship and cruelty aboard the dredge, the young fellow dived overboard, tried to swim ashore, and never reached land. The parents had taken out an insurance policy on his life when he was seven years old, the premiums being only five cents a week and the amount of the policy correspondingly small. Proof of the claim was immensely difficult, but dogged perseverance won at last, and nearly seven and one-half years after the boy's death his poor parents received the insurance money. As late as 1919 the Society obtained a pension for the needy English-born widow of a Civil War veteran deceased some years previously. The applicant's memory had failed and only from other sources could the lawyers piece together convincing evidence of a marriage between the young English girl and the soldier in blue in "the days of lavender and old lace" more than half a century before. Over a month's time went into collecting data and preparing and submitting the application, bright with its red- and gold-sealed county clerks' certificates. Then followed an eager wait of several months, ended by the good tidings that the pension had been granted.

Really contentious cases, where the Society's opponents offer active resistance, may present additional difficulties. Sometimes short cuts can be found, however, as in one instance where an Italian laborer had died, leaving his family nothing except a three-dollar claim for unpaid wages. The employer refused to hand over the money, believing that no action could be brought against him without the expensive process of having the widow appointed administratrix. But the attorney in charge of the matter obtained evidence that the decedent had told his wife she might have the money if she could collect it, and that the employer had said he would pay the woman provided she could establish her identity. On this basis he erected a theory of oral assignment, brought suit in the widow's name, and won a clever victory.

Yet only too often a tedious struggle must be dragged through to the end. When Howard O. and Reinhart A. Kaempf, boys of nine and ten respectively, paid their ten-cent retainer fee, the Society settled down to a fourteen months' battle to recover from an uncle acting as their guardian $1700 which the two youngsters inherited on their father's death. The file of papers in the case grew into a volume almost four inches thick; the first guardian was removed and a successor substituted; part of the misappropriated funds was laboriously retrieved; and finally, when the original guardian made a flat default, he was clapped into Ludlow Street Jail to reflect upon the inadvisability of misappropriating trust money.

In Stockman *v.* Potter Wall Paper Mills the greatest difficulties ended with entry of judgment, the defendant being a sound concern of excellent financial standing. But it was a long, weary pull to reach the judgment stage. About 1900 the wallpaper mills employed the plaintiff, an old man who had twenty-five years' selling experience and an established trade in the western part of the country. Three or four months later they discharged the salesman and instructed him not to visit his customers. He brought action for breach of contract in 1901, but his case languished under a New York lawyer who thought that it called for too much work and promised too little compensation. Reduced to desperate straits, poor Stockman attempted suicide in Cleveland. His life was saved, and the authorities communicated with The Legal Aid Society, requesting assistance on his claim for damages. The lawsuit had been so ill handled that the Society was forced to pay out $30 for costs in order to get it moving ahead. At length, after a further delay of three years, the case was reached for trial toward the end of January, 1907. Four days of strenuous work in court led to a plaintiff's verdict and judgment for over $2000.

The two claims last described involved considerable amounts of money. But it must not be supposed that smaller claims are slighted. Even the most minute sum may mean a great deal to a poor man. Thus the report for 1896 runs as follows: "Hattie Schoep claimed 75 cents for washing. The amount was collected. We also had two cases for even smaller amounts, one for 60 cents and another for 50 cents, which sums were collected and paid to the complainants." Next year: "The smallest case actually carried through to judgment this year was an action for $1.77. Our client bought a jar of pickles from a large manufacturing house in Washington Market. He . . . never received the pickles. He came to us in very great excitement; we wrote to the firm, and they answered that they knew nothing of so small a claim and would pay no attention to it whatever. We brought suit and got judgment; execution was issued and the money was finally recovered."

Such instances are not confined to the Society's early history. In 1921 it finally broke up a prolonged oppressive attempt to make a woman pay an apparently unjust claim of $12.50. From time to time for nearly nine years the plaintiff had been bringing actions which he discontinued as soon as a defence was offered. He hoped that some day the applicant would fail to defend and suffer a judgment by default. At length the Society blocked the proceeding by procuring not only the dismissal of the last action but also a judgment for costs. In 1925 a client laid claim to $10.50 in wages. The defendant, without any real excuse for not paying the entire sum, offered only $8.50. This amount was rejected and an action pressed to a successful outcome. One of these tiny claims may well close the chapter, for it vividly proves the Society's influence. A recently arrived immigrant hired a cheap room and paid $1.25 as his first week's rent. After two days the landlord evicted him, kept the money, and disregarded demand letters. Suit was commenced and collection made. On receiving his money the applicant exclaimed: "I now begin to believe that not all is 'bluff' in America!" For him the assertion of equal justice to all had changed from a copy-book phrase into reality.

V

LEGAL REFORMS

THE ideal corollary to relief against past evils is prevention of like evils in the future. All public-spirited lawyers are nowadays carrying on such preventive practice. They strive by sound advice, by enforcement of existing laws, and by procuring the enactment of new laws to keep others out of pitfalls from which they have rescued or tried to rescue unfortunate clients. The Legal Aid Society, with its wholesale experience and consequent knowledge of the tides of affairs within the community, has often had the honor of contributing to the accomplishment of important legal reforms. A chapter touching upon some of its efforts in such matters is an illuminating supplement to the tale of particular cases just told.

There is good reason to believe that Mr. v. Briesen from his very earliest connection with the Society realized its rich constructive possibilities. His first clear expression of these possibilities came after the bucket-shop fight of 1896–1897. The evil tendencies of the New York bucket shop have always been painfully apparent. As an open temptation to gambling of the most intriguing type it not only swallowed up many a poor fellow's small savings, but also turned uncounted dupes into paths of dishonor and crime. Revived business confidence following McKinley's election in 1896 caused great increase of activity by bucket shops and so-called "investment agents" who acted as solicitors for these concerns. The dice were double-loaded against their victim. If he guessed wrong about market fluctuations, his margin was wiped out; if the bucket-shop proprietor guessed wrong to any substantial extent, his business usually blew up and the theoretically fortunate customer found himself again a complete loser. Cases by the dozen poured into the Society's office, the clients generally being without adequate remedy in the civil courts. Mr. Goeller, the Attorney-in-Chief, was deeply disturbed but saw no way out. The growing trouble passed him and reached Mr. v. Briesen. From now on the story becomes one of activity by the president rather than by the regular legal representative of the Society. But that makes it none the less appropriate. For more than a quarter-century the v. Briesen office was an effective supplement of the Legal Aid offices. To it came many commonplace clients and a very large proportion of those whose cases presented peculiar difficulties. Mr. v. Briesen's great gift to American law was never bare for lack of the giver. He thought and talked and wrought legal aid. When the life of this big-hearted citizen is finally written, its readers will learn of a hundred touching instances where he and his sons struggled for the poor with tenacious ingenuity which would not admit defeat.

On the present matter, Mr. v. Briesen says in the report for 1897: "Individual claims for advice regarding all relations of life and business receive our Attorney's attention, and as a matter of fact the work is gradually entering fields of a public, or semi-public character. For example . . . it was determined . . . to start a crusade against [the] bucket-shops. At first it was found that many persons in authority deemed the effort hopeless, but with the assistance of such unselfish lawyers as Philip Tecumseh Sherman, Stephen B. Stanton, and others, who undertook (free of charge) to gather the necessary evidence, it finally became possible to obtain the necessary warrants and to raid, with the aid of the police force, two of the worst places in the city. The magistrates who issued these warrants were Messrs. Mott and Brann. The public officer who was most zealous in the success of these efforts was Assistant District Attorney Charles Zaring. The police officer who prepared and executed the raids was Detective-Sergeant Frederick W. Wade. These names are specially mentioned because it is thought that particular praise is due where here it is given."

This, however, is only a bare outline. Although Mr. v. Briesen failed to receive from Wall Street quite the full coöperation which he felt his plan deserved, members of the Stock Exchange contributed $500 toward expenses. This helped solve the difficulty of obtaining evidence. Still more important, a certain bucket-shop operator chanced to be in such a position that it was discreet for him to work with the attacking forces on their problems of fact. But there was also a legal difficulty. The New York statute books had long contained a section making it a misdemeanor to keep a room for purposes of gaming or betting. In January, 1889, though, the Supreme Court decided that the section did not include bucket-shop activities. Annotators promptly affixed a summary of this case to the law, and the magistrates boggled over the decision when confronted with applications for warrants. Even judges are not all wise. They did not know that in June, 1889, the legislature had so expanded the law as to abrogate the Supreme Court's restrictive interpretation, and were hard indeed to convince. The ultimate victory may have seemed small and temporary. Quite the reverse was true; instead of being wiped out, it grew with time. The eyes of the police were opened to the possibility of pressure under existing law. Risk of prosecution has gradually squeezed the bucket shops into furtive seclusion, from which they dare not flaunt anything like their old brazen attractions.

Next should be described the great instalment crusade of 1902. A quotation from the New York *Tribune* for May 7, 1905, gives an excellent introductory summary: "Apart from its thousands of personal cases, the Legal Aid Society can and does do much civic work. Up to a few years ago the society was approached over and over with cases of poor men who had been imprisoned for owing on goods bought on the instalment plan. Almost invariably the imprisonment was wrongful, and finally the society decided to take more aggressive steps than merely to have the individuals released, and what is known as the instalment crusade followed. It soon appeared that certain instalment dealers traded upon the ignorance of immigrants, chiefly Italians, induced them to buy worthless jewelry, brought suit and obtained judgment without proper notice, and then caused the arrest of the purchaser, who in eight cases out of ten borrowed money and pawned his effects to pay the judgment and any fees called for, rather than go to jail. These arrests were much like marauding parties. The instalment dealer, a marshal, two or three assistants, would go at night to the tenement of such a purchaser, drag him out of bed, use threats, and sometimes violence, until the man, in fear of being dragged off, paid up — often much more than he owed, with exorbitant costs. Often the marshal was not really an officer of the law, as required, but only some impersonator used to frighten the poor purchaser." By way of explanation it should be added that the city marshals are officers extensively used to serve process and levy execution in small lawsuits; the mayor appoints them and may remove them for cause. The *Tribune* might justly have taken more credit to itself. For during the war against the instalment dealers a certain young *Tribune* reporter named Frank Simonds, later to acquire fame in a vaster and more dreadful war, worked and fought shoulder to shoulder with the Legal Aid forces. It was a current pleasantry at the time that this rising newspaper man stood eagerly ready to "cruise" for the Society's "crusades." Mr. Simonds's unsigned contemporary news stories furnish us a brilliant running description.

On April 7, 1902, he opens fire with a first-page article stating that a mass of evidence tends to involve some city marshals in instalment frauds, and describes the cases of several victims then languishing at Ludlow Street Jail, the New York Marshalsea. Tadero Rosario, a barber, bought a jim-crack watch at the insistence of an instalment dealer, paying $2 down and signing a paper with some printing which he did not and probably could not read. Later a pawnbroker told him the watch was not worth two cents. But the dealer refused to call the trade off and Rosario was suddenly jailed under a body execution for $51.14 issued after default judgment in an action of which he received no notice. Pasqualo Gulda, also a watch buyer, was summoned to court on an excessive claim, put off with several adjournments, and finally enticed out of the court-room by a marshal while his case was called and he was defaulted. Execution issued with such speed that the watchful marshal deposited his prisoner at the jail inside an hour. Daniel Cassese, a one-legged man, was hauled from bed at five A.M. and dragged away to prison. His creditor had previously told him he might consider the debt settled, and he had never heard of the commencement of a suit. The object in jailing these and other instalment purchasers was probably not to squeeze money out of them. Usually they had none. But the arrests and incarcerations were well calculated to terrify relatives and friends of the victims into paying exorbitant sums for their release.

Almost from day to day for over two months Mr. Simonds sketched the developing situation, recounting many new cases — those of defendants illegally held at marshals' offices and other fouler places of confinement in the instalment dealers' control, of men actually pulled from sick beds and cast into prison, of men whose defaults on instalment contracts had been purposely induced by the collectors' failure to call, of at least one man deliberately arrested for another's debt, and of a purchaser imprisoned upon an utterly false affidavit that he intended to leave the state. Legal Aid representatives watched the courts, where a marked diminution of instalment cases resulted. R. C. Ringwalt of the East Side Branch spent much time at the Ludlow Street Jail getting the facts from frightened prisoners and their weeping families, and trying to put fighting spirit into them. This was not easy, for some dealers bullied and browbeat their victims in the jail itself. Incidentally, Mr. Ringwalt's safe where he stored the documentary evidence gradually gathered was broken open and rifled. Luckily the important documents had just been transferred to a more secure place. The number of jail commitments shrank notably for some days, jumped again as the sharks showed their teeth, and then shrank permanently.

The pressure was telling. A judge against whom suspicion had been directed found it advisable to make a statement wherein he vaguely deplored the general conditions of life in his district. A city marshal whose activities had been questionable voiced a plaintive disclaimer. One of the larger instalment dealers undertook to make no arrest until a lawyer from the Legal Aid had seen the case. Another dealer was forced in court to accept the return of four watches and was denied costs. Further civil cases went against the instalment men, and one justice recommended that certain matters proved before him be submitted to the grand jury. Mayor Low approved and the Governor signed a bill limiting the power of arrest in instalment cases and enabling the mayor to suspend a marshal against whom a municipal court justice preferred charges. The University Settlement Society went actively to work on the situation, and the Educational Alliance aided in publicity. District Attorney Jerome, living personally among the people of the East Side, began to reach out for a good test case to prosecute. Three of the more notorious dealers were prosecuted criminally for extortion in King's County. The case of Rosario, summarized at the beginning of this account, became the basis of a damage suit for false arrest. Mayor Low removed a city marshal on charges brought by The Legal Aid Society. The air began to clear. One instalment dealer brought a libel action against the *Tribune* for a particularly stinging Simonds article. This case went all the way to the Court of Appeals on preliminary points, and by the time it was sent back for trial, in 1904, victory in the main campaign had plainly declared herself. During the session of 1903 the powers at Albany enacted a law making it impossible for an instalment dealer to arrest a purchaser unless he first obtained a net money judgment of more than $100 exclusive of costs. Never again was the old Ludlow Street Jail to become the scene of such a revolting, sordid, and pathetic drama.

This crusade and the anticipation of others like it led in 1903 to revision of the Society's purpose clause. The alteration included an addition frankly avowing the function of reform. Since the general phrasing of the clause was tinkered and smoothed, the entire revised sentence is here reprinted with the addition italicized:

> The purpose of this Society shall be to render legal aid, gratuitously if necessary, to all who may appear worthy thereof and who are unable to procure assistance elsewhere, *and to promote measures for their protection.*

The instalment fight has suggested a general topic which must be followed further. It is noteworthy that many instalment purchasers were, or claimed to be, victims of "snap judgments" — that is, judgments in cases the pendency of which had never been brought to their notice. Of course it is a dictate of the most rudimentary fairness that a defendant must have timely information of any suit against him, so that he may prepare and present his defence. The plaintiff is supposed to give him this information by serving him with process, and no court will move a case forward to judgment until duly assured that process has been served. In the Municipal Court of New York City, which carries the bulk of legal aid litigation, service of process may be made either by a marshal or by "any other person over the age of eighteen years and not a party to the action." The marshal proves service by his written return or certificate, any other person by affidavit. It follows that the "snap judgment" connotes a false certificate or a perjured affidavit.

This sort of judgment has not been confined to instalment cases, but crops up again and again in the Society's experience. An example or two will be useful. About 1911 a woman employed a person holding himself out as a rabbi to conduct a Jewish funeral on the East Side, agreeing to pay the very substantial sum of $30. After the funeral it developed that the man was not a rabbi at all, and he accepted a lesser sum in settlement. Later the "rabbi" brought action on his original bill, suing, not the woman, but her aged and infirm father. The reason for this move lay in the fact that at the time no execution permitting arrest could issue against a woman. The case proceeded entirely without the old man's knowledge until a marshal appeared to make a levy. The Legal Aid Society then came into play for the defendant, and had the judgment and execution vacated. Later in the same year a mercantile concern which also dabbled in small loans obtained grossly excessive judgments against four city employes for loans made to them. The men stoutly maintained that they were given no notice whatever of the proceedings until their wages had been garnisheed after entry of judgments. Once more the Society had the judgments set aside and the executions vacated. The plaintiff tried hard to save its extortionate recoveries by appeal on a technicality, but lost again before the Appellate Term. These two matters exemplify an abuse of judicial process which has at times been alarmingly frequent.

The foregoing cases indicate the kind of relief which can be had against the snap judgment in the particular litigation. But something more is essential. The process server should be made to smart for his falsehood. If he be a marshal, a complaint to the mayor is clearly indicated. To be sure, the latter may turn a deaf ear.

This, however, is the kind of risk which must be faced in all matters of official discipline. Every governmental device stalls hopelessly unless the men administering it have the skill and will to make it go. If the process server be an ordinary private citizen, the problem changes. This man has no office to lose. Two punitive steps are possible, however. *Ex hypothesi* he has by his false oath committed perjury, for which statute provides a heavy penalty. Moreover, his action so interferes with proper judicial procedure as to constitute a contempt of court. In 1910 and 1911 reluctance of the District Attorney to commence, or his ill-success with, prosecutions for this kind of perjury, and obvious unwillingness of the justices to cite false process servers for contempt, were coupled with a number of cases involving lying affidavits of service. The Law Committee, seriously troubled, began to study methods of relief. But even at this time Mr. McGee held to the opinion that persistence would make the two existing remedies adequate, and during 1910 he succeeded in obtaining one fifteen-day commitment for contempt, which unquestionably had a salutary effect. This is a legal point to be watched. Perhaps New York is already sufficiently armed against the abuse, subject only to the character of the men who must enforce the penalties. Perhaps further steps must ultimately be taken. Certainly if reform changes from the potential to the active, The Legal Aid Society's experience records will be invaluable in shaping the measures to be pursued.

Still another line leads off from the instalment crusade, namely, the whole question of imprisonment in non-criminal proceedings. When Arthur B. Reeve examined Ludlow Street Jail in September, 1909, he found thirteen prisoners being watched and served by a staff of twenty-two — one warden, eleven keepers, three cleaners, five cooks, an engineer, and an engineer's assistant. A few of the prisoners were probably active members of "The Alimony Club." This shifting group of husbands who prefer jail to squaring their obligations to their wives keeps up its numbers well. Just before Christmas, 1927, fifteen "members" then at Ludlow Street Jail were moved to new quarters on West Thirty-Seventh Street. The "Club" did not strike Mr. Reeve as particularly pitiful or deserving of relief, although he probably heard about a few cruel commitments in these matrimonial cases. Neither was he greatly moved by the plight of employers committed for non-payment of wages, about whom more will soon be said. But he did vigorously deplore the other laws permitting plaintiffs to arrest defendants. These laws have always borne most heavily upon the destitute, as persons of even moderate means can supply bail which enables them to enjoy the very wide present-day "jail liberties."

Mr. Reeve pointed his comment by describing several typical instances of hardship, including the famous Charles H. Miller case. Miller, a paperhanger by trade, invested his savings in mining stock, depositing the certificates with a Wall Street brokerage firm to furnish margin for later purchases. Certain occurrences awakened Miller's suspicions about this firm, and he sued out a warrant against its manager on the ground that the man was about to convert Miller's securities and leave the jurisdiction. The manager was arrested, locked up for some eighteen hours, bailed out, and finally discharged by a magistrate. Whereupon he commenced against Miller an action for malicious prosecution. This form of action permitting the defendant's arrest, the manager had Miller seized and imprisoned for lack of $2500 bail.

From June 1, 1907, until March 25, 1908, Miller lay in the Ludlow Street Jail. He had retained lawyers, but they handled his case ineffectively. The poor fellow lost hope and his nerves began to give way. In November, 1907, he learned by chance of The Legal Aid Society and sent it a pleading letter. Prompt investigation showed that Miller had a good defence, his half-hearted lawyers were ousted, and the Society's attorney was substituted. Previous misconduct of the case blocked the way to a speedy trial, but a motion for reduction of bail to $500 succeeded. The Society produced the necessary bond, and Miller at last left jail. Although only forty-five, he looked like an old decrepit man. His hair was gray, his health broken, and he tottered on the edge of a mental collapse. Nearly twelve months later the malicious prosecution action went on trial, was bitterly fought for two days, and resulted in a complete victory for Miller. But beyond this he had no redress.

Such is the seamy side of arrest on civil process. Few persons considering it will fail to sympathize with the Society for having advocated further restriction of the procedure, or to applaud the legislature for having heeded such advocacy. The so-called body execution is now much less easily obtainable than it used to be. Many would go further and abolish it entirely. With these persons The Legal Aid Society feels bound to part company in one large class of cases — the wage claims which have always formed the greatest numerical item of its practice. It cannot be denied that wage earners may abuse their power of arrest. In 1910 a little East Side tailor employed a helper for a few days of rush work. The man was incompetent, and the tailor discharged him at the end of the first day. Having refused to accept one day's wages, the helper sued for the wages of a week. The tailor blundered into the wrong courtroom on the trial day, and judgment went against him by default. Then came a marshal to levy. Finding no property of the defendant's, he returned again with a body execution granted on the helper's false representation that he had worked a full week. And away to Ludlow Street Jail would have gone the little tailor had not a friend advanced the amount of the judgment. This friend sent the tailor to the Society, which prepared and served papers to vacate the judgment. The plaintiff, knowing the jig was up, lay low, and the case was dismissed.

But the foregoing instance is a rare one. The employing class by and large has money enough to defend itself against unjust claims. On the other hand, many an honest wage-earner would never get his money at all without the body execution. This does not mean that actual arrest for a wage debt is normal or usual; the possibility of such arrest generally suffices. In the Society's early days only a female wage-earner was entitled to arrest an employer if he failed to satisfy a judgment. This law indicates the influence of the Working Women's Protective Union. It provided a very practical comparative test. The Society found much difficulty in collecting wages for its male clients but observed that female workers were invariably paid. The report for 1892 contained the recommendation of Messrs. v. Briesen and Goeller that men be put on the same basis as women; a similar suggestion appears in the 1895 report; not until 1902 did the change of statute actually come. A prompt paean of praise arose from the East Side office, which forthwith whipped into line more than one astounded employer who had hitherto successfully boasted that he was execution-proof. The statute originally required action to be commenced within 30 days after the completion of the term of employment, and astute employers developed excellent technique in "stalling" until the time limit had passed. The year 1907 saw the 30 days extended to 60 on urgent representations of the Society and other interested organizations. Some amusing cases arose, notably that of an Italian operatic impressario on the lower East Side. He owed a trio of his girls the sum of $11.50 for wages. But he "packed a gun" and the girls were thoroughly afraid of him. Thus speaks the *Legal Aid Review:* "The . . . Society finally obtained a body execution. . . . Here, however, the problem of its enforcement against a perambulating arsenal had to be solved. Luckily the City Marshal proved equal to the task. [A contemporaneous newspaper account here insists that the marshal bore down upon the fiery Italian with "three strong arm men"!] The manager was locked up in Ludlow Street Jail, where no Italian opera is given. He remained in custody only a few hours, when money was forthcoming with which to satisfy the three claims."

Indeed "Liberty or Ludlow" had become a serious choice for male employers, who usually found it worth while to pay and embrace the first alternative. But the female of the species — the boarding-house keeper, the milliner, and so on — was not yet deemed by the courts to be subject to arrest on a wage judgment. She took contemptible advantage of her position, and on September 1, 1915, found in operation a new law subjecting women as well as men to body execution under any wage judgment not exceeding $100 exclusive of costs. The jail penalty runs not longer than 15 days without privilege of the jail liberties, quite enough to make most defendants produce the "roll of bills" which this kind of employer seems usually to carry on his person. But sometimes more pressure is required, as witness the following case. Acting for eleven employes of Mr. B., the Society sued and recovered eleven wage judgments, each carrying the possibility of arrest and aggregating about $500. Property executions being returned unsatisfied, B. was marched off to jail on January 26, 1923. In February he sued out a writ of habeas corpus, claiming that the eleven commitments ran simultaneously and that he was entitled to release at the end of 15 days. He lost. Then he claimed that the judgments were "snap judgments" and should be vacated. He lost again. On March 15 he once more sued out habeas corpus, taking the ingenious line that statute forbade arrest on an execution over 20 days old, that if the terms of confinement ran successively he was in substance being arrested on stale executions for the last nine terms of 15 days each, and that he therefore became entitled to release after serving the first two 15-day terms. He lost a third time. Having then served 60 days, with 105 days on seven judgments still in prospect, he surrendered and paid these judgments. The money was available to B. all the time, but only the most unusual pressure was capable of extracting it. And even so, the first four judgments remained unsatisfied. For determined individuals of this kind, 15 days' confinement is all too little. Luckily they are rare specimens. At least the Society is firm in its general conclusion that some power of imprisonment on wage claims should be retained.

On this general conclusion an immediate question arises. If the wage debtors subdued by actual or threatened arrest have funds or property from which to satisfy the judgments, why does not the marshal discover and levy upon these assets? In part the answer must be that much property is of the kind termed "portable" by the redoubtable Mr. Wemmick, and although easily available to the owner can be effectively concealed from the eyes of strangers. More largely, the answer is that money makes the mare go; that a marshal is compensated for his work with executions principally by a very small percentage fee depending upon the sums collected; that he has other easier, pleasanter, and more profitable types of work than enforcing the little claims of the Society's clients; and that, being human, he will therefore sidestep this latter task. Truth to tell, this answer carries even further and makes us fare worse. The city marshal dislikes the small body executions, and shirks them also. Thus for the Society the task of collecting by legal process from stoutly recalcitrant debtors often approaches the point of practical impossibility. Here is a vital problem upon which the Law Committee has expended its best energies. One attempted expedient is the use of sheriffs in place of marshals, since the functions of these two classes of officers somewhat overlap. But the sheriffs are not much more effective, usually refuse to work without fees on free or pauper summons cases, and frequently reject body executions. Another possibility, which has a hard practical ring, is a statute assuring the marshal a minimum five-dollar fee for *any* collection on execution. A third plan is to procure better disciplining of the marshals either through a chief city marshal or through justices of the Municipal Court, any of whom may now, by merely preferring charges against a marshal, cause his automatic suspension pending a hearing before the mayor. Some justices are willing to coöperate under this third plan, but the attitude of others can be guessed at from the fact that they have not helped the Society effectively to counteract an obstinate and unjustified refusal on the part of certain court clerks to permit the issuance of body executions as required by statute. Again it would seem as though The Legal Aid Society were encountering a problem of men rather than of legislation, and that it must settle down to a pertinacious educational campaign. For if our poor are to respect the law, they must be shown that legal decisions are inexorably enforceable. Meanwhile, Mr. McGee emulates Diogenes in his search for a vigorous, self-sacrificing marshal. The type is not imaginary, having appeared during the Society's early history in the form of Marshal Einstein, and more recently had a reincarnation in Marshal Henry H. Lazarus.

Wage collection has cut such a figure in the preceding discussion as to suggest an inquiry into the workman's resources when his wages prove inadequate to meet an emergency, or fail altogether because of sickness, injury, or death. The classic haven in time of trouble was the pawnshop, more recently enlarged by adding the lender who advances money on the security of furniture or other chattel property not immediately surrendered into his possession. There has also developed a class of lenders who take for security assignments of wages to fall due later on, thus enabling the borrower to anticipate future earnings. Finally, we have the modern beneficent system of workmen's compensation. This system entered New York quite well developed, and the Society has not had over-many reasons for suggesting changes. Still, some important recommendations were made. In 1924 Mr. McGee strongly urged a shortening from 14 days to 7 of the "waiting period" for compensation in cases of disabling injuries. This change was promptly made, becoming effective January 1,

1925. The Society also opposed discrimination against non-resident dependents of alien workers killed by New York industrial accidents, and has argued that the time limit for giving notice of injury should be calculated from the date of disability rather than from the date of the accident. On this latter point, there are plenty of actual cases where disabilities develop so long after the original mishaps as to leave victims remediless under the latter form of time limit.

But despite growing humanitarianism the small-loan question still remains as an extremely complex and difficult problem. Up to 1904, conditions in New York with respect to these minor financial transactions had seemed moderately satisfactory. During that year, unwise tinkering of the usury statute made the field more open and attractive to "loan sharks," who began to appear in considerable numbers. Profound forces not at once generally appreciated lay behind this social phenomenon, and it is probable that, even without the particular bit of statute changing, the serious problem which soon arose would ultimately have had to be faced. A few years later reliable estimates placed the annual business of small-loan concerns in Greater New York at $30,000,000, and their monthly profits at about 10 per cent on the investment. Manifestly they both had and were exercising powers of extortion, and possessed an established strength of resistance to remedial measures. This local situation was but one item in a bad state of affairs embracing the whole country, and its solution — so far as a satisfactory solution has been reached — is closely related to similar achievements in the other states. Clearly this is no place for the history of the great national crusade wherein the Russell Sage Foundation played a leading part. It is, however, proper to indicate what The Legal Aid Society did to make effective the New York phase of the attack.

First, it supplied concrete experience showing the nature and extent of the difficulty. Second, it joined with others in formulating and advocating the proper legislative remedies. This necessitated active criticism of many proposals either ill-advised or actually ill-intended. For relief could not come from any simple scheme, and some more elaborate plans had dangerous possibilities. Merely to enact that all loans carrying over 6 per cent interest should be illegal would have been both harmful and absurd. Poor people, lacking sound collateral, cannot reasonably expect to borrow at gilt-edge mortgage rates. Yet borrow they must in many a time of illness, death, or other emergency. It is far wiser to recognize these disagreeable facts than to pass impractical laws which drive the needy to illicit money-lenders who exact not merely high interest but also a kind of insurance premium to cover risks of prosecution and repudiated obligations. Specifically, it was an inadequate policy to try solving the salary or wage-loan problem (as New York did at the beginning) solely by combining with old-fashioned usury laws a provision that wage assignments should be invalid unless assignees gave employers prompt notice. So far as this played the employés' fear of discharge for anticipating their pay against a merely careless desire for quick money, it had merit. But where the wish for ready cash arose from dire need and not from passing whim, this very fear gave crooked lenders a terrifying club which they used constantly for their own profit. Before the end of the fight, employers were publicly urged not to bear down too harshly upon wage assignors, and to the extent that this request was heeded it tended to minimize the psychological effect of the notice statute. New York, as a first effort along wiser lines, has now adopted a system whereunder specially licensed lending concerns, subject to rigorous supervision, may advance small sums at interest rates supposed to yield a reasonable profit, but no more. Violations of the restrictions, and small lending by unlicensed concerns at more than the old-fashioned "legal rate" of 6 per cent, carry with them the possibility of forfeiture and criminal conviction. Here enters the third and most active function of the Society. It must be the watch-dog, or at least one of the watch-dogs, of the law, protecting individuals from imposition, fighting out test cases, gathering and reporting evidence for prosecutions.

No sooner had the regulatory scheme above outlined gone into effect than the sharks tried to evade it. When Mrs. Elizabeth Riordan on April 28, 1910, applied to the London Realty Company for a $50 loan with chattel-mortgage security, she was required to give a mortgage for $65, and from this sum to pay the company's attorneys $10 for their services in examining title and drawing the papers. By way of scenery, she also had to execute a written retainer of these gentlemen as *her* lawyers for the purposes of the transaction. Mrs. Riordan defaulted and the company brought a foreclosure suit. The Society defended on the ground that the veiled attempt to charge more than the legal rate of interest had discharged the debt and avoided the security. Up all the rungs of the New York judicial ladder went this little case, and in 1913 the Court of Appeals decided for Mrs. Riordan. It was simpler to break down the plan of a lender who had forced a municipal employé to pay $5 in advance for a loan of $50, and then pay a $5 fee on each of ten successive monthly renewals. This shark lost his principal and suddenly found himself the pursued instead of the pursuer, with an action pending against him under the usury law for twice the excessive interest paid. The Star Finance Company (suspected of being simply another name for a certain notorious old-line money-lender) combined the two plans by causing an attorney's fee to be collected for each monthly renewal. But there was nothing new here, and in 1914 the Society beat this concern soundly under the Riordan case. Then the Star ceased to twinkle in New York, informing applicants that its business had been turned over to the London Finance Company of Boston, Massachusetts. Receiving this news, John L. Shattuck, an employé of the New York police department, on March 3, 1914, took advantage of the Star's obliging offer to receive his application and forward it to Boston. He asked for $25, signed a note for $27.50 carrying 3 per cent interest per month, and also executed a confession of judgment. He soon received $25, which he did not repay. About August 11, 1914, the Boston concern took judgment by confession for $43.70 and levied on Shattuck's salary. Then appeared the Society with a motion to vacate the judgment for usury, and another bit of judicial ladder-climbing began. On November 13, 1917, the Court of Appeals decided in Shattuck's favor, evidently adopting the view of an intermediate court that the Massachusetts coloring of the deal had been "a mere subterfuge for the purpose of evading the usury laws of the state of New York."

This result was scarcely surprising, as the Society had in the lower courts won two earlier cases from the State Loan Association of Chicago, a former New York organization which had migrated westward when conditions became too unpleasant at its old home. This association had a very plausible interstate scheme. The borrower in New York executed nothing but an application and a power of attorney. Under this power an agent in Chicago signed the necessary papers and, in case of default, entered a confession of judgment. But there is no real novelty under the sun, and the plan just described was rather like an earlier subterfuge connected with loans secured by wage assignments, which subterfuge the Court of Appeals had held bad in 1912. So the Illinois people got nowhere upon judgments confessed either in New York or in the Chicago Municipal Court. Incidentally, Chicago seems to have been hard set upon teaching New York about small-loan sharpness. For in 1916 or thereabouts one E. Hollister Wrightson of the western metropolis brought against Mrs. Virginia Williams an action which developed remarkable features when the Society investigated it for the defendant. Mrs. Williams, living apart from her husband, had nearly three years previously been out of work and in great need of money. Responding to a loan concern's advertisement, she received a call from an investigator. Ultimately she decided not to borrow. But she unwisely signed certain papers which the investigator took away with him. Next appeared a collector, who demanded $30 with interest and a fat attorney's fee. Later came a sheriff, who seized the best pieces of Mrs. Williams's furniture under a writ of replevin. At the trial a joint mortgage was produced, executed in Chicago not only under a power of attorney from Mrs. Williams but also under a similar power from the absent Mr. Williams, who remained discreetly invisible during the trial. The evidence indicated that the husband had received and used the money advanced. In the end, the plaintiff was soundly defeated and the defendant duly indemnified for the improper seizure. This, of course, was an extreme case. But a dozen other tricks and dodges might be told as showing what constant vigilance is needed to protect the small borrower in New York.

Before closing a chapter indicating only by fragmentary illustration the numerous lines of constructive social betterment which legal aid has pursued, a word should be said about the harassing puzzles of domestic relations. Back in the old reports of the Society are statements showing that these questions then seemed much more black and white than they do now. This abuse was to be suppressed, that reform supported, and so on. But with the huge growth of practical experience inside the walls of the poor persons' law-office has come a tone of honest doubt and hesitation. Further restrictions upon marriage? Perhaps; but we must first examine more carefully the collateral dangers of such restrictions. Uniform laws for marriage and divorce? An attractive theory; but could it be practically and beneficially imposed upon the many jurisdictions of this country which have for long years grown used to their own peculiar law? New legislation to give relief against abandonment and the like? Surely; but let us never forget that the poor, even more than the well-to-do, need such relief, and that it is the normal tendency of such laws to carry an expense scale putting their practical benefits far beyond reach for the mass of the people. And when the Society comes down to the question of legal action in a specific domestic difficulty, it feels always bound to ask itself: is this a luxury or a clear necessity? For the torrent of these cases has long tended to be absolutely overwhelming, and the most deserving alone can receive intensive treatment. Thus in an instance of flat desertion, where the wife has been left to support herself and the children, a divorce of itself will not better her economic position although it may give her a greatly desired feeling of freedom. She is likely to be denied help in obtaining a decree. But let the errant husband interfere with the wife's efforts to make a living, or threaten to take the children from her, or bring divorce proceedings himself to head off a claim for separate support, and the Society will promptly swing into action on the wife's behalf. So where a very young Jewish girl had married an Irishman, and found herself cut off by her own family when the man deserted her, a Legal Aid attorney sought an annulment and by the time he obtained a decree had persuaded the girl's father to take her into his home again. A more shocking and obvious case for intervention was that of a fifteen-year old wife whom a vicious husband forced into promiscuous immorality. The marriage was annulled on the ground of non-age, the child removed from contaminating influences and placed under the permanent guardianship of a kindly relative.

Of course the Society never commences a divorce or annulment proceeding without exhausting every possibility of reconciliation. These attempts at pacific adjustment so often succeeded that in 1923 Mr. McGee tried what may be termed an experiment in anticipatory advice. After due deliberation he composed and published a "Decalogue for Husbands." Then, the spirit of inspiration again moving him, he produced a corresponding "Decalogue for Wives." The admonitions of these instruments were simple, sound bits of common sense, that rare but always accessible quality so often overlooked in human dealings. The two decalogues swept the country. For weeks the newspapers reprinted them, quoted them, and commented upon them. There was some adverse criticism and not a little natural levity, but on the whole the twenty points were warmly received. Perhaps no other single act in legal aid history has attained such quick and wide publicity. The publicity was complimentary yet at the same time pathetic. It showed the wide respect held for The Legal Aid Society and its advice. It proved the soundness of Mr. McGee's judgment as to what would catch general interest. And it indicated the touching eagerness of many puzzled and troubled people for help in their common personal difficulties. The problem of happy family life is nowhere near being answered, but we may hope for further guidance from the great law office which has seen and aided so many domestic troubles.

VI

THE SEAMEN'S BRANCH

"HERE'S $5 you got, an' $5 you have to get, an' $5 you never had—an' so you owe me $15!" This was the song of the crimp, a song without any rhyme or much reason, but singularly effective when a runner droned it off to a simple sailor-man, his simplicity largely increased by potent South Street whiskey. The crimp was one great reason for The Legal Aid Society's arrival on the waterfront, and the Society in turn is a leading reason for the present-day absence of the crimp and his whiskey and his song from the South Street neighborhood. A crimp is a man-seller—"one who, for a commission, supplies . . . sailors for ships by nefarious means or false inducements." He has other less disagreeable names, but the reader will easily discover him in the following summary of the sailor's human adversaries toward the end of the nineteenth century.

Suppose that a ship anchored off New York after a long voyage. Forthwith runners for the seamen's boarding-houses came over the rail armed with hard liquor and soft words. Then or shortly afterwards the crew was paid off, during which financial ceremony the runners danced eager attendance. Next they guided the men to their respective boarding-houses, where each sailor's money was at once subjected to melting influences. By way of concrete illustration: William Hopley came ashore with no less than $110 in cash. He fell promptly under the simultaneous ministrations of a boarding-house master and a tailor or seamen's outfitter. The latter persuaded him to buy for $35 a suit of shoddy clothes. The sailor's money was in his overcoat pocket. He fumbled out two $20 bills. The tailor snatched them and briskly made off. With a cry of dismay Hopley jerked free from the overcoat, tossed it to his boarding master, and gave chase. Returning from an unsuccessful pursuit he received the overcoat — but its pockets were bare as Mother Hubbard's cupboard! Lacking any witness to support his story, poor Hopley could do no better than compromise for half the missing $70 with the boarding master, who was of course injured innocence personified. Incidentally The Legal Aid Society obtained a $5 judgment against the tailor so that the mariner's whole experience left him only $35 short. This was a case of gorgeous and unusual opportunity. But old-time boarding masters, like forceful generals, *made* their opportunities. One extremely simple plan was to have a newly landed sailor deposit his wages with the boarding-house proprietor, who undertook to dole them out upon request. Soon enough the depositor went on spree and got delightfully drunk. When he recovered and asked for cash, the boarding master blandly informed him that during his period of exhilaration he had demanded and received all his money! In passing, it should be observed that sailors' boarding-houses existed under a license system and were supposed to be carefully scrutinized and somewhat regulated. Most unwisely, though, it had been arranged that the sole emoluments of the particular licensing commissioners should come from the fees paid for licenses *which they granted. Verb. sap.!* The early attorneys at the Seamen's Branch, at least the first of whom was assistant secretary to the commissioners, decided that many or most of the sailors' boarding-houses were in improper hands.

Miscellaneous sticky-palmed and plausible gentlemen had their innings with Jack ashore. Illustrations are legion, and one which contains entertaining elements may be given. Two seamen, just paid off, while wandering about town entered one of those extraordinary places of amusement called anatomical museums, and fell into conversation with the quack doctor who conducted it. Surrounded with his grisly exhibits, he wrought in the men great fear of the ills of the flesh, and persuaded them (at $3 per capita) to have him examine into their condition. The result may be imagined. Both poor fellows were ill — very ill; they could be cured, but it would cost one $90 and the other $120. They should, and did, pay down $25 each to cover a week's treatment and medicines. Once out of the doctor's sphere of influence the two tottering invalids began to feel certain comforting suspicions. So did their boarding master, who sent them to the Seamen's Branch, which sent them to a physician at the Marine Hospital, who returned them with the report that they had suffered from nothing worse than museum-induced hypochondria. Thereupon, it is good to record, the hand of legal retribution descended upon the quack doctor and squeezed him most effectively.

It can be imagined that no man's pay would last long under such affectionate attentions as this, particularly before The Legal Aid Society branched out toward the sea. Hence for the latter part of his time ashore the seaman was reduced to a financial zero, dependent for pocket money, for food, and for lodging upon his boarding master. This worthy normally proceeded to obtain his lodger a berth on a new ship, working either directly or through one of the numerous waterfront shipping masters. Under the careful chaperonage of a runner, the man went to sign shipping articles. Here he found himself quite divested of any effective bargaining power. The articles were cast in fixed form, which he must take or leave. It was frequent practice to make men sign on for very long terms running into years. This opened the possibility of desertion and forfeiture of pay. Sometimes the rate of compensation was ridiculously low, either for the whole period or for so substantial a time that the sailor was likely to desert in disgust before the higher rate began. As late as 1905 an American youngster signed from New York to Liverpool at one shilling per month. On reaching his destination he was compelled to do a week's shore duty without pay. Being thus put in severe financial straits and having become most anxious to get home, he was easily persuaded to sign new articles which he did not read or have read to him. These articles, as was customary upon English vessels, provided that the boy should be paid off only at a port in the United Kingdom. Consequently, when he asked at New York for his discharge, his clothes, and his pay the request was refused. At a hearing before the British consul the attorney for the Seamen's Branch showed that the boy was an American citizen under twenty-one years of age and therefore entitled to rescind his contract. The consul accepted this argument and the boy was immediately discharged, but presumably without wages.

To come back to the time of signing articles, the foregoing paragraph suggests that the sailor had to take or leave the articles presented. There was extremely little chance of his leaving them, with the runner nudging his elbow. For unless the man signed on, he knew in the old days that the incensed boarding master would, at the mildest, take revenge by seizing his outfit and putting him on the street. At worst, he might well be shanghaied. On every turn the runner carefully looked out for the boarding master's interests. When articles were signed, he obtained from the seaman what is called in America an allotment note. A Federal law has long and wisely forbidden advance payments of wages to seamen. But this same law, at the time of which we are speaking, permitted advance allotments for the benefit of the seaman's family and of his creditors or so-called creditors. The latter part of this provision was played to the limit. Even though a boarding master had given a seaman very little in the shape of supplies, food, or shelter, he would present a fat bill and insist upon payment. From the money thus collected he paid any shipping master concerned in the transaction a fee for the latter's services. Statute forbade the taking of "blood money" from sailors for obtaining them employment, shipping masters being supposed to receive their entire compensation from the owners. But under the cloak of boarding masters' claims it was simple, and for many years a common practice, to violate the statute.

Our sailor now puts to sea. In the course of a long voyage he might suffer unjust brutality from the captain or officers of his vessel. Mr. Justice Henry B. Brown of the United States Supreme Court wrote thus in 1901: "One of my earliest experiences was to make a voyage to Liverpool upon a sailing vessel from New York. During that voyage I became a witness of scenes which I have never been able to recall without a shudder. The treatment of the common sailors was so inhuman that I should have thought it impossible it could be tolerated in a civilized country; but the difficulty was that the law placed in the hands of the master a despotic authority over a crew of ignorant men, whom he seemed to take a delight in abusing and beating. The very possession of this arbitrary power seemed to be provocative of a desire to misuse it. This desire, of course, was fostered by the isolation of the vessel, the impossibility of communicating with the shore, or [and?] the [lack of] opportunity of securing legal redress." Also, while many captains were honest men, some played unfair games upon their crews. For example, a seaman given shore-leave at an intermediate port would request part of the money coming to him. The captain, however, might be persuaded by one of the shore sharpers to refuse any cash advance, instead turning his man over to these designing gentry and promising to meet their bills out of the man's pay. The long and short of such a transaction usually was that the sailor got some very tawdry entertainment, clothes, and supplies while the sharpers grossly overcharged him and split their excess profits with the master. Sometimes, one blushes to state, captains did not even stick by their ships. In one case which the Society handled, the skipper of a coaster sailing from Maine to New York became so fearful about the vessel's seaworthiness that he landed and made the trip by railroad, while his crew at very considerable risk completed the voyage! They arrived exhausted, half starved, and, naturally, unpaid. The skipper denied responsibility. When the ramshackle boat was sold, she produced only about half the sum due for wages.

The foregoing account shows that an old-time sailor was safe neither at sea nor ashore from men who very well knew their own interests and cared nothing about his. Long before the end of the century this had been realized and several benevolent organizations were at work along the New York waterfront. During the mid-nineties these societies banded together into a Joint

Conference to promote helpful legislation for seamen and obtain proper enforcement of existing protective laws. The Conference itself did not desire to undertake direct aggressive work. Hence the Protestant Episcopal Church Missionary Society for Seamen in the City and Port of New York (now the Seamen's Church Institute of New York) in 1897 employed a representative to seek out and advise sailors and protect them from robbery and outrage while in port. This good beginning proved not entirely adequate. The Society and the Conference sought to locate a responsible legal aid organization which would coöperate along the lines indicated above. An investigating committee reported The Legal Aid Society as the only body which could promise satisfactory service. The consequence was, of course, establishment of the Seamen's Branch, the earliest and in many ways the most interesting and important of the Society's ramifications in New York. Its novelty caught attention and invited support. Almost at the beginning William G. Low, whose generous contribution to the security fund has been described, first lent and soon gave outright a fund of $5000 to help sustain the work. The police commissioners detailed a uniformed officer for duty at the Branch, this being the first strictly public recognition paid the Society. All over the world seafaring men learned of the venture. New York became uniquely distinguished for its legal protection of sailors, and even as late as 1914 seamen said that nowhere else upon the fringes of the seven seas were their rights so fully guarded.

The chairman of the Conference's investigating committee was J. Augustus Johnson, a gentleman then in his early sixties, not too much bound down by business or professional connections, and intensely eager to better the lot of the seafaring man. Mr. Johnson's previous career has peculiar significance. After being educated for the Bar he entered the consular service in 1858 and remained for twelve years, first as consul and later as consul general at Beirut, Syria. Under the treaty of extraterritoriality with Turkey the consul general acted as judge in all cases involving American citizens. Numerous complaints by seamen against their masters, before Mr. Johnson, drove him to conclude that, while the dictatorial powers enjoyed by a ship's captain are necessary for discipline and safety at sea, inadequate safeguards had at that period been provided to protect the men before the mast against abuse of these powers. He determined that as soon as circumstances permitted he would devote himself to the improvement of maritime law bearing upon the condition of the sailor. In this activity we find him engaged at the time of the founding of the Seamen's Branch. He was admirably suited for the work thus voluntarily undertaken. He had energy, enthusiasm, and human sympathy. His government connections made him an effective advocate of reform legislation before administrative departments and legislative committees at Washington. He was a tower of strength to The Legal Aid Society. He was perennial chairman of the Visiting Committee which oversaw the activities of the Seamen's Branch. His working hours were very largely devoted to the interests of the Society and the welfare of its clients from 1899 until his death some fifteen years later.

At first glance it would seem that, as to many attacks upon sailors' persons and property, the Seamen's Branch had to deal with problems parallel to, and only of the same difficulty as, those encountered by the main office in its civil and criminal practice. The reader will correctly assume that it was no more legal to commit assault and battery on a seaman, to cheat him, or to retain his wages, than it was to treat a landlubber likewise. Indeed, more than this can be said. Congress, recognizing the peculiar nature of the seafarer's life and his somewhat peculiar personal characteristics, had long been building up a protective code for his benefit. Some of its features were taken over from similar laws enacted by Great Britain and other leading maritime countries, and therefore carried with them a presumption of soundness and efficiency. We have already briefly noticed the act forbidding advance wage payments to seamen, and shall have occasion to discuss it further. Additional acts provided for substantial damages to a sailor who was wrongfully discharged or whose wages were improperly withheld. It has for many years been a rule of general sea law that a hand injured in the course of his duties is entitled to "maintenance and cure" as part of his pay. Also the Federal statutes contain special procedural provisions for facilitating lawsuits by wronged seamen. On the whole, our laws seemed to place the sailor in an exceptionally favored position.

But this very fact suggests that these artificial advantages were conferred to offset natural disadvantages. Nor are the latter far to seek. The seaman, possibly more than any other human being, is a person of frequent and erratic movement. His whole life is one of varied journeying. Travel takes him to strange countries perhaps more often than to his own. In the Seamen's Branch the proportion of alien applicants for relief has persistently run very high. What could be more exotic than a crew of thirty-seven Lascar seamen, clothed for the tropics, shivering in Battery Park on a piercing December day? Abdul Rahman, their serang, found his way to the Branch with a plea for warmer clothing, which was ultimately supplied by an advance of wages from the vessel's agents plus a donation from the Protestant Episcopal Missionary Society. Such strangers are ignorant of American legal processes, and neither they nor even United States seamen have the resources or the time to wait in New York upon the somewhat deliberate movements of the Federal courts which handle maritime disputes. Early in January, 1914, a naturalized American citizen lost part of one finger by accident on a British steamer. There was some doubt as to his proper legal remedy, and further delay when correct action had been determined. Eighteen months after the accident, the case was still far from trial. The client had run up a bill at a South Street boarding-house fully equal to the maximum recovery possible, while his destitute family had been forced to sell their household effects and move from Buffalo to another city where a relative was willing to receive them.

Here, then, even more than at the Society's other offices, we find that quick settlements and many of them have always been imperatively necessary. Along that line the attorneys in charge at once began to work. One feature of the situation greatly favored them, so far as they sought to dispose of claims which permitted the libelling of vessels. A libel ties up the ship in custody of a court officer, subject to the willingness and ability of owner or master to release her by giving bond. Hence lawyers of a shady type had greatly enjoyed enforcing and rather overplaying small claims by libelling ships (in the vernacular, "sticking plasters on them") when they were about to sail and delay of any sort was most inconvenient. So a large number of the more respectable shipping concerns had as early as 1901 recognized in the Seamen's Branch a power for justice from every point of view and were settling most complaints promptly upon notification of the claims. This attitude was amusingly exemplified in 1908 when a bellicose scow captain appeared with a claim for $48 and urgent demands for "a plaster." There were questionable and difficult features to the case. The Branch knew the scow owner, had a high opinion of him, and granted him time to investigate. This did not suit the applicant, who went off asserting that he would get a *good* lawyer. He then proceeded to retain successively three attorneys without making any real progress. After about two weeks the owner had determined what ought to be paid, and sent the crestfallen captain back to the Branch to have his papers drawn for a $45 settlement.

As to cases of assault and battery on shipboard by masters and officers, the age of deep-sea brutality was distinctly beginning to pass in 1900. During that year and for some time afterward tales of terrible cases involving even murder and maiming of seamen came to the Society. No doubt there are still sporadic instances of vicious cruelty. But even as early as 1901 the authorities were making object lessons of the more flagrant cases, the average English officer found it wiser to put a sailor in irons than to strike him, and officers of the American merchant marine thought twice before resorting to violence. More than once, a man coming to the Seamen's Branch with charges against a bucko mate could be told: "The mate has been here to see us. He'll settle for $10. Does that satisfy you?" Usually it did. Money in hand was worth more than a lawsuit, with the chance of being detained indefinitely as a witness. Many such disputes, and also controversies as to adequate provisioning and so forth, have to be fought out before the consul of the nation to which the vessel in question belongs. These consular hearings are of course prompt, and at them the Society has had a satisfying measure of success, although in some consulates seamen are forbidden to bring lawyers and are thus placed in a disadvantageous position when opposing the better-educated, more astute ships' officers. It is also possible, where conciliation fails to settle a dispute between master or owner on one side and any of the crew on the other, to avoid court delays by mutual written agreement for submission of the matter to a United States shipping commissioner. This would be a more frequently invoked procedure if either party might effect such submission irrespective of the other's attitude; but Congress has never felt it advisable to accept The Legal Aid Society's recommendation for this change in the law. It is of course a cheering possibility that the glut of petty prohibition cases before the Federal courts will force a reorganization incidentally helpful to the small affairs of seamen.

But despite all delays and difficulties, the Seamen's Branch has had to make itself a fighting record by putting through enough court cases to prove that painful consequences flow from refusing reasonable settlements. Some shipping offices used to have a pleasant method of holding up wages which seamen had earned while working in port. Typically these men would have signed articles and actually joined their ships before the port pay fell due. If they could be put off for a few hours, the ships would sail and they might never get back to make effective claims. Hence at nine o'clock nobody in the shipping office had power to pay the bills; at ten the paymaster had just gone out; at eleven the money had just been sent for; and every moment brought sailing-time closer. If poor Jack was wise, he went promptly to the Seamen's Branch. A few sharp lessons taught the shipping firms to pay on the nail when The Legal Aid Society took the field, and Fabian money-saving tactics were discarded. Detention of sailors' clothing presented a serious problem, as this deprived seamen of the equipment for their trade, without which they could not face exposure to ocean weather. In 1895 a Federal act exempted the clothing of seamen from attachment and provided a money penalty for its detention. With this act the Branch brought down one or two high-handed boarding masters, but something more severe was needed to make quick work of practically every case. So in 1904 the Society, working through Mr. Johnson, persuaded Congress to turn the detention of mariners' clothing into a misdemeanor punishable by fine or imprisonment or both. The result was immediate and has been lasting. Polite utterance of the dire words "Federal crime" leads almost unfailingly to prompt surrender.

The Federal statutes provide that, where a seaman who has signed articles is unjustly discharged before the voyage begins or before one month's pay is earned, he may recover not merely what wages he has earned but also an additional sum equal to one month's wages. The Society deemed it important to discourage the practice of leaving sailors in the lurch, by getting a favorable decision or two under this provision. In 1906 a proper test case arose. Five seamen who signed on with the schooner *Charles K. Buckley* were told to meet the captain next day at 38 South Street. The men kept the appointment, but the skipper did not. Instead, he ultimately signed on a fresh crew and put to sea. After a good deal of waiting and inquiry, and some unsuccessful negotiation with the captain, the five men went to the Seamen's Branch. Their suit came on for trial almost exactly a year later. Possibly absence of the ship from port may account for the delay. At any rate, Judge Adams decided in the men's favor, allowing them a month's wages each. The Society thus served general warning on masters and owners inclined to repudiate shipping articles. But a significant fact should be noted. Judge Adams gave judgment reluctantly because he did not think the men had suffered much. Legislators are prone to forget that the mere enactment of severe penal provisions will not always accomplish the intended object if courts believe the penalties exaggeratedly harsh. The particular statute left Judge Adams without any alternative, and in 1925 Judge Campbell had no hesitation about awarding a month's pay even though the man claiming it had not experienced any hardship; but under another section of law covering seamen's wage payments the same problem as to practical enforcement arose and caused more trouble.

This is the section requiring that sailors be paid off within specified time-limits after their discharge. Here the penalty provision used to be that any master or owner failing "to make payment in the manner hereinbefore mentioned *without sufficient cause* shall pay to the seaman a sum equal to one day's pay for each and every day during which payment is delayed beyond the respective periods. . . ." The Society tried for years to obtain an unqualified favorable decree under this so-called "waiting pay" clause. The case first chosen was that of the brig *Havileh*, libelled for unpaid wages and sold in 1904. A mariner named Nathaniel Pitt duly proved his wage claim before the United States Commissioner and demanded waiting pay. At first the Commissioner absolutely refused any allowance on the latter score, but ultimately awarded two days' waiting pay, holding that the filing of a libel at the end of that period prevented further accrual. This decision Judge Adams confirmed, to the considerable disappointment of the Seamen's Branch. Richard D. Currier, attorney for the Branch from 1903 to 1906, came to the conclusion that wherever a judge had any reasonable excuse for doing so he would avoid the rigors of the statute by squeezing through the exit provided in the words "*without sufficient cause*." Mr. Currier himself felt sympathy toward this attitude. No wage case was likely to come up for decision until several months after the original refusal or failure to pay. Meanwhile the claimant would normally have obtained work on another ship. So waiting pay might mean double pay for a very substantial time. Hence Mr. Currier recommended that the arbitrary measure of damages be repealed and the judge's discretion substituted. Perhaps it might have been still better to allow waiting money for a definite minimum period, further awards to depend on the circumstances of each case. But when Congress did alter the law in 1915 by the LaFollette Act, it took exactly the reverse direction and *doubled* the waiting pay. Naturally enough, a number of later decisions have refused the increased waiting wage, particularly where financial stringency made prompt payment difficult or impossible. Yet in 1925 the Society actually recovered the double wage for a group of clients under circumstances which might have sustained a finding that the original refusal to pay was based on "sufficient cause." Although the awards added up to a substantial aggregate, the respondent was solvent, and apparently for the first time in the history of such proceedings before the United States District Court for the Eastern District of New York payment in full was exacted. It took twenty-five years, but a clean-cut precedent went into the court records at last.

Other interesting cases handled by the Branch have had intensely moving human elements, although their significance has not been so broad as that of the matters just discussed. When in 1904 a man honorably discharged from the navy fell among thieves who stole his money and discharge papers, it followed not unnaturally that he was first arrested on suspicion of desertion and later committed to Blackwell's Island on a vagrancy charge. Meanwhile, though, his wife and children in Boston, Massachusetts, were deprived of support. Another sailor, given a shorter term on Blackwell's Island, learned of the ex-naval man's troubles and reported them to the Society, which soon had the unlucky prisoner discharged, collected his back pay from the navy, and restored him to his family. A few years later the Seamen's Branch received a call from Henry Beer, who had shipped for three years on a tramp steamer then bound to South America, come ashore to buy supplies, and been left behind when his vessel sailed some nine hours ahead of time. Beer had a good record and was anxious not to be logged as a deserter. Since the ship must coal at Norfolk, Virginia, he might catch her there by taking the train. But he had no money. The attorney in charge, liking Beer's looks, bought him a ticket for Norfolk. He caught the steamer and gratefully repaid the money.

About the end of 1911 a young seaman shipped from New York to New Orleans and back on a sailing ship. After three or four weeks the vessel put in at an island to take aboard some cargo. The young fellow having been sent ashore with a comrade, the ship sailed away and left them marooned with an old negro and a group of men who spoke only Spanish. The negro insisted that the pair had signed papers by which they agreed to stay on the island and work for a year at $10 per month. Hard labor, bad food, and fever made their existence miserable. After three months a storm drove a schooner to take shelter in the island harbor and on her the maroons made their escape. When they finally reached New York and consulted the Seamen's Branch, investigation showed that the two men had been shipped without any agreement and without the knowledge of the master or owners of the sailing vessel. The latter, however, ultimately made a settlement satisfactory to the victims of this peculiar adventure. Two or three years later the Society helped at the other end of a somewhat similar case. Miguel Bonaparte and R. Pardeza, natives of Porto Rico, had in 1901 been moved to Hawaii by Americans interested in the sugar plantations. They lived happily enough in Hilo with their families until work became slack about the middle of 1913. Then they shipped on the bark *John Eno* for a voyage to the United States and return. At Philadelphia the master left them behind. For two months they vainly sought employment, then walked all the way to New York and spent six December days and nights actually in the streets. Finally directed to the Seamen's Branch, they were rescued from their ugly predicament. Through a shipping agent who, oddly enough, had helped to bring about the emigration of these very men from Porto Rico, the attorney got them booked as passage workers on the only ship leaving the North Atlantic ports for San Francisco and Hawaii in the next six weeks. And so a grand family reunion was accomplished.

The significance of the foregoing paragraphs can be easily summarized. These incidents show that the Seamen's Branch succeeded in giving sailors a fair measure of protection against, and of recompense for, legal wrongs either threatened or actually committed by ships' officers, ships' owners or agents, and miscellaneous miscreants on land. But the heart of the Society's problem at the port of New York lay in pernicious activity by shipping and boarding masters who directed and controlled the crimping industry. Of all the matters hitherto discussed, only one — enforcement of the prohibition against detaining seamen's clothing — struck this industry at all directly, and the blow thus given was very slight. Here, then, rather than in any effort previously described, was the acid test of success by the Seamen's Branch. The exponents of crimping were powerful and well entrenched. Their aggregate exactions from individual victims were beyond calculation, but in 1901 Mr. v. Briesen says: "It has been estimated that shipping coming into this harbor had . . . been taxed . . . more than $5,000,000 per year [by the crimps]." So profitable an industry was bound to fight hard against extinction. Yet in the huge profit lay a seed of weakness. By exploiting all with whom they came in contact, masters and owners as well as foremast hands, the crimps stripped themselves of friends and allies. Rifts appeared even in the industry itself. Boarding masters informed against shipping masters who struck them as too grasping; the Irish crimps informed against the Germans; internecine feuds developed among the Irish themselves. The Society began to procure convictions. In October, 1900, a captain and apparently a shipping master as well were convicted of taking an unlawful shipping fee ("blood money") from a sailor. In 1901, Irish boarding masters exposed to the Society a German runner's violation of the Federal act forbidding lodging-house keepers to board incoming or recently arrived vessels and solicit seamen as lodgers. The runner was arrested and held for trial. At about the same time the Seamen's Branch caught an Irish shipping master taking blood money and had him haled before a United States commissioner.

Matters often wore an uglier and more difficult aspect for the Branch lawyers. During 1901 a deputation of ruffians came to the office and threatened Clark H. Abbott, the first attorney in charge, with a beating if he did not ease off his pursuit of law-breakers. It was unsafe to sneer at such threats. In June, 1899, Rev. Carsten Hansteen from the Scandinavian Seamen's Mission conducted a service on the ship *Abbie S. Hart*, and was attacked by some of the Cherry Street crimping gang as he started to leave the vessel. The crimps restrained the officers and crew from interfering, beat Hansteen brutally, and might well have killed him had he not managed to escape into his launch alongside. So tight was the shipping combination that the Norwegian consul could not procure sufficient evidence to justify prosecution. The Society therefore felt obliged to employ a special police officer for Mr. Abbott's protection.

The immediate cause of the threats may have been the attorney's direct attack upon the shanghaiing or kidnapping of sailors. This criminal practice unquestionably went on at New York, but was very difficult to expose. In April, 1901, two mariners named Campbell and McKay entered a State Street saloon and had a drink which evidently contained more evil ingredients than the demon rum. They came to aboard the steamer *Ems*, lying off Stapleton, Staten Island. Luckily enough,

Mr. Abbott was looking for two other men supposed to have been shanghaied, and in his search visited the *Ems*. He discovered Campbell and McKay, proved that they had never legally signed articles, and took them back to land. About this time or a little later the British ship *Westgate* took on a crew at New York. According to a subsequent statement signed by fifteen of her men, they found before sailing that the crimps were collecting extortionate advances and allotments aggregating $54 per man. The sailors protested and refused to go to work until they had seen the British consul. Pretending to go ashore for the consul, the captain returned with a man named Glennon "and eight boarding masters and Cherry-St. pugilists." The roughs forced the crew, one by one, to go aft to the mate's cabin and sign a paper authorizing payment of the full $54. Those who refused to sign were assaulted and thumped into submission. Then, says the statement: "Glennon's bullies compelled us to turn to by force, and told us if we tried to go ashore they would lick our bloody heads off. . . . During the time this was going on the captain was walking the poop with the pilot, and the chief officer was standing on the main deck, both within sight and hearing, and neither one said nothing."

The Federal laws against crimping and illegal boarding of ships were clear enough, if only evidence of their violation could be obtained. During the day constant vigilance reduced illicit boarding to a minimum. Even when an incoming ship anchored outside the harbor she could often be seen from Mr. v. Briesen's Staten Island residence — "the first house on your left as you enter America," he jokingly told Prince Henry of Prussia. Here Mr. v. Briesen frequently watched arriving ships through a spy-glass to make sure that the "hawks" did not get aboard. During 1901 Mr. Abbott was of opinion that the Society's efforts had practically broken up illegal boarding. R. C. Ringwalt, his successor, who came to the Seamen's Branch fresh from the instalment crusade, found this view perhaps too optimistic. But he also found new and powerful allies working with him. President Roosevelt, a sturdy friend of legal aid from his Police Commissioner days, and Collector of the Port Stranahan used government tugs to increase the scope and effect of the Staten Island spy-glass, and the Collector a little later permitted the Branch attorney to board any ships in the harbor to carry out his duties.

Both Abbott and Ringwalt agreed, however, that The Legal Aid Society greatly needed a launch for its marine work, particularly after dark, when criminal activities had better cover. As Mr. v. Briesen explained, the activity of the Seamen's Branch soon forced "the pirates and the crimps" into "working during *the night*, boarding ships *at night*, to get the seamen off or to sell their human merchandise. Mr. Abbott and his assistants, though amply occupied during the day, have spent many a night on the waters of the bay to intercept these rascals, and were frequently successful. But . . . vessels are not to be easily obtained at night to take our officers where they should be able to perform their duty." While efforts to raise the necessary funds proved unsuccessful, in 1904 the Episcopal Church Missionary Society generously lent its launch *Sentinel* to the Legal Aid lawyers whenever necessary. This loan came in the nick of time, for the Society was getting firmly at grips with crimping, and the turning-point of the struggle was not far ahead. It will be remembered that in 1904 Congress made criminal the detention of seamen's wearing apparel; simultaneously the demand or receipt of a shipping fee from a sailor was also made a Federal crime. Incidentally a Congressional commission began a general survey of American mercantile marine conditions, including the treatment, comfort, and safety of seafaring men. Needless to say, Mr. Johnson followed this survey carefully and made numerous contributions. In 1906 shanghaiing in addition became a Federal offence. By that time the Society's activity had led to a wide campaign against maritime kidnapping. The fight spread to other ports and to such areas as Chesapeake Bay, where outrageous conditions existed on the oyster boats. Still later the same movement manifested itself in the suppression of peonage, the land equivalent for shanghaiing.

The Society gave prompt and effective publicity to the new laws by issuing its famous "Sailor's Log," a convenient and well-indexed little pamphlet containing not only full reprints of statutes but also succinct advice to the seaman about his rights and obligations. The first edition is dated January 1, 1905; the second edition, August 1, 1906. A third edition, long urgently needed, was at first regretfully deferred for lack of funds, and is now being held back because of extensive pending amendments in the laws affecting mariners. This book did more than sweep the country; it swept the seafaring world. Requests for copies came from every corner of the globe. In 1911 a letter to the "Seamens Legel Aid Socitity" from Seattle asked for "one of thos smal books in wich is given the rights of Seamen towards the vessel and master paing of wages and shipping rules. I had one of thos smal books wenn sailing on the Atlantic Coast two years ago, *and it has saved many a quarrel bedween Officer and mann.*" Precise knowledge replaced the annoying inaccurate haggling of the old "sea lawyer," and if men learned clearly about their rights, they also learned no less clearly about their duties. There was some opposition, of course. Said Richard D. Currier, the Attorney who compiled both editions: "Perhaps the greatest compliment paid the book is that given by a seamen's society, which devotes much time to distributing libraries on vessels. This society began to send out a copy in each library. Soon a great protest was raised on the part of captains who complained bitterly about the book, because they stated that it was teaching the sailors too much law. One captain went so far as to threaten to throw a whole library overboard unless the pamphlet was removed." Rather than defeat the general usefulness of its libraries, the society in question omitted the "Sailor's Log" where such protests were made.

With the 1904 and 1906 legislation, the Society again went out for test cases. The first blood-money case was tried in January, 1905, and lost. It was a costly disappointment, as the District Attorney detained the four prosecuting witnesses in jail for nearly two months. Such detention was unfortunately necessary because of both the wandering character of the witnesses and the practical certainty that the criminal interests would tamper with them if at large. Judge Thomas, who presided at the trial, thought the evidence ample for conviction. But this was cold comfort after the jury had the final say. A number of subsequent prosecutions broke down when witnesses could not be held long enough for the slow-moving Federal courts. At best, proof of the crime was difficult, for illegal fees were usually hidden in superficially valid allotment notes running to boarding masters who openly claimed all the money as creditors but secretly divided with the shipping masters. Finally, about October, 1907, the Society simultaneously encountered both a shanghai case and a blood-money situation involving several seamen and two crimps. While the former seems to have fizzled out, the latter resulted in a pair of convictions on October 8, 1907.

A little more than one year later Mr. McGee, then attorney in charge at the Seamen's Branch, discovered that an employment agent had made two Spanish coal passers pay him $5 each for jobs on the Morgan Line ship *Creole*. Carefully guarding the Spaniards against improper influences, the United States District Attorney went to work so effectively that the agent changed an original plea of "not guilty" to "guilty," was fined, and received warning that if convicted again he would get the maximum penalty. The year 1910 saw a still more telling blow. On information obtained by the Society two of the oldest and most notorious shipping masters in the whole port of New York were convicted for taking from sailors illegal fees under the screen of allotments payable to a boarding master. Of four original complainants against these men one mysteriously disappeared pending trial. Thereupon the prosecution discreetly guarded the remaining three by putting two in the Tombs and the third on a job where he could be reached when wanted. Either before or during trial two complainants were attacked on the street, but escaped serious injury. After the conviction, the licensing commission refused to renew defendants' license and so put them out of business.

For some years the crimps remained very quiet and comparatively inactive. Their trade had not quite died, however, and late in 1914 the United States Attorney, with help from the Branch, struck it again. This time the defendant was a man named McNamara, who had been associated with one of the 1910 defendants. On conviction, the judge fined him $750 with the alternative of a like number of days in the penitentiary. Incidentally, His Honor caused one of defendant's witnesses to be arrested for perjury and, when the man pleaded guilty, gave him a four-month sentence. Next year the LaFollette Act repealed the statutory provision allowing seamen to make allotment notes payable to their creditors. Thus ended a legal device which had not only tended to make sailors debt slaves, but also caused masters and owners much trouble from desertions incited by boarding-house keepers who would enrich themselves through fresh allotments after signing the deserters on with other ships. Hit so hard and often, crimping broke down, and with it went shanghaiing, although there appears to have been no Federal conviction at New York for the latter crime. The Seamen's Branch had won its great fight.

Meanwhile an entirely distinct reform was being carried forward. On January 28, 1908, Mr. Johnson thus reported:

"The published accounts of loss of life and cargoes by the breaking up of tow-lines at sea should call attention to the unnecessary risks incurred by the existing system of barge transportation.

"Subject to no inspection old schooner and sloop hulks are too often cut down for barge service when unseaworthy. The too great length of tow-lines invites disaster in foggy weather to passing vessels which run across tow-lines and barges connected by invisible hawsers. The unseen barges at the end of the line swing around with fatal effect against the side of the passenger and freight carrying craft and the snap-the-whip effect of a long line of barges when rounding a point of land or a lightship is a well known cause of disaster.

"But it is not the wreckage caused by storms alone to which I call attention. The unprotected barge and scow in all weathers should no longer pass unnoticed. It would seem incredible but it is true that barges and scows in use on our rivers, lakes, harbors and sea coast are not supplied with bulwarks, steering appliances, small boats, life preservers, line buoys or other protection, common to other vessels. Their decks, without freeboard, when loaded, frequently greasy from garbage, and icy when all awash are not over 12 or 15 inches wide. Men slip off unseen in the darkness or fog to their death, unprotected by side ropes or stanchions which could be provided at slight cost.

"After much observation and inquiry I learn that the expenditure of less than fifty dollars on each barge would save more than fifty per cent. of the lives annually lost on these boats. The barge crews are sometimes limited to one or two men. They are seldom registered, and when lost, reports cannot be sent to their homes, because their names are not known and the dependent families await in vain the return of the breadwinners and add to the list of dependent widows and children supported by the public.

"It cannot be that the directors and stockholders of the towing companies will allow this unnecessary waste of human life to continue when these facts are known to them. Public sentiment and ordinary benevolence should induce them to correct these omissions. If not, Congress should provide by legislation for adequate inspection and safety appliances as it has already done for vessels and railways carrying passengers for hire."

Less than a year later Mr. Johnson was able to quote reasonably satisfactory Federal legislation on all points mentioned above, obtained after a good deal of pulling and hauling with shipping interests. The usual fight for effective enforcement followed, the Society finding not only numerous private vessels but also the New York City municipal dumping scows operated without proper equipment. Having felt the squeeze of the 1908 laws, ship owners dragged the matter back before Congress and accomplished some modification and partial repeal. In the long run, however, much of the legislation stood and the sailorman's lot was substantially benefited. As early as 1912 Congressional discussion began to touch many of the points finally embodied in the LaFollette Act of 1915. While carefully abstaining from expression of opinion about technical matters not covered by its experience, the Society warmly urged enactment of certain provisions which have now become law. Prominent among these were the restriction of allotment notes already mentioned, abolition of imprisonment as a penalty for desertion, a section compelling part-payment of wages to sailors on demand at intermediate ports of loading and discharge, and provisions for better living quarters, more adequate sanitary protection, and fully adequate boats and other safety apparatus. This last matter received terrible emphasis in the *Titanic* disaster.

Mr. Johnson of course was prime mover and chief legal aid representative with respect to all these affairs. But his son, Tristram B. Johnson, ably assisted him. This young man, who by 1911 had become Solicitor of the Navy Department, bade fair to carry on the work for seamen when his father should be forced to lay it down. Fate decreed otherwise; the father survived the son. On July 16, 1911, the younger Johnson was struck and killed by lightning while playing golf. His parent never relaxed the struggle for maritime justice, but the tragedy undoubtedly hastened his death, which occurred February 27, 1914. As Mr. v. Briesen said, "his spirit hovered over all the men at sea, and on shore from sea," and he "will continue to live in the hearts of hundreds of thousands of his fellow men, to whom he extended his kindly thoughts and his ever ready helping hand."

Then came the World War. For seamen it was a time of toil and peril and death. Yet, to quote Mr. McGee, "the War in two years has gone a great way toward remedying the shortcomings of a century." Ships had to be run, and men must be had to run them. Sailors found work on every hand, wages rose, the dignity and freedom of marine labor increased. Seagoing men learned their own value to the general economic scheme. Never again will exploiters find them the simple, easy victims of old. Of course, reaction came when the conflict ended. Depression set in during 1919 and 1920; 1921 was a year of disaster for mariners. Ships were tied up; shipping companies went bankrupt; wages dropped; overtime was largely eliminated; the sailors' union, trying desperately to hold war-time gains, fought and lost an important strike. The Seamen's Branch itself was hard hit by fire, and had to rely upon the generous Seamen's Church Institute for temporary quarters while arranging its burned and water-soaked records. But the work went on. By 1923 a slight betterment of shipping conditions made itself felt. Pay on American vessels rose a trifle. By 1925 the Branch was breaking records in numbers of clients, in amounts collected, and in gross earnings from commissions and fees. Such activity is not an unqualifiedly healthful sign. It was known to mean that some shipping proprietors, for reasons best understood by themselves, were fighting claims which would have been settled a few years before without court proceedings or even the interposition of a lawyer. Still, action is better than inaction, and the Seamen's Branch once more knew that it was contributing vitally to the welfare of a living industry.

Here the account might end. No reader can fail to perceive that much must yet be done to put seafaring labor on a par with that of landsmen. Even a satisfactorily comprehensive American maritime workmen's compensation law is lacking and being debated at the time of writing. That particular lack cannot be blamed wholly upon legislators. Disconcerting and puzzling United States Supreme Court decisions have precluded effective local legislation and complicated the problem presented to Congress. But before leaving the Seamen's Branch, one cannot resist summarizing its peculiarities and merits. Here law and adventure have joined forces. The office itself has always been near the waterfront, with the tang of salt water in the air. The curious clients served and cases presented; the comings and goings of early attorneys by boat about New York harbor, often under cover of night; the boarding and searching of strange vessels; the very real element of personal danger; the hours passed afloat by Mr. Johnson and Mr. McGee in first-hand observation to assure the effectiveness of the safety laws — this is no dry-as-dust practitioner's activity.

It has called for brave, self-sacrificing, earnest men, and year after year they have responded. Frank Simonds, when telling of the instalment crusade, pointed out Mr. Ringwalt's physical strength and courage. Soon after, Mr. Ringwalt went to the Seamen's Branch. Although it is now years since his connection with the Society ended, he is still remembered as one of its best assistant attorneys. Another newspaper in 1909 said Mr. McGee "looks as though he would make a bad opponent in a fight," and Mr. v. Briesen wrote of him as one "who is rendering invaluable service and who holds out promise of a brilliant future." Year by year these men and others like them have slowly built up an object lesson of the modern practical jurisprudence, which asks not whether a rule of law reads well and responds theoretically to the needs calling it forth, but whether it *actually works*. Here, in a field big enough to run beyond any mere pocket experiment, yet not so big as to exceed the scope of accurate observation, a mixed code of statute and judge-made law has been enforced, tested, patched, cut, and greatly expanded. It has been shown that Congress as well as the state legislatures will act in aid of the poor — in aid, moreover, of a class very largely voteless. And into the whole resulting legal fabric, old as well as new, the breath of life has been forced. Law in theory has become law in action, the kind of law which those who go down to the sea in ships may trust and revere as a practical force actively operated for their safety, welfare, and peace.

VII

"EAST SIDE, WEST SIDE"

ON March 13, 1881, Loris Melikoff persuaded Alexander II, the Czar Liberator, to publish in the official journal a new liberal scheme of government. That very afternoon, with grotesque untimeliness, the Czar was assassinated while driving. Professor C. D. Hazen tells how a bomb thrown at his carriage wrecked the equipage: "Alexander escaped as by a miracle, but a second bomb exploded near him as he was going to aid the injured. He was horribly mangled, and died within an hour." Like the shots at Concord Bridge, those two explosions were heard round the world. Nowhere did their echo ring more loudly than in the offices of The Legal Aid Society. For under Alexander III "began the inhuman persecutions of the Jews which have been so dark a feature of recent Russian history. The great Jewish emigration to the United States dates from this time." As early as 1891 the first waves of the immigration were reaching the Society's doorstep. Yearly the number of Russian applicants increased, and with this increase the interest of the Legal Aid workers in New York's East Side area became more and more intense. Truth to tell, that area by reason of its population had always been regarded with unusual concern. In 1870 the Irish filled the lower, the Germans the upper, part of the East Side. Gradually the Germans pushed out the Irish, then in turn were extruded by the influx of Russian, Polish, and Austro-Hungarian Jews. The newcomers soon began largely to absorb the Society's energies. In 1893 a special appeal for contributions to meet this new demand was prepared, but withheld because of bad business conditions. The report for 1894 states that most of the litigated cases occurred in the courts around which these people had settled. Two years later the report expresses an ambition to become "the Family Lawyer of the great East Side." In mid-October, 1899, a branch in this area was opened and a serious effort to realize the foregoing ambition began.

The East Side Branch (originally called the University Settlement Society Branch, because of the liberal support given by that society and its members) started work at 57 Rivington Street. This address lay in a community notorious for ignorance and poverty. It was the front-line trench of legal aid activity. The very office-hours were significant. They included Saturday afternoon and evening, and seemingly at times Friday evening, as well as every regular business day. Clients here were so tied down to their tasks of earning meagre livelihoods that only entirely outside working-hours could many snatch time to consult a lawyer. The office needed the gift of tongues, for applicants spoke "various and surprising languages." Yiddish was the most common medium of communication, and phonetically spelled Yiddish correspondence sometimes proved insolubly puzzling to every member of the staff save the office-boy! A grateful Polish client obligingly furnished forms of routine questions translated into his language. With these forms and a printed calendar, one of the attorneys could make shift to extract the essential facts bearing upon a wage claim. From beginning to end of the Branch's activities a large majority of its applicants were aliens, with so high a Jewish percentage that one attorney called the office a Hebrew legal aid society.

Many applicants did not deem precise veracity essential or even desirable. Many had punitive inclinations. Arthur G. H. Lester, attorney in 1902, wrote: "The spirit of compromise does not exist with them. I arranged to settle a wages claim of $45.00 for $43.50. The client refused to accept this amount; he said he would get the $45.00 if it cost him $50.00 to do so." A year later the succeeding attorney, Samuel Goldberg, added: "It is undoubtedly true that our clients are naturally litigious. The Hebrew . . . does not know any other redress than that offered by a court of law."

Yet at this Branch there were peculiar reasons for enforcing a general policy of reasonable compromise. The clients lived from hand to mouth and needed their money without delay. The local courts were frightfully congested. Rigidly, albeit with the utmost difficulty, the attorneys kept litigation at a minimum, insisted upon fair settlements, weeded out unjust claims. One client presenting a wage claim against a large construction company was faced with the employer's assertion that he had stolen building material worth more than all he had earned. Under careful examination the man admitted having been caught carrying the material away, and left the office with the cheery remark: "Well, I am ahead of the game anyway!" For every instance of such downright dishonesty a dozen cases were refused in the early days because passionate applicants would not give fair and reasonable statements of their losses. The attorneys felt driven to suggest that as a general test of good faith the registration fee be raised from ten to twenty-five cents, that still larger fees be taken in particular instances, and that the 10-per-cent commission charge be imposed upon all collections and not merely upon those exceeding $10. With modifications, these experiments had a measure of success. Constantly, too, the Branch dinned into the ears of applicants the rule that actions would not be brought where there was indication of the defendants' financial irresponsibility. Parenthetically, the East Side attorneys refused to enforce body executions where wage defendants were genuinely penniless. It would have been fruitless and cruel to imprison men who were not concealing assets.

This course of training in honesty, accuracy, and practicality proved hard to administer, but results soon made their appearance. The famous "demand note" worked well, even on the East Side. Responsible local employers appreciated contact with honest, unselfish attorneys and came fully halfway to meet claims against themselves. Where an apprentice painter worked for seven weeks, expecting to receive pay for the last five, and his employer conscientiously asserted that the only compensation promised had been free tuition in the trade, a situation full of opportunity for recrimination and disagreement arose. But the attorney perceived that the seven weeks had immediately preceded the Passover, thus falling in the busiest and best-paid painting season, and brought the parties peaceably together on a moderate compromise figure which yielded the apprentice some money, yet left the master feeling he had not been gouged. Another employer was persuaded to pay something for services rendered, although his employé had broken his contract by leaving in the middle of the stipulated term. A third case, which balances the second, showed the client entitled by express agreement to $15 for some electrical work; the materials and time expended, however, came to very little. The defendant submitted to the attorney's judgment, and the claimant acquiesced in an award of $10. A fourth and more striking case ended happily when the Branch so thoroughly and pleasantly convinced an employer of his liability for wages that he not only paid in full but left $5 at the office to be used for some deserving family. Meantime, churlish and unfair defendants were given a warning object-lesson by the Society's record of almost uniform success in the litigation it felt free to handle. So the report for 1900 could say: "We have found . . . that the East Side defendant is very apt, like Davy Crockett's coon, to come down; that is, when he has enough property to make him afraid of a judgment."

One terrible reflection of the treatment which the East Side Jews had suffered was their exaggerated suspicion. The loss of a case, even a day or two's delay, would bring from a client bitter charges that the Society had "sold him out." Utterly unfair as such accusations were, no understanding person could help feeling distinct sympathy for the accusers. Robbed, beaten, and outcast in Europe, they were going through a continuation of the same process in New York. Among their most shameless despoilers were shyster lawyers frequenting the inferior courts. The worst aspect of this legal victimization will be treated more fully in the chapter on the Society's criminal court activities. For the present it will suffice to say that during its first months the Branch did comparatively little business because the people believed that this office was simply another wolf in sheep's clothing! Such was the standing of the East Side legal practitioners. This element of mistrust soon disappeared, and the working staff found itself hard driven to keep even with the rush of applications. Volunteers added their strength, and more paid workers had to be assigned. In the calendar year 1900 the Branch dealt with over 2500 cases, ten years later with over 5000, and in 1917 (the last full year of its existence) with nearly 4400. The earlier quarters on Rivington Street and on Orchard Street proved inadequate. "The small cramped rooms," says the report for 1905, "were filled with such crowds all day long that the air became stifling and the attorneys did their work amid such surroundings at the risk of positive injury to their health." Mr. Lester paid with his life for loyalty to legal aid. He died in 1904 from a disease contracted while acting as head of the Branch. Not until July 1, 1905, however, was it possible to escape this menace. The office then moved to really adequate quarters on the ground floor of the University Settlement Building. Later moves carried it first to Grand Street and finally to Delancey Street.

Even aside from bad lawyers, East Side dwellers had a host of cheats to combat. It will be remembered that the instalment frauds of 1902 and earlier years flourished among them. These frauds affected the Italians rather than the Jews, the latter being too alert for the sharpers. But even where a poor man refuses to let his money be stolen — or has no money to steal — a harsh employer can steal his labor. The East Side Branch was always a great wage collection bureau, and with good reason, so long as practices like the following were attempted.

In 1904, Hon. George F. Roesch, Justice of the Fourth District Municipal Court, sent to the Branch forty-two Hungarians so incapable of speaking English that an interpreter was necessary. Each of the men, to quote the report for this year, "had paid a fee of two dollars to a man named S. Roth, a keeper of an intelligence office, and he promised to obtain a position for each of them. The next day he sent all of them to work as common laborers at excavating on Broadway and 136th Street, City. These ignorant people went to work without knowing who was to pay them. All the assurance was given by Roth. The majority of them, after working a few days, were discharged, and were told by the man in charge to go back to Roth. They came to Roth; he demanded an additional fee of seventy-five cents, and after receiving that amount he sent them back to the same place. The men then worked several days more and demanded their money, but there was no one to pay them.

"With these facts in our possession, we started to investigate the case, and as a result we discovered the fact that the man in charge of the excavating and Roth shared the fees that were paid by these men. It was Roth's duty to send the men and the foreman's duty to accept them and give them work. More than a hundred men were misled in this manner; and Roth's business was steadily increasing. He no longer gave receipts to those who paid him; he no longer kept a register. He was too busy. License Commissioner Keating was immediately apprised of these facts, and we preferred charges against Roth. A hearing took place before the Commissioner, and Roth's license was suspended; besides, he was compelled to return three-fifths of the fees collected by him.

"We also brought proceedings against Michael Fortunato, whom we discovered to be the contractor, to recover the wages of these men. In each case we succeeded in a recovery of a judgment which carries with it a body execution. Our action against Roth did not deter other keepers of intelligence bureaus from sending men to Fortunato. About four weeks after the complaint against Fortunato, about two dozen men came into this office and told this amazing story. A certain intelligence office advertised for men who wanted work at fifteen cents an hour. The advertisement requested the laborer to bring one dollar and a shovel. No man was barred. Any one could qualify. All of them paid one dollar to the intelligence bureau, and as they had no shovel, each one of them had to pay an additional seventy-five cents for the shovel that they obtained at the office. These men were then sent to Fortunato. He would keep them half a day and then discharge them without pay. These men would then return to the office and there receive back three-fifths of their fee and twenty-five cents for the return of the shovel for which they no longer had any use. In this way a profit of ninety cents is made on each man.

"This intelligence office keeper profited by Roth's experience and I have no doubt that he was informed of all the proceedings that were held before the Commissioner. He faithfully kept a true register of each case, and gave each laborer a receipt for the fees received by him. He was also careful in the management of his business, and no evidence could be obtained that he shared the fees with any one. In this way, he fully complied with the present law, and nothing could be done to revoke his license. The only way this swindle was stopped was by having the matter fully published in all the Hebrew newspapers."

These were not isolated instances, as witness an item in the New York *Sun* for March 3, 1905, about the troubles of other Russians, Hungarians, and Austrians with one William Bradley:

"On the East Side Mr. Bradley is looked upon as a person of first importance because in snowstorm periods he is in a position to give work to practically all who apply. In the busy season he has as many as 10,000 men working for him on the snow removal contract. The pay for shovellers is supposed to be 20 cents an hour.

"About forty men called on Mrs. Mary Grace Quackenbos, the attorney for the society, at her office and said that the 'snow commissioner,' as Mr. Bradley is called over there, had not dealt fairly by them in the matter of wages. Each man had with him a ticket upon which was punched the number of hours he was supposed to have worked. The men were credited with seven, eight, and nine hours each, although some of them said they had worked two and three days.

"Mrs. Quackenbos could do nothing then but settle with Mr. Bradley's lawyers for the face value of the tickets. It was declared that some of the tickets were counterfeits although they are about as difficult to imitate as bank notes and most of the men holding them could neither read nor write. Nevertheless those who held the tickets said to be bogus got no pay at all.

"When more complaints were made to the society about Mr. Bradley last month it was decided to take the matter to the municipal courts and in the last few days a batch of free summonses has been issued. The men in every case have been instructed not to accept any sum less than the full amount due them. The cases will come up in the Fourth, Fifth and Thirteenth district courts just as soon as Mr. Bradley can be served. According to the process servers of the society it is an extremely difficult task to get at him. Mr. Bradley has a dozen or more offices in New York and he is a very busy man."

No wonder, then, that East Side distrust was hard to overcome. But the Branch made headway. So confident did one female applicant feel of its integrity that when she was wrongfully excluded from rooms for which she had paid advance rent, she left her three weeping children in the office and her van-load of furniture outside the door while she went about finding a new home! Slowly the unceasing campaign of civic education ripened and bore fruit. Many small signs showed a healthy change of local attitude. Thus Mr. McGee in 1913: "In this section we meet misery and poverty to a larger extent than anywhere in the city, but here a contented poverty finds no place. The employer of to-day was the poor immigrant of a few years back; the push-cart merchant of to-day has his eye open for a business location — well has the east side been called 'the most progressive spot in America.' The defendant receiving our notice of claim recalls the effective results brought about by the Society when he himself was our client. He immediately ceases to dictate to his employee, and calls at the office ready to submit to a just settlement of the claim. To some, our demand letter has the effect of a court order." The wheel had turned half-circle. It was only a question of time before these defendants of the newer generation, having risen yet higher socially and financially, should become members of The Legal Aid Society and contributors to its work. Through all the confusion and darkness and distress, here, as in the other offices, ran a bright gleam of hope, visible from the first to such men as Mr. v. Briesen, and with passing time becoming ever more plain to less discerning eyes.

So much for the general aim of the Branch, the objects sought and to some extent accomplished. Something further may be said as to the nature of the cases which engrossed the attorneys' attention. Against the background of a thoroughly typical and miscellaneous practice the office found from the beginning two kinds of claims especially emphasizing themselves. First in number and perhaps in importance came the wage disputes, of which something has already been said. But one peculiar aspect of the matter deserves further expansion and emphasis. The attorney in charge during the early part of 1901 was Philip J. McCook, now a justice of the New York Supreme Court. He saw the special problem in its sharp and distressing outlines: "What can be done for the ignorant apprentices at the different trades? Nearly every week one or more of them comes in for relief. The story is nearly always about the same: $8 to $15 paid as a fee to learn cigar or cigarette making or machine operating, with an agreement by the master to teach for four weeks and then to employ steadily with pay; permission to work in the shop but no real lessons given; discharge at the end of four weeks; refusal to pay wages or to return the fee. The complainants are invariably 'greeners' who are just over [from Europe], know nothing of our ways, and spend this, their last cent, to fit themselves for earning a livelihood. Often they have made the contract in reply to an attractive advertisement in a Yiddish daily." A cruder aspect of the same thing was presented where shifty and knowing individuals persuaded greenhorns to pay them substantial sums for positions as janitors, porters, and the like. The positions were really forthcoming, but might have been had direct from the employers without any fees or through respectable employment agencies at much lower fees. To take a glaring example, one immigrant paid $28 for a job as street-car conductor, which he held for only three days before the transit company found he could not read English and naturally enough discharged him. Even the body execution for unpaid wages offered no cure in these situations, since the claims were not strictly wage claims. Two resources remained: frequent warnings to "greeners" about these frauds, given with the greatest possible publicity; and criminal proceedings against persistent offenders. In 1915, vigorous moves by the District Attorney caused substantial recoveries for victims of the "apprentice" swindle and a considerable loss of enthusiasm on the part of the reprobates who had been practising it.

Next — and from some points of view transcending the labor problem in importance — came family troubles. They had at least two manifestations with which the Society could come definitely to grips, even though it did not pretend to have a general solution for domestic difficulties. One of these the Main Office knew before the establishment of the East Side Branch. Says the report for 1897: "Your President was informed during the past year that a practice of granting divorces exists amongst certain Jewish rabbis, especially in the thickly settled eastern portions of the city. The question came to the President's attention by the visit of a Russian Hebrew, who stated that he had emigrated from Russia about a year ago, had left his wife and three children there, had here found a girl he liked better than his wife, had gone to the rabbi to get a divorce, had obtained the same, and had thereupon proceeded to marry the girl. He then learned that his Russian wife, with her children, was coming to America, and called at the office of the Society to see how he should protect himself against them." Mr. v. Briesen's reaction to this application was that to be expected from a man with militant respect for the law and the matrimonial tie: "The advice he [the applicant] received was that the Society would seek to locate him in Sing Sing prison if possible." Nor was this particular marital adventurer nearly as bad as certain others. The Society encountered one Rosner, who "was in the habit of marrying a woman, disposing of her bank account, then obtaining a Jewish 'Ghet' and marrying another woman, who soon suffered the same fate. [The applicant for relief] was the fourth who had this disagreeable experience. 'Mrs. Rosner' through our office made a charge of bigamy against the man and he is now awaiting trial, which will doubtless end in his conviction. The money is still in the bank, so that 'Mrs. Rosner' will not lose it."

Referring to the instance first spoken of, Mr. v. Briesen goes on to say that "this was not an isolated case, but . . . in hundreds and possibly in thousands of instances this same kind of crime is being inflicted upon innocent women and helpless children. It appears that under the Mosaic law the rabbi has the right to separate a wife from the husband at the latter's request, and that when such right is exercised it has the effect of a divorce. Of course, where the religious law is identical with the law of the State, as it was in Judea, such a power given to the priest is lawful, apart from the question of humanity and wisdom; but in the United States, where the statutes are not controlled by religious prescripts of any sect, a procedure such as that here referred to is intolerable, and every effort should be made by public officers and lawmakers to nullify it."

The second matrimonial offence painfully prominent on the East Side was abandonment and non-support of women and children. William Michaelson, attorney in charge of the Branch for 1905, calls it "a problem of paramount importance" and adds a statement showing its unusual difficulty: "The frequency of this offense on the lower East Side is startling, and the staff of the East Side Branch have devoted much attention to minimizing it. But the complete inadequacy of the number of attorneys and attachés available for the work admitted of but little progress towards this end. In cases of the abandonment of children and the flight of the father from the jurisdiction of the State of New York we were, until September of this year, practically powerless. Before that time the abandonment of children in New York was merely a misdemeanor. Consequently, when a father abandoned his child and left the State, it was impossible for us to reach him from this city. The new law, making this crime a felony where the abandonment is of a child under the age of sixteen years, makes possible the extradition of offenders of this class. Naturally, where the absconder is at a distance we can do little or nothing. But where the parent abandons his children, and remains within the State, concealing himself somewhere in this city (and this is the case in most instances) this Society could bring relief to the deserted family were we in possession of proper means for tracing and running down the fugitive. For this purpose there should be attached to the East Side Branch an investigator or special detective, and I recommend the earnest consideration of this urgent need."

We have seen the marked effect of the World War upon the Seamen's Branch. On the East Side the industrial depression of late 1914 and 1915 caused a considerable flare-up of employment frauds. Then came the feverish industrial awakening and the practical disappearance of such problems. But others at least temporarily took their place. Having more money than ever before, the East Siders became attractive victims to all sorts of dishonest salesmen. Also people "going up in the world" must have better living accommodations. Financially ascending clients of the Branch found to their grief that landlords and real-estate agents were ready with trick receipts and leases which left the new tenants in most uncomfortable positions. Not infrequently the glib salesman or the grasping manager of real estate overreached himself and got on the windy side of the law, so that the Branch could effectively help his sorrowing dupes. Yet, after all, the "new rich" must do a good deal of learning by hard experience. Fortunately, however, East Side conditions were good for quick learning. The older residents rarely gave lightning any chance to strike them twice, and the practical cessation of immigration prevented new crops of callow victims.

The War furnished occasion for closing the Branch. From the beginning of 1916 the Society's straitened resources forced consideration of retrenchment. The East Side office was kept going literally from month to month until exactly thirty-one days before the Armistice, and then discontinued. This seems a confession of defeat; in fact, it is more like a proof of victory. There was no desertion of helpless people. Nineteen years' education had taught the East Side a great deal about self-protection and fairness to others. The check on immigration, instead of ending with the War, became permanent. Mass ignorance and "greenness" are largely conditions of the past. East Side clients could continue relations with the Society by coming to the Main Office, and many did so. More cheering still, East Side conditions had caused development of other legal aid institutions exactly fitting local needs. As the neighborhood became crowded with Jewish immigrants, The Educational Alliance entered the field. It tentatively opened a Legal Aid Bureau on the East Side about April, 1899, thus antedating the East Side Branch itself. Reorganized with good financial backing on

October 13, 1902, this Bureau has since carried out vigorous work upon a large scale. It did much to eradicate the illegal Hebrew "ghet" and enforced many claims for support against wife and child deserters before the National Desertion Bureau came into existence. This latter is an extremely effective organization with wide affiliations, formed in 1911 and incorporated in 1914. Its work entitles it to the highest praise. The two bodies between them now handle approximately 7500 cases per year. Hence the story of the East Side Branch is a satisfactorily rounded-out incident in legal aid history, not ended until the ground won could be left well garrisoned by competent allies of the Society.

The third of the early branches, the Women's Branch, was an interesting experiment. It seemed possible that women, and particularly women involved in marital or other domestic difficulties, would prefer to consult a lawyer of their own sex. In addition it was believed that an office located (as this one was) actually at the United Charities Building, on the corner of Twenty-second Street and Fourth Avenue, would coöperate very effectively with other charitable agencies. The Branch began work on an unusually economical basis because Miss Josephine Stary and Miss C. Annette Fiske, who played Box and Cox as attorney in charge from 1899 through 1901, donated their services.

Opening about October 15, 1899, the Women's Branch gathered headway rather slowly. Up to January 25, 1900, only 90 applicants had appeared. But the full calendar year 1900 showed increasing impetus, as 760 cases were handled. Three features of the practice are noteworthy. First, applicants who were citizens heavily outnumbered the non-citizens. Clearly this Branch was tapping a district very different from the

East Side. Second, over one third of the applicants were men. Third, the bulk of the work consisted of general advice and wage-collection cases. Only 81 cases involved domestic difficulties, not an overwhelming proportion although somewhat above that prevailing at the Main Office and the East Side Branch, and of course vastly above the proportion at the Seamen's Branch. Next year (1901) no possible doubt could be raised as to the activity of the Branch, for over 1600 cases came in. Miss Stary justly urged that no single lawyer could adequately handle this mass of work, and suggested the possibility of volunteer assistance from women in New York who held law degrees but were not really active practitioners. Once more the bulk of the applications fell under the heads of general advice and wage claims, with domestic difficulties forming barely 7.5 per cent of the aggregate as compared with 10.6 per cent the year before. The 1901 tabulations fail to give the relative numbers of male and female clients. It is, however, significant that both Miss Stary and Mr. v. Briesen emphasize the value of the Branch, not because of its service to women, but rather because of its close articulation with other charitable and municipal organizations and departments. Cases of distress brought to this office could be comprehensively looked into and dealt with.

The year 1901 was the last full year of existence for the Women's Branch under that name. Before the end of 1902 a so-called "Up-Town Branch" succeeded it, the office now being at the West Side Neighborhood House, 741 Tenth Avenue near Fiftieth Street, with Carl Stedman Brown as Attorney in charge. For the sake of clearness it may be added that in 1905 the Up-Town Branch assumed its present name of West Side Branch. Some difference of opinion exists as to the reasons for discontinuing the Women's Branch. Financial necessity undoubtedly played a part. At the new location and under the new name the Branch received substantial assistance from the John D. Rockefellers, senior and junior. Miss Stary has stated positively that the money reason is the sole and complete one. Yet that does not account for the alteration in personnel which put a man at the head of the office. In 1902, women applicants at this Branch were still nearly twice as numerous as men. The *Bulletin* of the Woman's Municipal League for November, 1908, says: "For a year or two a Woman's Branch was conducted at the United Charities Building, but experience showed that it was unnecessary and unwise to provide an office exclusively for women, and the location was not favorable." Still another cause of the change may have been the nature of the clients' cases as indicated above. Family difficulties, on which a woman's advice was deemed peculiarly important, had become a minor item, albeit a substantial one. Some of the best modern authorities on legal aid practice are absolutely opposed to specialization along lines of sex. It is scarcely likely that the experiment of a women's branch office will be repeated.

The first years of the reorganized Branch were comparatively calm and uneventful. As the report of the Society's Attorney-in-Chief for 1902 puts it: "The Seamen's Branch and the East Side Branch have distinct problems of their own; the problems of the Main Office, as far as its routine of work is concerned, and of the Up-Town Branch, are only those of all philanthropic effort: to do [their] work in such a way as not to be an injury to the applicant, or to any other person." Three years later Miss Bertha Rembaugh, the attorney in charge, said: "The West Side Branch is located in a region which makes it freer than almost any other branch from special problems. We have no sweatshops or fake employment agencies and no large non-English speaking population. The cases that come into the office are for the most part merely the product of the ordinary wear and tear of the life of a large city, and present questions of legal rather than of economic or sociological difficulty." "The applicants," said an earlier attorney in charge, "have been for the most part self-supporting men and women. They have come to us simply because they lacked means to defray the extra and unusual expense of employing private counsel for prosecuting small but meritorious claims." It must not be supposed, however, that the office force sat placidly by with folded hands. Quite the reverse. During the year 1905, Miss Rembaugh and her associates dealt with very nearly 3700 applications. The work increased fairly steadily until, from 1912 to 1918 inclusive, the annual number of cases never fell below 5000, and three times exceeded 6000. So the Branch, without furnishing any such striking and arresting examples of service as were to be drawn from the waterfront and the East Side, proved over again under modern conditions what the original office of the Society had proved years before — namely, that even a community of perhaps more than average prosperity, with distinct self-sustaining power, may profit vastly from the presence of an efficient legal aid organization.

A running history of the Branch's life should properly begin with grateful reference to the Rockefellers' extremely generous and long-continued support. This leads naturally to a really ludicrous incident occurring in 1907. Mr. v. Briesen had never made any secret of the help given by the oil magnate and his son. No great amount of public comment resulted for some years. But in late October of 1907 renewed mention of the matter caught fair and square the eagle eye of the press. The consequence was a series of brief and semi-exclamatory newspaper items bearing such headlines as "John D. in New Rôle; Friend of Lowly," "New Light on Rockefeller," and "Rockefeller Pictured as Seeker of Justice." Most of these journalistic squibs exploded far beyond the bounds of New York City and of the Empire State. In the Society's clipping-book are articles from Georgia, Alabama, Louisiana, Texas, Washington, Colorado, and Michigan. And herein lies an amusing sign of the public attitude about the year 1907. Nowadays we are happily aware of the good uses to which wealthy men constantly put their money. But turn back the calendar twenty years and you are in the days of "trust busting," "malefactors of great wealth," and other popular catchwords giving the man in the street a caricatured impression of the typical "captain of industry" which supplied its subject with horns, cloven hoofs, and a tail at the very least. Hence the emphatic news value of a brisk story which linked the Rockefellers with an organization already distinguished by the warm and active friendship of Theodore Roosevelt, the trust-buster *par excellence*. It seemed utterly anomalous, and the public loves anomalies.

Without special problems as the Branch may have been for most of this period, its types of clients presented some peculiarities and their surroundings gave particular emphasis to some special legal difficulties. The ratio of citizens, and therefore of English-speaking clients, continued to run high. Many women applied for aid, clearly because the office was amid theatres, hotels, and boarding-houses employing female artists and servants.

Here, too, the Society put itself temporarily in direct touch with a section of the mobile Irish community, dwelling throughout the tenement-house district west of Eighth Avenue. A large group of negroes also lived near the office, and great numbers of them became clients. Year in and year out the wage claim was the staple basis of complaint. Wage matters involved certain difficulties that may be described briefly in their chronological order of development.

First came the masked corporate employer, of which complaint is made in the report for 1903 and very often thereafter. The trouble arose from "the frequent incorporation of a . . . business which is on its last legs and which, perhaps, has been practically looted by the promoters. In this case . . . the remedy of execution against the person is unavailable. Bodies of fifty or more angry employees will file claims against a supposed hotel proprietor. Investigation discloses the fact that our clients, unknown to themselves, have been working for a corporation which has nothing but its title left when the crash comes. Not a few of these justly indignant and exasperated clients have figured in the police courts for assaults committed upon the officers of the delinquent corporation." Parenthetically, it may be remarked that this plan of passing along legal responsibility to a worthless debtor was commonly employed in the theatrical business. Also that it may equally well be worked the other way about. The Main Office in 1904 acted for a talented young German mural decorator, who, having prepared a dozen or so pastel pictures for the store of a thoroughly solvent jewelry corporation, was told that he must seek compensation from a "senior contractor," then in bankruptcy. The Society saw the point otherwise and pinned the corporation's president so hard and fast on cross-examination that a really enforceable judgment promptly followed.

But to return to the specific West Side question. The wage creditors of an insolvent corporation were not, at least in theory, left to take their claims "out of the hides" of the company's officers and thereafter to face unpleasant consequences before a police magistrate. New York law had from the middle of the previous century provided a somewhat varying measure of personal recourse for such claimants against the corporate stockholders. Theory and practice, however, did not fully square with each other. For enforcement of stockholders' liability, it was a condition precedent that the employé should serve notice of his claim within thirty days after termination of his services to the corporation. But who were the stockholders to be notified? The employé often had to guess at this unless he might inspect the stock books. And such inspection was not granted as of right to a corporate creditor until he had reduced his claim to judgment. So it became a race with time to get judgment against the corporation before the thirty-day limit ran out. The reader may properly conclude that no great ingenuity was necessary to keep the plaintiff from winning the race. It must not be imagined that the stockholders' liability provisions were entirely futile. Now and then personal judgments proved obtainable. Yet this instrument of legal redress, even in the Society's vigorous hands, has not lived up to its promise. An additional reason for its frequent failure to produce practical results may be remarked in the fact that personal judgments against stockholders do not carry body executions. These difficulties are still alive, and fully deserve legislative consideration.

Second, passing mention should be made of the wage exploitation carried on for a time by female boarding-house proprietors in the bailiwick of this Branch. Knowing that body executions could not issue against them, some of these women made employés miserably uncertain of getting their pay. But, as has been indicated by a previous chapter, this abuse of a privilege duly brought an adequate cure in legislative extension of the right to arrest on civil execution.

Third, as the moving-picture industry began to rival the "legitimate" theatre, there arose a class of middlemen whose activities frequently caused just complaint. These were the agents who supplied minor actors to the studios. In 1917 this sort of thing was reported: "The assistant director of one of the leading moving picture firms telephoned [an] agent directing him to send twenty-five artists of a certain type to his studio to be put to work. The agent issued a call to about two hundred men to report to his office for selection. 'A' . . . was . . . happy when the agent selected him and directed him to the studio of the company. He there put in a hard day's work and received a slip O.K.'d by the assistant director, stating that his work had been . . . satisfactory in every respect. 'A' on presenting this slip, upon which no amount due was stated, received from the agent $2.75 as his full day's pay. Now, the truth of the matter was as follows: The film company had instructed their assistant director, *who was really in partnership with the agent*, to procure these men at a wage of $5 per day; the assistant director telephoned his partner . . . and the agent sends the men . . . [who] receive only $2.75, the agent and the assistant director splitting the remainder between them, thereby depriving the film company of a $5 performer to [whom] they were entitled and cheating the poor actor out of his just wage." Clearly this was a swindle hard to discover and punish unless the film producers were ready to help. In 1917 the industry was too young and too little interested in its own integrity to stand by the hard-worked minor actors.

Fourth, there was continued trouble with out-of-town summer hotels which engaged their help in New York before the beginning of the season, persuaded these people to advance their own boat or railroad fares to the summer resorts, and on arrival set them to work under conditions vastly more unfavorable than had been promised at the time of employment. Many disgruntled employes would throw over their jobs and return to the city considerably out of pocket. Even the Society's long arm was unable to compel reimbursement from the distant hotel companies. Common sense, displayed in advance by the servants, has seemed the only relief to be counted upon. No wise employer will furnish transportation to a prospective servant without having formed a deliberate favorable judgment of the applicant's probity and responsibility. No servant is wise who advances his own travelling expenses until he has likewise passed judgment upon the employer.

Some troubles of the West Side were cured by time and changing economic conditions. For example, in and about 1914 a swarm of clever advertisers preyed upon boarding- and lodging-house keepers during slack seasons by promising to supply boarders or tenants for fees of $5 or some such sum. Here the printed word entered the bargain; the typical advertiser's receipt for his fee included a promise to recommend to the victim such persons as applied to the advertiser — simply that and nothing more. No duty of pursuing "prospects" was undertaken, nor were the results of recommendations guaranteed. Almost without exception the fees turned out to be money ill spent. Nor was there any effective legal remedy. But by 1919 all this had gone. The city was packed to bursting, and those with rooms needed no aid in getting tenants. So, from one point of view, the overcrowding after the War was by no means that uniquely disagreeable ill wind which blows nobody good. The Branch, though, had also to face the ugly side of congestion and profiteering. In its district were worked out many practical applications of the Sanitary Code provision requiring landlords to furnish tenants with reasonable heat. The law promptly developed two weaknesses. Complaining tenants might win a momentary victory, only to have their vengeful landlord dispossess them at the earliest possible moment — no light penalty for rebellion. In addition, foresighted landlords could take advantage of a clause allowing them to contract out of liability to furnish heat. Their commanding position usually compelled acquiescence in such contracts. Considerable reinforcement of these weaknesses, and a distinct general bettering of the tenants' position, came in 1919, when the legislature enacted the famous laws restricting rent increases and profoundly modifying powers of eviction. These laws went to the verge of constitutional authority and perhaps to the verge of sound economic doctrine. The United States Supreme Court sustained their validity by a hair-line 5–4 decision, the favorable majority rising to 6–3 on a later case brought after the death of Mr. Chief-Justice White and the choice of Mr. Taft as his successor.

This legislation crammed the inferior courts with rent and tenancy cases for years, and forced the judges to heroic effort merely to keep their heads above the mountain of work. Not until 1923 did the calendars approach a normal state. Advantageous and even essential as the housing legislation may have been to the community, it placed a heavy burden upon the Society's clients, who suffered at least ten times as often from non-payment of wages as from trouble with their landlords. The disproportion at the West Side Branch was even greater than these average figures. So, while the report of this Branch for 1920 warmly praised the Lockwood Committee Housing Acts, the report for 1922 bitterly laments the choked calendars which compelled attorneys and witnesses "to return to court three or more times in order to obtain trials in small wage claims." The moral of this and the somewhat similar experience in the English county courts is obvious. If such social legislation ever again plays a leading part in metropolitan welfare, it should be supplemented by special and adequate judicial facilities.

One small incidental touch concerning the business of the Branch casts a sidelight upon changed standards of living. In 1918 and again in 1926 women applicants appeared who had been grossly defrauded when buying coats from fur dealers. The first fur coat was priced at $100, the second at $225. Both cases were taken and pushed through to satisfactory adjustments. Now in 1876, or perhaps at any date prior to the World War, an applicant able to lay out such a sum for such a garment would hardly have been considered a proper Legal Aid client. But prompt recognition of the new economic basis and attitude was entirely wise. If fur coats had so come down in the world as to be within reach of these ladies, it is nevertheless reasonably certain that proper charges of the ordinary lawyer and miscellaneous expenses of litigation as ordinarily conducted still remained considerably higher than they could afford. The Society, alas, will scarcely find its occupation gone because of any diffusion of wealth or comfort which we have yet seen or are likely to see.

Attention has already been called to the large and quite constant activity of the Branch between 1912 and 1918. The attorneys can hardly have failed to note, though, that the business of the latter year measured by number of applicants showed a drop of 1000, or over 16 per cent, as compared with 1917. And when the applicants for 1919 again dropped off even more notably (the 1918 figure was about 5000, that of 1919 under 3500), obviously a time for stock-taking had come. To be sure, the 1919 collections in money were reassuringly substantial, but what was happening to the clients? In fact, the Branch had slipped into the trough between two waves. A change was coming upon the West Side, and at the halfway stage legal business for the poor temporarily slackened. For the first signs of this change one must look back some years.

We left the Branch at 741 Tenth Avenue, in surroundings described as semi-residential. On July 27, 1910, a fire burned out this office. Most of the current files escaped and insurance money replaced the furnishings. But the Branch had to move. It now hung out its shingle on the northwest corner of Fifty-ninth Street and Columbus Avenue, one block from Columbus Circle. The new address was on or near half-a-dozen elevated and surface lines, as well as the subway. The 1910 report significantly speaks of the environment as a growing business neighborhood. Business continued to grow apace, and residential characteristics correspondingly to decline. Hideous traffic hubbub drove the office from its corner to the New York American Building, Columbus Circle, in 1913. About 1919 this part of the West Side crossed the Rubicon and committed itself to mercantile development. Between 1918 and 1921 whole rows of flats and tenement-houses were given over to business purposes, and away went the former resident clients of the Branch. That is half the story; now the second half is unfolding.

Columbus Circle has turned into a commercial centre of first importance; on the way, Mr. McGee thinks, to "becoming the hub of New York City." The local inferior courts, gradually shaking themselves free from the tangle of landlord and tenant cases in 1923 and the following years, enjoyed only a brief respite. By 1926, cases were threatening to pile up again despite splendidly effective work on the part of Justices Noonan and Crane. "As far east as the East River, and west as the North River," wrote Mr. McGee, "old type flats and tenements are fast disappearing, being replaced by monumental office structures. The rebuilding movement extends as well both north and south from Columbus Circle, resulting in the concentration of thousands of people from various sections in the commodious offices already constructed. Preponderant among this influx of population is the salaried or wage earning class in whose behalf there is increasing call for the services of the West Side Office. . . ." In the last six months of 1926 over 3600 applicants came to the Branch — more, it will be noted, than came during the entire "dull" year 1919. Thus the Branch has twice changed its spots. Beginning as an experiment with distinct sociological color, it became more nearly an ordinary law-office for a resident clientele; and now it has altered to a law-office for a non-resident clientele of clerks, salesfolk, and the like. Legal aid is booming on the West Side. Its greatest days and its largest problems are yet to come.

VIII

1901–1914

WITHOUT a brief summary at this point, the variety of matters touched upon by the preceding chapters might cause confusion. Beginning with the general forces giving rise to legal aid work, and particularly the background from which that work emerged in New York City, we have traced the early development of the Deutscher Rechts-Schutz Verein and its gradual metamorphosis under Mr. v. Briesen's impelling hand into The Legal Aid Society. To fill in and color this outline examples have been given of activity both on individual cases and on large classes of legal difficulties where "preventive law" came into play. Three branches, pushed out from the central stem, have had their stories carried through to the time of writing. The account now returns to the general progress of the Society as a whole, picking up this main thread at the organization's twenty-fifth anniversary.

There should have been a birthday party, and there was. On March 23, 1901, officers, members, and friends of the Society met at the Waldorf-Astoria Hotel. For the excellence of the repast we must rely upon the reputation of that famous hostelry. For the quality of the after-dinner speaking, however, we may consult a pamphlet recording verbatim this part of the entertainment. One's immediate impression is that these banqueters of the very early twentieth century were hardy listeners indeed. They absorbed a programme filling nearly thirty closely printed pages. The last two speeches carry internal evidence that midnight had struck ere they began. Yet even at this point the audience was breaking in with laughter and applause. The reason is not far to seek. Not only will the addresses bear the hard literary test of being read in cold blood a quarter-century after their delivery, but the Society's activities were impinging upon so many points of the body social and politic that many speakers were needed fairly to indicate its scope.

Hon. Charles S. Fairchild as chairman first called upon Mr. v. Briesen to open the topic generally. The Bench was represented by Hon. Joseph M. Deuel, before whom came a substantial amount of the Society's litigation; also Mr. Justice Brown of the United States Supreme Court sent an interesting letter already quoted in the chapter on the Seamen's Branch. Rear-Admiral Francis J. Higginson, too, talked emphatically about sailors' needs. Hon. St. Clair McKelway delivered a polished address from the viewpoint of a publicist and philosopher who felt that the forces of public opinion vivify all formal law, and saw in The Legal Aid Society a significant manifestation of those forces. Most appropriately, consular representatives of seven European countries voiced official gratitude for services to their nationals. Among these gentlemen was the Russian consul-general. As to him a suspicion may be pardoned that his really graceful tribute implied feelings not openly expressed — sentiments of rather ironic thankfulness that New York could and would receive so many of the Jews whose departure from the Czar's empire was being relentlessly hastened!

The high note came from Theodore Roosevelt and Dr. Lyman Abbott. Those who have seen both will remember how marked was the physical contrast between the two: one, a sturdy man of destiny, pulsing with energy, hard-hitting, outspoken; the other, a fragile-looking seer, in whom the light of faith burned as in a translucent lamp. Yet on this topic each at his own angle struck the same chord. The Vice-President of the United States, in a characteristically vigorous and pointed speech, referred to the Society as one great safeguard "against the men who would in the effort to undo existing injustice plunge us into a chaos which would mean injustice of an infinitely worse type. . . . The men who are fighting the battle against violent revolution in the existing social order are the men who are doing their best to abate the injustices of the existing social order. A failure to recognize these injustices, a failure to exert every effort to abate them . . . is in many cases equivalent to aiding the effort to overthrow by violence the good and evil alike." True words, with almost portentous intimation of an impending menace. Inside six months an anarchist's bullet slew McKinley and made the speaker President. Almost at the end of the evening Dr. Abbott urged that the first necessity in any civilized community "is law formulating justice and protecting the right of persons and of property. I dare to say that it is the foundation of religion. It is more basic than the church. . . . 'What doth the Lord require of thee,' said an old Prophet, 'except to do justly, to love mercy and to walk humbly with thy God.' Do justly comes first. . . . What we have to do in all our national work . . . is, first of all, to see that justice is done. Charity comes afterwards." There rang out again the Legal Aid pledge of faith. By these words the efforts of the nineties were pointed forward into the new century.

The names mentioned in connection with the silver-anniversary dinner show that the Society was gathering unto itself new friends. One of the most faithful and influential was Theodore Roosevelt. Upon becoming Police Commissioner in 1895, he took pains to acquaint himself by first-hand observation with what he later described as "the awful crime and misery that welters around us." During his investigations case after case appeared wherein an outside, non-official force had lightened the load of injustice. They were common-place, work-a-day cases: a German peasant girl had come to America, worked as a servant for two or three months, and been turned off without her wages; a glazier had been left unpaid after finishing a job; a man had been arrested for some offence committed by another. These matters never involved enough to cause the corrective forces of law to be set in motion by the regular means. But usually they were affairs of vital moment to the poor victims caught up on the wheel of circumstance. And under such conditions the "outside, non-official force" time and again struck the inert law into life. Jacob A. Riis introduced the Society and Mr. v. Briesen to the Police Commissioner, and a fast friendship resulted. After succeeding McKinley, Roosevelt accepted election as an honorary vice-president of the Society, thus setting an example followed by three subsequent Presidents of the United States. Always he stood ready to help legal aid.

Then there was Joseph H. Choate, the Nestor of the New York Bar. When Louis Windmüller, the kindly business man who was Legal Aid treasurer from 1902 to 1913, approached Mr. Choate for a contribution, the latter roared in mock indignation: "What, you take the bread and butter out of my mouth, and then expect me to support you!" Whereat, to Mr. Choate's secret joy, the embarrassed treasurer painfully explained the Society's non-competitive attitude, being quite unaware that his hearer had been a member since 1893. On that occasion, ignorance was not bliss. Mr. Choate was for some fifteen years an honorary vice-president; in 1913 he sent the Society a check for $1000 "to celebrate my eighty-first birthday," and was thereupon elected a life member; and by his will he gave the Society $10,000. Nor were his contributions all, or even principally, measured in terms of money. From him, as from many other leaders at the Bar and in the life of the community, Mr. v. Briesen obtained invaluable personal support.

Likewise the legal personnel shifted and enlarged. Mr. Schurz, the fourth Attorney-in-Chief, resigned in 1901 because his wife's illness in Germany necessitated an indefinite absence from the country. He had, as a matter of fact, been away for several months during 1900. On this occasion Miss Rosalie Loew (now Mrs. Travis H. Whitney) had filled his place with signal ability. Therefore she naturally became fifth Attorney-in-Chief. Her appointment was a striking occurrence. Women had for years been graduating from law schools and passing the examinations for admission to the Bar. But obtaining official permission to practise and securing practical opportunity to display one's legal ability are very different things. As might have been expected, legal conventionalism hampered the advancement of female lawyers. Now, The Legal Aid Society was essentially unconventional and willing to experiment. So we find women practitioners on its staff from a fairly early date. Whether Miss Loew was the first of these is perhaps debatable. Certainly, though, she was the first to achieve definite prominence, and no other woman has ever approached her attainment in the New York legal aid field. With her, joining the Society's staff was not at all a question of "any port in a storm." Her father had an office at the same address. She could not but observe the work of the "poor man's lawyer." Observation aroused enthusiastic approbation, and led to participation. In August, 1897, she took charge of the District Court practice, and the report for that year warmly praises her ability and self-sacrificing energy. No wonder! In 1901, after succeeding Mr. Schurz, she "is at her office nearly always from seven o'clock in the morning till late in the evening. Her work hardly ever stops before ten o'clock at night. During this time the vast correspondence of her office, the personal consultation with clients, arguments in court and the keeping of accounts had to receive her personal attention."

The matter of accounts deserves special comment. The new Attorney-in-Chief found the office without any accounting system that reflected its financial state. She was no accountant, but by the light of nature and common sense devised a simple system meeting immediate needs, which was continued for some years. The auditing committee, appointed for the first time at the end of 1901, commended Miss Loew's system as eminently practical and sufficient. This committee recommended certain minor accounting changes at the Branches. In 1902 the committee reported that "there now exists in every office a simple and adequate method of keeping the books"; also that the multifariously harried Miss Loew had been furnished with a bookkeeper. In 1906 came a comprehensive reorganization of all the Society's accounts by a trained accountant.

For over three years Miss Loew's dynamic personality drove forward the legal aid practice. With the enthusiasm and courage of youth she fought for servants and sweatshop workers, faced and sometimes triumphed over corruption in official quarters, and made herself a terror to dishonest lawyers. She was profoundly interested in the delicate problems raised by family difficulties, especially as they affected the welfare of children. Efforts to accomplish matrimonial reconciliations sometimes succeeded, sometimes failed. Once she tricked an estranged husband and wife into a meeting at the office. Tempers flamed up, and Miss Loew "thought it prudent for their sakes to sit between them. In three minutes I was the storm center of the strongest domestic gale I had ever seen. The man, poking his fingers into my ribs, shouted in my ear: 'Now listen to her, lawyer lady; did ye hear that? A nice woman you're tryin' to make me live with!" On the other side the wife was nudging me with her sharp elbow and shrieking: 'Listen to that lunatic, will you! I'd rather die than live under the same roof with a maniac!'" No happy family reunion followed. It may be added with a certain appropriateness that for part of Miss Loew's administration a volunteer medical committee helped out the legal work, "particularly in examination of persons alleged to be insane, whose incarceration we were asked to prevent, and in examining clients in negligence cases." Miss Loew married Mr. Whitney during her term of office. Toward the end of 1904 she tendered her resignation, to take effect February 1, 1905. It was accepted with great and outspoken regret, the one compensating factor being the continued interest of both Mr. and Mrs. Whitney in the Society's welfare.

The sixth Attorney-in-Chief was Cornelius P. Kitchel. His administration, running from early 1905 until nearly the end of 1906, showed steady progress in numbers of clients and amounts collected for them. Generally quiet in external aspect, the period was characterized by internal reorganization. No law-office of any kind, and most particularly no office on such a huge scale, is likely to escape considerable accumulation of deadwood in the shape of somnolent or defunct cases. Knowing this, Mr. Kitchel attacked his files and had a rousing legal housecleaning. He also put rigidly in force a still-existing rule that no letters save those of purely formal nature should leave the main office without the knowledge and approval of the chief Attorney. The immediate reason was a threatened libel action based upon an unfortunate choice of words in a letter written by an assistant. The action came to nothing, although at first it caused Mr. Kitchel a certain amount of uneasiness. The next Attorney-in-Chief was Merrill E. Gates, Jr., who served until the beginning of 1910, when Mr. McGee, the present incumbent, succeeded him. It will thus be seen that Mr. McGee's term of office already greatly outruns that of any predecessor. As he is still a young man, the Society may hope to profit from his vigor, tact, and experience for many years to come.

Among the most pleasant features of the period between 1901 and 1914 were honors bestowed upon Mr. v. Briesen. His hobby of equal justice for all was making its mark in the world. The small organization which he took over in 1890, at a time when it was little known even among New Yorkers and seemed balancing on the verge of extinction, had become a great American institution. Magazine and newspaper articles carried news of it to the four corners of the country, and also across the ocean to Great Britain and Europe. Its deeds, too, spoke in no uncertain terms abroad as well as at home. In 1905 Mr. v. Briesen received from France the Cross of the Legion of Honor. In 1908 the Kaiser sent him the Cross of the Order of the Prussian Crown. Next year Mr. v. Briesen was received by the Kaiser at Potsdam. Nor was this kind-hearted prophet without honor in his own country. On February 24, 1910, his associates gave him a great silver loving-cup to commemorate his twenty years as president. On June 4, 1913, his alma mater, New York University, conferred upon him the honorary degree of Doctor of Laws in recognition of his learning, philanthropy, and distinguished public service.

It remains to speak briefly of some tendencies and developments during this period. The work grew and grew. Cases dealt with in 1901 were 15,880, in 1914, 40,430. Amounts recovered for clients in the same years were $78,173.97 and $134,895.59. The strain on the legal staff was almost inexpressibly heavy. Such expansions were made as finances permitted. Miss Loew persuaded many students from the Columbia Law School and the New York Law School to serve part time as volunteers. Harvard Law School and Princeton University men worked for the Society in summer. From 1908 on, the Board of Trustees issued a formal certificate to every law student rendering satisfactory gratuitous service for six months. Still, as a great authority on legal aid has remarked: "You can't drive volunteers." Full-time paid workers were best from every point of view. In obtaining them, the financial shoe pinched and kept pinching. For convenience and clarity, the Society's finances are discussed comprehensively in a later chapter. But the matter is here mentioned lest the reader forget that the problem was always a pressing one.

However hard it was to obtain money for the Society's use, methods were bettered, old offices rendered more efficient, and new ones established. For a time at least an investigator, who was also a special police officer, worked from the Main Office in sifting cases and procuring evidence. This took a burden off the attorneys' shoulders and gave them added assurance against imposition. To meet the needs of the growing body of Italian clients a competent interpreter was sought for and obtained. These small matters, chosen rather at random, are mentioned to show the administration's alert sensitiveness to possibilities of improvement. Much more important was the establishment in 1903 of a quarterly magazine called the *Legal Aid Review*. This publication has ever since continued to put before a broadening constituency the facts, the hopes, and the fears about legal service for the poor. Brief statements of actual cases appear by the hundred in its columns. Articles upon the work of the Society and of its colleagues in America and abroad have been printed. Through the numbers of this periodical can be traced the growth of a world movement. Another publication, made possible by the generosity of Charles F. Wiebusch, had important effects. This was a small book or pamphlet for servants, compiled in 1908 by Miss Helen Arthur and George H. Englehard. The pamphlet followed generally the lines of the famous "Sailor's Log," with variations appropriate to the different subject-matter. It received widespread favorable comment. A new edition has been desirable for many years, but rising printing costs and limited revenues stand in the way. Certainly the Society could well use a special endowment for purposes of initiating and renewing such publications as fast as demanded by changing laws and social conditions.

Actual experience puts hope for such endowment within the bounds of practical possibility. Since May 8, 1905, an endowed extension of the Society known as the Harlem Branch has been actively operating in the general neighborhood of Lexington Avenue and 125th Street. This Branch serves a huge, densely populated area including Harlem and the Bronx. For years prior to its establishment poor persons living and working in this territory were largely cut off from legal aid. The half-hours and hours required for transportation to the more southerly offices made consultations with their lawyers during the working-day next door to impossible. Conversely, those claims which did trickle down from the northern area consumed an amount of the attorneys' time utterly disproportionate to the volume of business. Lawyers could not journey to the northern courts any more rapidly than clients could journey to the Main Office or the southern branches. When, therefore, Mr. v. Briesen was notified that a charitable lady who insisted upon anonymity stood ready to contribute no less than $5000 per year for support of the Harlem Branch, he knew that a momentous forward step could be taken. The Branch promptly realized expectations. Gathering swift headway, it was for a long series of years second only to the Main Office in number of clients. Most happily for its sound progress, Carl L. Schurz served until 1917 as chairman of the directors' visiting committee. His kindliness, sagacity, and energy had great influence.

The early applicants here were thoroughly assorted. They included many native Americans, but the English language could never have sufficed for much of the business done. Julius Heynen, attorney in charge during 1906, reports with pardonable pride that he and his legal associates can speak Czech, French, German, Moravian, Magyar, Slavonian, and Yiddish, while an assistant on the staff commands Italian. At the beginning it was supposed that this office would be resorted to by the great colonies of Italian laborers in the Bronx. Certainly substantial numbers of these people came, but on the whole the dominant groups were Americans, Russians, British, Germans, and Austro-Hungarians, in about the foregoing order numerically. Almost from the first, it was noticeable that the source of many applicants was the Bronx rather than Harlem. Not infrequently the Bronx has supplied a majority of clients for a whole year or even longer periods. So the reports advocated again and again establishment of a Bronx branch, both to take the excess load off the Harlem attorneys and to develop fully the legal aid needs of the more remote district. Unfortunately the necessary funds have never been available.

In the evil day of the uncurbed loan shark the Harlem Branch had to do what it could for an extremely large number of distressed small borrowers. As these complaints gradually diminished, the attorneys became increasingly aware that their district reeked with petty frauds more or less successfully applied against the poor. In this respect conditions became even worse after the negro influx began about 1917. Insurance sharpers gaily exploited to the full the colored man's reckless inclination to purchase superficially liberal policies at very low premiums. So crammed were these contracts with conditions and exceptions that their coverage was mainly illusory. Even when the underwriters could not slip away through the jungle of verbiage, they dodged payment with persistent ingenuity. Defeating such tactics is always heavy work, the more so because similar undeserving evasion may be repeated through any number of subsequent litigations. More pleasantly and profitably, the Harlem attorneys, pursuing the Society's time-honored policy of pacific adjustment, devised and enforced to the satisfaction of all parties certain specialized settlement machinery which will be adverted to at the close of the chapter.

Russian clients were visibly affected by the Communist fever just after the War. Not a few came to the office expressing the utmost contempt for capitalism and all its works. Whereupon special efforts were made to show the applicants that their rights could and would be enforced by the mechanisms of the existing capitalistic order. Deeds spoke louder than agitators' words. At this Branch, as elsewhere in the Society, curious and pitiful manifestations of human nature occurred. One will suffice as an indication of many others. The client was a married woman, deserted by her husband in 1913. Seven years later came a letter from England, whereby a relative of the husband's informed the client that she was widowed. An enclosed photograph of a coffin being lowered into a grave added some touch of verisimilitude. Rather suspicious, and desirous of obtaining a widow's pension if the report were true, the Branch wrote both the mayor of the English town and a British firm which had been the husband's employer. It then appeared that the relative's letter had been a hoax; the man was alive and employed in Calcutta. Again the Branch wrote, this time to the husband direct, explaining the deserted woman's difficulties in supporting herself and the absentee's infant daughter. The husband responded with a remittance and expressions of deep contrition. He asked the woman to come with the child to Calcutta. Reconciliation seemed on the way. But it was not to be. The man, rendered despondent by illness, killed himself during the tedious long-range negotiations. It remained only for the Society to protect the widow's and child's interests in the deceased's property.

For the maintenance of this useful Branch credit can now be given where credit is due. Mrs. Elizabeth Milbank Anderson, one of New York's greatest woman philanthropists, was the donor. Albert G. Milbank, the lawyer through whom she contributed, thus reports her explanation of the original gift: "She told me that she was a great believer in the motto that one should be just before being generous, not only in its usually accepted meaning but because she felt that there was nothing more demoralizing to the community than for any member of it to be deprived of the privilege of asserting or defending his rights through lack of funds. She selected The Legal Aid Society as the best medium to insure against this happening in a great city like New York. She attached quite as much importance to 'legal' justice as to 'social' justice." Mrs. Anderson died February 22, 1921. But the Harlem Branch was still adequately sustained. Her will gave the Society $50,000 for its continued maintenance. That sum, added to $50,000 previously given by the Memorial Fund Association which she had founded and liberally financed, provided a sufficient endowment.

The later history of the Branch to date calls for no great detail. Its grist of cases diminished during the period from 1921 through 1926. In 1921 the Brooklyn Branch passed it, and for some time remained statistically leading by a varying margin. The West Side Branch also passed ahead in the statistical race about 1922, and has within the last year or two run far beyond Brooklyn as well. Mr. McGee's reports show frank uncertainty as to the reasons for decreasing applications in Harlem. He suspected, without enough positive evidence to turn the suspicion into certainty, that the cause might be lack of recent commercial development for some distance north and south of 125th Street between the East River and Eighth Avenue. Disputes requiring legal service arise more often where clients work than where they live, and of course the inclination is therefore to seek the Legal Aid office nearest the place of employment. But in 1927 all such reasoning with respect to the Harlem Branch could be put aside. Business at this office rose 60 per cent, its roaring flood bringing nearly 6500 cases during the year.

Not long after the Harlem extension, another much-needed branch made its start. The reader will remember that early Legal Aid work had been fragmentarily carried on in Brooklyn by kindly disposed practitioners. Somewhat later the famous Plymouth Church, under Dr. Hillis, established a legal bureau, open from 8 to 10 o'clock each Thursday evening, at which three young lawyers named Cavo, Badger, and Noble gave gratuitous service. Louis Stoiber, a director of The Legal Aid Society, helped supervise the bureau. These various volunteers between them disposed of hundreds of cases. Yet lawyers at the Main Office knew to a certainty that the Brooklyn poor had not hundreds but thousands of meritorious claims, and that no member of the Bar earning bread and butter by private practice could possibly offer them more than tantalizingly inadequate assistance. In 1906 over 1600 applicants came to the Main Office alone from Brooklyn, which then had a population of at least 1,300,000 and was by 1910 to have 1,600,000. Unquestionably there were in so huge a community people sorely needing legal help who had never heard of the Society or who, having heard of it, could not spare time to cross the East River for consultation. Indeed, not a few might find the small item of carfare an insurmountable barrier.

So, after much thought and discussion, the Brooklyn Branch opened at 186 Remsen Street on January 2, 1907. Its leading supporter among the directors was, as might be expected, Mr. Stoiber, who supplemented a pledge of $500 from William H. Childs by promising the remaining funds needful to run the office for two years. Mrs. Whitney and Frederick W. Hinrichs also were active, the former becoming chairman of the directors' visiting committee at the Branch. Mr. v. Briesen took an unusually great share, even for him, in steering the new office and helping it on difficult cases. One anecdote of the first day's work survives. When the advertised opening hour arrived, there was not a stick of furniture in the room, the dealer who had taken the Society's order having broken his promise of timely delivery. But window sills were made before chairs, and by 10.30 A.M. three clients had been carefully, if somewhat unconventionally, interviewed. The Branch was a going concern immediately.

It kept going with accelerated speed. Soon the attorneys found themselves overburdened. They were expected not only to serve a great population, but to cover a bigger territory than any other office of the Society — Kings, Queens, and portions of Nassau Counties. Before the end of 1907 they had regretfully to reject practically all litigation in Queens. Through 1908 the business grew quite steadily. Yet lack of applicants from many quarters of the borough showed that the office was not universally known. It was only beginning to meet an intense need. Meanwhile, money support sadly lagged. Early in 1909 a financial vacuum compelled the directors to close the Branch. For the first time in its history, Legal Aid beat a forced retreat. The experience stung and rankled. Mr. v. Briesen and his coworkers buckled down to money-raising. A special committee composed of Henry Escher, Jr., Mr. Stoiber, and Mrs. Whitney threw all their power into the struggle. On March 10, 1910, the Brooklyn Branch began again on work which has never since halted or paused.

The Society's presence had to be advertised afresh, and in this the local newspapers gave most effective assistance. Before long the old familiar cry went up: Williamsburgh needed a Legal Aid office of its own. A few years more — Brownsville needs an office; then Queens County; and later, to ring the changes, are recited the demands of Woodhaven, Springfield, Ridgewood, and the area between Long Island City and Flushing. But this is legal aid of the mellow future. The Brooklyn Branch is still single and without far-flung sub-stations.

At first this office did much work for recent immigrants from Southern Europe employed on borough constructions of various types. About 1912 a definite shift manifested itself. Negroes and Germans bulked large among the clients. At a later period domestly difficulties were exceptionally numerous. Significantic enough, these painful cases had very clear connection with the worse type of instalment-furniture salesmanship. The glib dealer places his furniture, not on the idea that it will "stay put," but rather to extract all the money possible from this temporarily enchanted buyer, then to "pull" the goods (that is, retake them for default in payment), polish over the scratches, and sell again, repeating as long as the articles will hang together. And who can blame a poor husband and wife, whose lares and penates have just been "pulled" by this far-from-painless process, for display of mutual bad temper? In 1919, on the heels of the War, many applicants came from the pathetic "new poor" — gentlefolk, taking fair and kindly dealing as a matter of course, who were getting their first rough rubs after falling in the world. These were good clients, honest, grateful, and confident of the Society's integrity. Next year, with bad times setting in hard, the Branch's practice jumped enormously. Wage claims increased 80 per cent compared to the twelvemonth before. Other claims, while not keeping pace, rose sharply. It was the old story of needy creditors and distressed debtors. Nor did this activity prove to be a mere flash in the pan. Through to the end of 1925 the business of the office ran never below 5200 cases per year and once reached nearly 6600. Of the wage claims, one deserves special mention, for it shows the Society's universal serviceability. The applicant was no horny-handed son of toil, but a refined, intellectual woman holding a Ph.D. degree from one of the leading mid-western universities. She had been employed for months on the translation and revision of a German medical book, furnishing both linguistic ability and scientific knowledge at one dollar per hour — a rate of wages which would send a Brooklyn bricklayer on strike. *O tempora, O mores!* And then the employer refused to pay her bill of $590.

With 1926 the work of this Branch dropped to about the pre-War level. However, as in the case of Harlem, one finds no indication that its bolt is shot. Still there remain over 4000 applicants annually, and out on the far borders of the broad territory in and near Brooklyn are districts and neighborhoods as populous as many a well-known city, awaiting that golden day of legal aid when lawyers for the poor will always be everywhere. Well may the Society echo Tennyson's "Ulysses":

> Yet all experience is an arch
> wherethro'
> Gleams that untravell'd
> world, whose margin fades
> For ever and for ever
> when I move.

The tale of new branches is not yet quite complete. In 1909 or 1910 a Criminal Branch was tentatively established. This, however, properly belongs with a later general account of efforts to better the administration of criminal justice. But the Immigration Branch does fit in at the present point. It will be remembered that toward the end of the first decade of this century immigrants were rushing into the country at a prodigious rate. Their coming gave rise to serious economic and sociological problems. Smug talk of "the melting pot" no longer satisfied those who questioned our national policy. Various restrictive or regulative devices were vigorously discussed. Aside from revision of the Federal law, New York was obliged to move for amelioration of immigrant conditions at her great port of entry. Bearing in mind the cause of the Society's organization, one is not surprised to find it an active participant in such efforts. About April 1, 1911, under agreement with the New York State Bureau of Industry and Immigration and the North American Civic League for Immigrants, it established a branch at No. 1 Broadway. The matters to be dealt with here manifestly included deportation, transportation problems, and tracing lost baggage. Also, as a substantial amount of "follow up" work was being done, the attorney in charge might expect a fair miscellaneous run of wage disputes, fraud claims, and all the other troubles likely to afflict ignorant strangers recently arrived from far countries.

Meanwhile, a special Committee on Immigration, headed by the indefatigable J. Augustus Johnson and functioning under sanction of the Society's directors, was attacking the whole vexed problem of immigrant regulation. On November 23, 1911, this committee offered, and the directors adopted, a set of resolutions advocating more flexible handling of immigration, with periods of probation in doubtful cases; thoroughgoing attempts both abroad and in the United States to give immigrants full information about industrial conditions and so forth; more thorough inspection by shipping concerns at foreign ports, with heavier penalties on these concerns for bringing ineligible immigrants; better accommodations for immigrants at ports of entry and elsewhere; and more comprehensive educational facilities for recently arrived foreigners. The resolutions specifically disapproved proposed literacy and physical tests. In taking this stand the Society entered upon hotly contentious ground, as appeared from the prompt resignation of one of its members, a gentleman of high standing connected with a large transportation company.

The Immigration Branch soon found the original location too far from its allies, the Bureau and the League. This office was therefore moved, and on March 14, 1912, reopened at 127 Madison Avenue, local headquarters of the last-named organization. Some months later the office moved again, this time to space furnished by the Bureau of Industry at 95 Madison Avenue. The volume of Immigration Branch business was never impressive, running under two hundred and fifty cases during its busiest twelvemonth. For this there was a special reason. The Bureau and League had never intended that the Branch should receive many direct applicants; primarily it was to take over cases already investigated by either of these two organizations and found not susceptible of friendly settlement. This operating method also explains the notably high percentage of actual lawsuits among the immigration cases. The method was not markedly successful. Failure to get expert legal advice at the very beginning of controversies caused much wasted and mistaken motion, and even complete disaster in such matters as wage claims, where the statutes provided that important legal steps, if taken at all, must be taken within definite time limits. Seemingly, too, the workers for the Bureau and the League did not have the tradition of relentless, driving speed which was always before The Legal Aid Society. Without very deep regret, therefore, Mr. v. Briesen announced consolidation of the Branch and the Main Office about the end of 1913 "owing to lack of funds." This year, however, had contained a spectacular immigration case. On July 30, 1913, the Society secured a writ of habeas corpus to stay deportation of a Greek boy about to be sent back on the liner *Olympic*. An attorney reached the pier with the writ, only to find the *Olympic* already in midstream. Racing by taxicab to the Battery, the lawyer chartered the tug *Crescent*, pursued the liner down the bay, and got his immigrant off quarantine, the vice-president of the White Star Line having by wireless asked the *Olympic* to slow down and wait for the *Crescent*.

As this chapter has already referred to the instalment-furniture business, it is appropriate to insert an account of the biggest furniture case, and in most aspects the biggest case of any kind, ever handled by the Society. For several years prior to 1914 Mr. McGee had been receiving information which made him increasingly suspicious of certain furniture concerns doing business under a scheme whereby each purchaser agreed to pay twenty-five cents per week until his aggregate payments amounted to $17.50, when he might have his choice of certain articles supposed to be worth this price. It will be observed that this is different from the ordinary conditional sale, where a purchaser takes possession upon making his initial payment; also that complete payment here required seventy weeks, an uncommonly long time to wait with nothing to show for one's money. But the dealers spiced the waiting period with an ingenious provision: every week a drawing was had among each "club" of customers, and he who held the lucky number received his chosen article immediately, without obligation to pay any further instalments. The articles thus drawn naturally came under envious scrutiny. So the sellers saw to it that these pieces of furniture were specially good. The majority of buyers, who won no drawings and persevered to the end in weekly payments, really were doubly unlucky. Their furniture usually turned out very inferior; many were even cheated by the crude trick of delivering a rug, table, or bed entirely different from the one selected.

Now, the seductive drawing feature of this plan constituted a lottery, and the conduct of a lottery was criminally punishable under New York laws. Mr. McGee finally presented the matter to the District Attorney, who promptly caused the issuance of warrants against the men controlling about a dozen of the offending concerns. Then arose a situation fraught with peril for the interests of 13,000 members of the "furniture clubs." If the defendants should be convicted and jailed in ordinary fashion, they would almost certainly go into bankruptcy, and the poor instalment buyers would emerge practically empty-handed from the resulting scramble. Mr. McGee rose to the occasion with a comprehensive settlement scheme. The defendants were to plead guilty, receive suspended sentences, and then, as far as lay within their power, to settle honestly with the furniture purchasers. Defendants, District-Attorney, and court accepted the proposal, and on November 30, 1914, liquidation began with a Legal Aid representative at each store to act as adjuster. Appeals from the adjusters might be taken to Mr. McGee for final ruling. This huge liquidating machine encountered troubles innumerable. Two of the defendants slipped from the path of rectitude, but were scared back into line by applications to revoke their suspended sentences. Merchandise creditors of the defendant dealers had to be appeased, lest their threats of bankruptcy proceedings be put into effect. These creditors actually did push three of the defendants into bankruptcy, but compromise of their claims prevented a general overturn of the apple-cart.

Most trying of all were the turbulent multitudes of excited, wrangling instalment buyers. They stood to lose in the aggregate about $160,000. None would save much of anything unless all yielded some fraction of their claims. This was hard indeed to hammer into the heads of poor folk who could only see that they were being paid off in furniture which could often be bought from a solvent store around the corner for much less than they had deposited under the "club plan." Some customers, it must be confessed, went so far as to decoy the dealers into delivering goods on promise of a small final payment at their houses, and once the furniture was inside slammed the doors in the delivery-men's faces. All in all, Mr. McGee had almost literally to ride in the whirlwind and direct the storm. But ride he did through situations that would have taxed the patience of Job himself. Occasionally mere patience lost its virtue, as at a meeting where the Attorney-in-Chief leaped on a table and by force of words and personality turned tumult into passable order. When the directors met in December, 1914, he could report over 4000 adjustments. By February, 1915, about as many more had been accomplished. Long before the end of 1915 some 11,500 adjustments were completed, and Mr. McGee could turn with a sigh of heartfelt relief to other business. The remaining 1500 or so customers either lost interest or else doggedly persisted in bankruptcy proceedings which brought very meagre returns. The Legal Aid Society has every reason to remember proudly its unique and successful disposition of a huge complication. And to this day some of the furniture dealers send Mr. McGee cards on Christmas!

So far, the furniture men have scarcely appeared in a favorable light. But by coming down to more recent times and shifting to the Harlem Branch we can give the story another aspect. After having trouble for years on end with the neighboring instalment-furniture houses, this Branch invited representatives of the six largest dealers in Harlem to talk matters over frankly. The upshot was a working agreement that whenever a customer complained to the office, the furniture concern involved would send a man to discuss the case, and both parties should listen to the attorney's suggestions. With surprising uniformity this plan led to satisfactory adjustments. Instances of real generosity occurred.

When the sudden death of a young husband left his widow ill, heartbroken, and so nearly penniless that she could not meet an unpaid balance of $14 on house furnishings, the furniture seller was legally entitled to foreclose his lien and seize the property. The seller did begin foreclosure proceedings. But he knew the Branch and had appreciated its fairness to him in earlier cases. So the attorney told the dealer the widow's story and asked an extension of time, adding that he personally had no doubt of the woman's desperate circumstances. Without hesitation the dealer answered: "Tell her to forget it — I'll close the account on our books and she does n't owe us anything. If The Legal Aid Society believes she is telling the truth, that is enough for me."

In many cases beside the furniture matters, the Harlem Branch has of late years employed the conference settlement method, obtaining mutually agreeable results eight or nine times out of ten. It devised a particularly satisfactory general scheme for clearing away disputes over the value of clothing, linen, and the like lost by laundries. Setting these values had always been a vexing problem, particularly in court, where definite legal evidence was required. The scheme reduced the whole matter to simple arithmetic. For lost shirts, collars, and cuffs the laundry paid ten times its laundering charge; for table linen, sheets, and other articles longer-lived and more expensive in proportion to washing costs, the settlement price was to be twenty times the laundering charge. Several laundries adopted this scale as part of their regular business policy, and claims against them absolutely vanished from the Branch's docket.

Too often, perhaps, this tale has been adorned with moral observations of one sort or another. But the bare facts of the narrative so frequently lead back to the topic of pacific settlement that comment upon the significance of the Society's practice in this respect is irresistible. It may seem trite to point out that a man with some legal claim which he is unwilling to surrender can proceed in two ways: (1) make an effort to settle with or conciliate his opponent; or (2) fight the dispute out. In fact he need never enter upon alternative (2) until the possibilities of (1) have been explored and exhausted. Also amicable settlement is more likely to succeed where a disinterested third party urges it and directs the efforts toward it. But trite though these statements be, our Anglo-American legal procedure has tended to belittle alternative (1) almost to the vanishing-point. Despite a great deal of talk about the sinfulness of stirring up litigation, our judicial philosophy has become a pugnacious one.[1] It has, officially, offered little save an arena for a fight confined within the bounds of decency and propriety. The spirit noted in the first chapter as pervading early English efforts at legal poor relief is to no small extent the spirit of the courts in general. Consequently, both here and in England, there is a lack of official domestic precedents illustrating conciliation as a judicial practice. And of course under our common law system,

> Where Freedom slowly broadens
> down
> From precedent to precedent,

the lack of existing authorities has a numbing effect.

Numbing, it would seem, not only to external development but to thought itself. On April 7, 1925, the

[1] Recent legal investigaiton indicates that conciliation anciently had a recognized place in English court procedure. But this has long since faded from judicial memory.

British Chancellor and Home Secretary appointed twelve persons a committee to report what, if any, further steps should be taken to provide legal advice for the poor and aid them in legal proceedings before the inferior courts. On January 2, 1928, the committee, with a dissenting minority of two, reported that next to nothing need be done officially so far as civil cases are concerned. This majority report discusses English legal aid (Poor Man's Lawyers) as follows:

"In most cases it appears that the Poor Man's Lawyer Centre [at each of ten large towns outside London] is open *on one or more evenings in the week* and a rota is kept of those members of the Bar or solicitors who have expressed themselves willing to attend on particular evenings. . . . If nothing more than advice is wanted [by an applicant] *the matter of course ends with the giving of advice. In certain cases it is proper that litigation should follow*. . . . It will be seen that the schemes are schemes *for providing free legal advice and for putting prospective litigants, where litigation appears necessary and proper, in touch with reliable solicitors who are likely to be willing and able to take up the case*. The witnesses before us were unanimous in saying that in an overwhelming majority of the cases advice only is required. Of course, *there are cases* where the advice is that litigation should be initiated or *where it is necessary that negotiations should take place, but all the evidence showed that these cases are very few when compared with those where the matter ends with the giving of advice*. . . . If in every important centre of population there was at work a Poor Man's Lawyer organized similarly to those already in existence, we are satisfied that the problem of legal aid to the poor would to a very great extent be solved." And a little later the report expresses apprehension that provision of free legal assistance, and remission of fees, for poor people in the county court might make the beneficiaries over-litigious.

For italics in the foregoing quotation the present writer is responsible. The italicized sentences and phrases, coupled with their context, vividly illustrate a "no compromise" attitude. Save for one fleeting reference to the occasional (and rare) necessity of "negotiations," neither Chancellor, Home Secretary, witnesses, nor members of the committee seem to see any middle ground between advice and contentious litigation. Admonition or battle — conciliation is nowhere. Now let us view the American scene, taking The Legal Aid Society's figures for 1915, one of its busiest years, when every office was working full-tilt. In round numbers, 2650 cases were rejected and 39,350 accepted. Of the latter about 10,700, or 27.2 per cent, required advice only. A substantial proportion, but far below a preponderance. *Fewer than 2500, or 6.4 per cent, were taken to court.* This scarcely indicates undue encouragement of the litigious spirit. *More than 26,150, or 66.4 per cent, were disposed of by conciliatory methods.* The stone which the English builders refuse is the very cornerstone of the New York structure.

This discrepancy between opinions on the eastern side of the Atlantic and actual successful practice on the western side of the same ocean challenges the English view. For it is scarcely conceivable that such radical legal or social differences exist as to render practically futile in England a procedure that settles two poor men's cases out of three in our hemisphere's greatest city. Indeed, Sir Edward A. Parry, speaking from long practical experience as a busy English county court judge, consistently urges the use of conciliation. F. C. G.

Gurney-Champion argues similarly in his book on "Justice and the Poor in England." But seeing is believing, and it would seem that the English have never seen skilled conciliation working steadily upon large numbers of controversies under modern conditions. Certainly Poor Man's Lawyer meetings held by volunteers "on one or more evenings in the week," without businesslike continuity, clerical assistance, or means of communication with applicants' opponents, cannot possibly give such an object-lesson. Therefore few men in all England have a practical conception of the opportunity which their legal system is neglecting. In America, thanks to Legal Aid, we have before our eyes a convincing domestic precedent to speed the day when peaceful, friendly settlement will become part of our official system for dispensing justice.

IX

THE WAR

EVEN before 1914, war and The Legal Aid Society were not utter strangers, for the organization had been actively operating during the brief conflict with Spain. But despite the vast ultimate consequences of that war, its immediate effect upon the Society's clients is accurately reflected by the fact that Mr. v. Briesen's report for 1898 makes not the slightest reference to hostilities. The story of 1914 and the following years is terribly different. Collateral effects of the world conflict have already been frequently mentioned. Its more direct effects manifested themselves promptly. Even before the end of August, 1914, wage earners by the thousand had been thrown temporarily out of work, often without being paid the wages due. These were commonplace cases, although in uncommon and disquieting quantity. Peculiar claims also abounded, as witness the following:

On September 2, 1914, two German firemen from a British tramp steamer reached the Seamen's Branch with a tale of woe. They had signed articles for three years about twelve months previously. Most of the crew were Russian or British. This hostile majority now made the lives of the "alien enemies" miserable. But the owners refused to pay the Germans off. The Branch attorney filed a libel claiming that war suspended such shipping contracts, particularly where the seamen were reservists, and had the pair discharged. More amusing was the case of the yacht *Alvina*, chartered in New York to bring home from Genoa, Italy, a number of wealthy

American travellers stranded by the fighting. After a crew of thirty-five had been signed on, the war exiles found other means of transportation and the *Alvina's* voyage was cancelled. Whereat her captain proposed to discharge his crew summarily. The Society began an action to recover under the waiting pay statute, which led to a satisfactory compromise. Then there was a German maidservant with this complicated grievance: Engaged in Germany during the early summer of 1914, after the declaration of war she started for America with her mistress, who agreed orally to pay the maid's passage back to Germany unless she herself soon returned there. Fearing to disclose her nationality, the maid destroyed her passport and posed as a Swiss while going through England. The conditions of work in America did not suit her, and the Society soon had in hand the double task of extracting passage money from the employer and a new passport from the German consul. Not many months later a bit of long-range passport work came up. A young American missionary had gone abroad before the war to a country which ultimately became one of the belligerents. According to the free and easy ante-bellum practice he took with him no proofs of nationality. Soon after the fighting began, this militant Christian found himself in real danger of being conscribed and becoming a militant of quite another sort. But his sister in North Dakota somehow knew about the poor man's law office at 239 Broadway. She wrote a pleading letter to the Society, which managed ultimately to arrange through the Department of State for issuance of a temporary passport to the young man and for his protection against impressment.

All this fell in the day's work. The Society, however, soon suffered a heavy blow by reason of war. Mr.

v. Briesen began his report for 1914 with these dismaying words: "Having occupied the presidential chair for twenty-five years this shall be my last annual report, since conditions have arisen that render it necessary that other, stronger hands shall henceforth be at the helm." We can only guess what anguish of heart went into this quiet sentence. The writer had determined to give up the dearest work of his life because he felt that his continued participation would jeopardize its future. The "conditions" referred to are these:

Mr. v. Briesen had soberly considered the complex mass of circumstances leading to the war, and concluded that Germany was far from being solely at fault. He frankly expressed this view in conversation and in published articles. Read at the present date, these articles seem calm and sane enough. One need not agree with them to grant their entire propriety. But America, or at least her eastern seaboard, was being riven into factions controlled by other forces than reason. Mr. v. Briesen knew that many contributors to the Society bitterly resented his attitude. He knew that legal aid work was sure to become increasingly onerous, expensive, and vital to public welfare as the conflict broadened and deepened. He could see that with multiplied demands upon everybody's generosity the support of his beloved institution must grow progressively more difficult. Irrespective of pain to himself, he chose to remove an element which might imperil the Society's continuance.

At the annual meeting in February, 1915, the President's associates pleaded with him to reconsider. "You, sir," said Judge A. J. Dittenhoefer, "have been instrumental in making the Society what it is. The name of v. Briesen is identified with the organization, and is known all over the country. . . . *Arthur v. Briesen has really been the Legal Aid.* I know none who could take office and fill it with more ability and success." At length, the father of New York legal aid agreed that if no other man could be found for president, he would serve, but only for another year. This year must have been to him a time of embarrassment and suffering. He was too frank and brave to be a turncoat or cloak his views. The whispering campaign went on. Written attacks upon him increased. At least one assailant sank to the contemptible level of an envenomed anonymous letter published in a newspaper correspondence column. At the Society's annual meeting on February 24, 1916, President v. Briesen firmly and finally laid down his office, saying that conditions had rendered its burdens increasing difficult. A directorship was pressed upon him, but even that he declined to accept at the moment. His name appears, however, on the list of directors for 1916. In 1917 he was made an honorary vice-president, his name immediately following those of Woodrow Wilson, Taft, and Roosevelt.

Thus passed from the Society's active workers the man who had the vision to foresee, the boldness to plan, and the patience to execute the great fabric of legal aid. In a very literal sense he devoted to the good cause thirty-two years of his life. "Appreciation cannot measure such life-long devotion," said his directors in their farewell resolutions, "nor praise enhance its success; but we who know the facts, his friends and associates, are unwilling to let the occasion pass without expressing these sentiments, approved by our fellow members, our clients, and indeed the whole community. RESOLVED, THEREFORE: That the Directors of The Legal Aid Society hereby record an obligation which nothing can repay, a regret universally shared, and a memory to be cherished as long as we live."

The blind spite which drove out this wise and kindly man is not the least of the great war's bitter tragedies. Although the United States had not yet become a belligerent, Mr. v. Briesen's assailants forgot all about his life's record, seeing in him only an outcast who trusted Germany and distrusted England and France. They forgot the young immigrant's early display of love for his new country when he limped off with the Union army in answer to Lincoln's first call. They forgot Roosevelt's statement on October 12, 1912, that Jacob Riis and Arthur v. Briesen represented "as high a type of the American citizen as this land can produce." It would be as easy to condemn these people now as it then seemed proper to them to condemn Mr. v. Briesen. But such condemnation is unjust. Who went through the tense days between 1914 and 1919 without passing some harsh judgment which now amazes and saddens him? Instead of blaming those who lost their heads, it is best to praise those who kept them. For Mr. v. Briesen had firm defenders always. The directors' resolution quoted above shows that. And another instance deserves recording here. On September 3, 1917, with this country heart and soul in the war, and when the hatred of pro-Germans past or present stood at its peak, a Special Conference of Delegates from Bar Associations, held in Saratoga Springs, devoted most of a morning session to legal aid. Elihu Root, a big man and a brave one, presided. Near the end of the discussion he spoke with earnest emphasis:

"Permit me to say a word of tribute for a lawyer whom I learned to respect and esteem through many years of association and co-operation in the work that we have been talking about. All honor is due to Arthur v. Briesen for his great-hearted, devoted and untiring labor, that in our free republic the poor might feel that the law was their protector and that justice was for them."

Mr. v. Briesen did not long survive the severance of his active connection with the Society. After a period of failing health he died suddenly on May 13, 1920. To mark his funeral, the Society's offices were closed for the first time on any working day in forty-four years. One may say that Justice mourned. Newspaper comment was restrained but kindly. The Brooklyn *Eagle* said editorially: "Twenty years from now, when the sores of war have become mere scars, Americans will have no trouble in doing justice to Von Briesen." In the sense immediately intended, this time limit was much too long. The petty hates and bitternesses incident to the great trial by battle have dropped away more rapidly than we dared hope. But in a fundamental sense, the time limit may prove too short. Only very, very slowly are we beginning to appreciate truly the profound influence for good which Mr. v. Briesen created in American life — to realize that he has left "a monument more lasting than brass, and more sublime than the regal elevation of pyramids, which neither the wasting shower, the unavailing northwind, nor an innumerable succession of years, and the flight of seasons, shall be able to demolish."

The Society was put in a delicate position by the resignation of its perennial President for the reasons upon which he rested his action. His successor must be a man of ability and prominence, certainly not open to attack on the ground of pro-Germanism, and yet, if possible, reasonably acceptable to those who had German sympathies. Wisely — or perhaps necessarily — the directors made haste slowly. Throughout most of 1916 Carl L. Schurz served as acting president. At length the Society's choice fell upon Charles E. Hughes. Of him little need be said to any American reader. A brilliant lawyer and of unsullied integrity, he had carried on the great insurance investigation, then become an effective reform Governor of New York, and later been appointed to the United States Supreme Court. From the high office last named he had resigned to run for President in 1916 on an "America first" platform, and at the time when his acceptance of the Legal Aid post was announced had just emerged from this extraordinary political campaign after losing to Wilson only by the barest of margins. He was, and has ever since remained, a notable and respected national figure. His willingness to undertake leadership of The Legal Aid Society was a striking testimonial to its importance in the community.

Mr. Hughes had scarcely settled himself in the driver's seat before the United States entered the war. Immediately legal aid problems multiplied and intensified. Something has already been said of the huge amount of work carried by the Society in 1914. The year's report shows 40,430 cases exclusive of the enormous furniture club matter. Nor did this stress abate. From 1914 to 1918 inclusive — the five "war years" — the organization took in the staggering total of 206,983 claims — almost one fourth of the matters handled during the Society's first half-century. Such unprecedented concentration of work in a quinquennial period would have burdened the officers and the staff heavily at best. On top of this, from 1917 on to the end of the next year the whole organization had to run shorthanded. In 1917 Allen Wardwell, the remarkably effective treasurer, went to Russia on Red Cross work; his temporary successor John T. Pratt also joined the Red Cross; both these gentlemen were directors, and no fewer than four others of the most active directors left for war service. Members of the attorneys' force and of the clerical staff constantly were dropping out to enter the army, the navy, or some other governmental employment. Money to sustain the Society's activities came harder and harder. Even most desperate tugging and hauling could not always make both ends meet.

And yet, as if by a miracle, the work not only ran full blast but expanded. The Selective Service Law roused to activity a pack of cheats and shysters whose conduct became so outrageous that the Mayor's Committee on National Defense and the War Committee of the New York City Bar asked the Society to intervene. As the worst manifestations of this trouble appeared on the lower East Side, a kind offer of free quarters in the building of the University Settlement Society, 184 Eldridge Street, was accepted. Here Mr. McGee established a special Bureau of Draft Information, open every weekday evening from August 2 through September 19, 1917. Before the latter date the first draft had been substantially completed, and such subsequent cases as were not dealt with by the new Legal Advisory Board, formed to help on the second call, went straight to the main office. Volunteers largely or exclusively handled this patriotic work. Mr. McGee chose them with great care, taking only persons thoroughly in favor of the draft. The total number of applicants to the end of 1918 was 1547. Compared with the enormous quantity of ordinary cases shown in the last paragraph, this figure seems low. But draft matters were unusually time consuming, as will appear from a brief description of their nature.

The simplest — and, one may add, the most respectable — type of case was a claim for exemption from military service on account of genuine dependency, alienage, or other ground recognized under the Selective Service Act. Every such claim had to be documented in proper form and supported by affidavits. Usually at least three witnesses, and often more, must be examined. Applicant and witnesses were ordinarily ignorant, frequently illiterate, and not seldom unable to express themselves clearly in English. Sometimes a case went on appeal from the Local Board to the District Board, involved application for rehearing (more affidavits!), or even necessitated presentation to the military authorities in an attempt to procure discharge of a wrongfully inducted man. Nor did the Bureau's task remain uncomplicated by irregularity, fraud, and cheating. Mr. McGee encountered and overthrew one super-patriotic young woman, employed by a Local Board, who firmly rejected all exemption claims, no matter how sound or correctly prepared. Little things like statutory provisions meant nothing to this ardent damsel. Still more serious, some Local Boards, either from carelessness or an easygoing desire to fill their quotas somehow and anyhow, certified man after man without giving hearings on perfectly good exemptions. The consequence was a flock of appeal cases.

As to fraud, one or two specific instances will tell the story. A young fellow of twenty-three desired exemption on the ground that he had dependents. Being told that they could not be accepted "unsight unseen," he departed and came back with a woman admitting sixty-two years of age, who was, so she said, the young man's wife. Inquiries for a marriage certificate, and hints that false affidavits led jailward, caused a second departure, never followed by another return. In actual fact, of course, Cupid's bow did twang lustily to produce a certain kind of war marriage — perhaps better called a draft exemption marriage. But these affairs of the heart did not appeal to the Bureau or the Main Office. Occasionally it was deemed proper to reject an applicant because he did not come clean-handed, although his claim seemed sound enough. Thus a Russian who had never taken out first papers, and was therefore exempt, lost his chance of help from the Society when it found that on May 12, 1918, he had tried to construct an evasive claim of dependency by marrying in haste. Now and then dependency matters came up rather the other way round. For instance, a man married long before 1917 claimed the dependency of his wife, who supported the claim by affidavit. Discharge from military service was allowed. Not long afterward the wife sought out Mr. McGee and told him that promptly upon getting out of the army, her husband announced his intention of avoiding all domestic obligations and had lived up to the announcement. This man, of course, had laid himself open not only to a non-support proceeding but also to revocation of his discharge.

Cheating and extortion may also be presented by illustration. The clerk of one Local Board persistently refused to furnish drafted men with the necessary blank forms, and equally persistently referred applicants to outside persons who furnished blanks and charged big fees. The inference is quite obvious. Mr. McGee broke up the practice. Notaries public capitalized the necessities of the ignorant by grossly overcharging for taking affidavits. This trick in its crude form was easy to punish, but could be guarded against attack by having the notary conduct his business in connection with a law office. Under the latter conditions, excess charges became "fees for legal advice." Still more pernicious were the activities of scoundrels who promised absolutely to get men exempted, extracted in advance as large fees as the traffic would bear, and then did one of three things: gave their dupes sound advice, so obvious that it should have cost nothing; gave them unsound and futile advice; or led them into perjury. Under either of the last two situations, punishment ought to have been swift and severe. But the necessary evidence was hard to come by. As an instance, on August 6, 1917, Mr. McGee personally interviewed a young man of Russian extraction who was insistent upon gaining exemption. During the conversation the fellow let fall that a purported lawyer on the East Side had promised exemption for $25, dropping his price to $16 when he found this to be all his prospective client had. The Russian paid over the money and received in exchange a perfectly worthless paper. With all his powers of persuasion Mr. McGee strove to obtain an affidavit. But the drafted man thought he had a bargaining point, became more and more excited, and finally burst out with a refusal to swear to any statement unless his questioner would get him exemption. This broke the back of Mr. McGee's patience, and the Russian literally flew out of the office, fortunately striking the doorway rather than the wall in his expedited departure. Such cases — and there were many of them before the Legal Advisory Boards came into being and received publicity — represented the most contemptible and dangerous type of knavery. The draft law inevitably put a heavy strain upon the loyalty and trust of the poor and ignorant. Every crook and grafter who gave them reason to distrust the honesty of the law's administration was lending aid and comfort to the enemy. If the Draft Information Bureau accomplished nothing more than a diminution of these traitorous swindles — and so much it certainly did — its existence was richly justified.

All this draft work turned out to be only a beginning of the Society's war service. It had steadily to combat fraud, or what amounted to fraud, in protean forms, while protecting the fighting men and their families. The chauffeur of one well-to-do citizen was inducted, but allowed to continue his work for three weeks between the receipt of the green card which told him to get ready and of the red card which ordered him into military service. His wife, clearly about to become a mother, informed the Harlem Branch that the employer refused to pay her husband's wages for the three week period above referred to. This was actually true, the theoretical ground being that the chauffeur "was in the service of Uncle Sam, and therefore I don't have to pay him"; the practical ground, announced exultantly, that "he can't sue me because he will be in France before long." But, oh, alas for "every man his own lawyer"! Even the army grants furloughs, and the Society so arranged matters that the ex-chauffeur, on his last furlough before going overseas, signed the necessary papers for a lawsuit. From then on events marched fast. At trial, the defendant to his vast embarrassment found himself called as the star witness to prove his opponent's case. Judgment — with a word or two anent body execution — brought full payment in time to help out on the expense of bringing the soldier's son into the world.

Equally pertinent is a Seamen's Branch case. Seventeen seamen were signed on an English liner for a voyage to Europe and return, to be paid off in the United States at $90 per man per month. Fifteen days later these men had escaped the U-boats and reached a European port. Here they were paid on an imaginary parity of the five dollar bill and the pound. The latter was in truth worth only $4.70, so each man got $42.30 instead of $45.00. A small trick, but the next ones were bigger and better. The ship remained in port for ten days, during which time each man received just fifty cents daily for food and lodging. They were then forced to sign on afresh for the return trip at one shilling apiece. But that return trip took them to New York, and when the smoke of the ensuing legal battle cleared away the Seamen's Branch had a good settlement for its clients.

Another seamen's controversy illustrates a wider problem and furnishes a remarkable illustration of the Society's wise methods in handling disputes. The U-boat programme subjected sailors to a double risk of life and property. Even when men were picked up alive, their outfits went into Davy Jones' locker. So insurance became the order of the day, and seamen's unions posted placards announcing that owners should cover the personal effects of their crews to the standard amount of $100 per man. The placards were misleading. No statute or general usage required such property insurance. Hence every man ought to have searched each set of articles he signed in order to be sure of coverage. This, of course, is exactly what every man did *not* do. A stream of sorrowing claimants, wise only after the event, flowed through the Seamen's Branch office. Many could not be helped at all. Now and then, though, a situation like the following arose:

An American schooner was torpedoed off the coast of France, the crew of nine being saved but losing their outfits. The local American consul took charge and spent about forty dollars per man for necessary clothing. Thinking this a gift from Uncle Sam, the sailors took what they were given without much exercise of personal choice. Unluckily for any such benevolent theory, the government reimbursed itself from the owners of the schooner, and the owners made appropriate deduction from each seaman's pay. Enter now the Society's lawyers, attempting to settle under a provision in the articles whereby the owners agreed to pay every member of the crew for loss of clothing and personal effects according to their value. Knowing of this provision, the men had given the master lists of their outfits. It must be confessed that these inventories were "padded" to amusing dimensions. The schooner seemed to have been as well laden with seamen's clothing as some believe the *Mayflower* was with antique furniture. *Per contra*, the owners hooted down any idea that a sailor's effects *could* be worth over $25 and refused to adjust the loss at better figures. It may be added that this contention largely ignored purchases by each man from the vessel's slop chest, for which on the average $15 was claimed. The Society filed a libel, but made no haste about serving papers. There was still room for settlement. Four libelants went to the owners independently and settled at $25 each. Four more retained another lawyer, who filed a second libel, served papers, and generally made the welkin ring. This group got $35 apiece, but each had to pay the lawyer $15. Meanwhile the Society, not knowing the dispersion of eight ninths of its clients, quietly continued pressure and dickering. Opposing counsel, also momentarily in the dark, offered to settle at $65 for each libelant. One only remained to take advantage of this offer. He paid as a fee 10 per cent of his $65, thus coming out almost exactly twice as well as his most favored comrade. The whole nine might have had the same terms by a little trust and patience. But it is only fair to add that unsound advice from their union secretary caused the second group of four to retain the outside lawyer.

The gentle art of persuasion often proved effective on the war cases. Soldiers, sailors, and their dependents could reasonably ask some favor above and beyond mere legal right. An instalment matter gives an example. The wife of a soldier in active service became unable to keep up payments upon a considerable amount of furniture which she was buying under conditional sale. So, although only a small balance remained due, the seller lawfully retook the goods, agreeing to hold them for a reasonable time on the chance that the woman's finances might improve. About a year later the soldier died and his widow began to receive a small pension. But, in the dealer's opinion, a reasonable time had long since elapsed and he had resold the furniture. Legally the poor widow's case was hopeless. Nevertheless, an attorney from the Society approached the dealer. At first the man seemed obdurate. Finally he melted to the extent of saying that the woman might choose some equivalent articles from his used stock. The melting process, once started, continued surprisingly. Within two days the applicant joyfully reported that the dealer had delivered, without charge, an entire set of furniture much superior to her original purchase, and capped the climax by absolutely cancelling any indebtedness.

Congress soon added the power of law to the power of persuasion in aid of service men and their dependents. The Soldiers' and Sailors' Civil Relief Act of March 8, 1918, provided that enforcement of legal claims against men in the fighting services might be suspended during the war, or alternatively that judgments thereon might be reopened within reasonable time limits. It also contained explicit clauses protecting soldiers' and sailors' families from hasty evictions by their landlords. On April 12, 1918, the Society won the first case in the Harlem courts involving these clauses. Its client was Mrs. Mary Creags, a poor sick woman deserted by her husband and with two sons in the army.

There remained, however, certain legal situations made very difficult to handle by war conditions. Of these some brief mention is advisable. They illustrate problems which Congress and the state legislatures ought to consider if we ever again suffer the calamity of a great international conflict. Many men drawn away on foreign service occupied fiduciary capacities as executors, administrators, trustees, and guardians. In the excitement of departure some of these men forgot to make provision for the persons whose property they controlled. More than one grave situation thus arose when a beneficiary or ward urgently needed funds. Along the same line, although less serious, were instances in which the departing soldier or sailor was himself the beneficiary. He would assume that a small inheritance held for him by the City Chamberlain's office could be drawn against as easily as a bank account. In fact, a special court order had to be obtained. All such cases when they came to The Legal Aid Society required quick action under high pressure, and sometimes even the utmost desire by judges and court officials to help out the applicants brought up short against a barrier of legal requirements which could not at the moment be fulfilled. During the war years, the Society's Surrogate Court work increased enormously. Not only did deaths in service and from the terrible influenza scourge vastly enlarge the number of small probates, but there were concomitant guardianship, adoption, and accounting proceedings almost beyond reckoning. So thick and fast did administration cases come that the courts were unable to maintain their excellent practice of drawing papers for applicants in these small and comparatively uncomplicated proceedings. The Society, wrestling mightily with the overflow, barely held its own. Miss Alice Dillingham, who had charge of the main office's Surrogate Department, earned Mr. McGee's warm praise by her effective and untiring efforts. One case that stands out as a distinctive achievement also exemplifies the kind of difficulty often surmounted:

Ordinarily a will must be witnessed and in written form. But there is an exception where the testator is a soldier in actual military service or a mariner at sea. Because of the exigencies of his position, such a person may bequeath personal property by nuncupative or unwritten will. In August, 1918, a man named Yarmolinski, with the American Expeditionary Forces, stated in the presence of two witnesses at Contres, France, that he wished his money in a New York bank to go to his cousin. Yarmolinski was later fatally wounded and died in March, 1919. Now it happened that one of the two witnesses, an army chaplain, methodically made a memorandum of the testator's statement. This memorandum or a copy of it finally came to the Society's hands. The chaplain was traced to Astoria, Oregon. He recalled the incident and could give the address of the second witness at Portland in the same state. The Society filed a petition for probate, issued notices to the dead man's next of kin in Poland, took the the testimony of the two witnesses before a Referee in Oregon, and obtained a favorable decree. This was the first nuncupative will of a World War soldier admitted to probate in the New York City courts.

Cases of mental incompetency among returned service men also featured the Society's work for 1918 and following years. In part these breakdowns were due to the unaccustomed conditions and fearful stresses of active military duty. In part they were due to causes entirely independent of the war, and had merely been dredged to the surface by it. On either hypothesis the incapacitated ex-service man was entitled to compensation from the government. But, being incompetent, he could not himself receive and disburse the government allowance. For that purpose a guardian or, to use the technical New York term, a committee must be appointed. Thus each of these cases involved not only negotiations with a Federal bureau but with New York officials as well, and generally a New York court proceeding to boot. Now committees had to furnish surety bonds for the performance of their duties, they often had to obtain court orders with respect to the use of the incompetents' allowances, and they had to file accounts. Between poverty and ignorance, let alone occasional cases of dishonesty, trouble arose at every step. Because both Federal and state authorities were involved, deadlocks might occur. In 1921 the Army physicians decided that a certain veteran was insane. Hence payments of compensation directly to him stopped. The man's sister brought a proceeding in the proper state court of New York to obtain an adjudication of insanity and appointment of a committee. But the jury found the veteran sane. The United States Veterans' Bureau at Washington stood by the decision of the Army doctors and refused to pay any attention to the verdict. Consequently the man's dependents remained absolutely without the immediate financial assistance which Congress had intended them to have.

This history is scarcely an appropriate place for analyzing difficulties brought out in the last three paragraphs, and suggesting solutions. It is, however, earnestly to be hoped that during and after our next great national emergency of this kind similar situations will find awaiting them legal and administrative machinery at once simpler, swifter, more flexible, and less prone to stop on the dead centre of internal opposition.[1] Certainly the social engineers who desire to create such machinery can glean much from the Legal Aid records by way of helpful suggestion as well as by way of criticism.

The year 1919 saw temporary war relief organizations rapidly leaving the field or at least cutting down their activities. But The Legal Aid Society, like the poor whom it serves, is always with us. It became a kind of universal successor to all legal problems of the temporary committees and societies. Having bridged the chasm between peace and war, it was now called on to reverse the process. Also, as might be expected, the "return to normalcy" gave victimizers of the poor fresh opportunities in new forms. Distressed Europeans appealed to American relatives and friends for remittances of money or consignments of foodstuffs. Individuals, firms, and mushroom export or finance corporations boldly held themselves out as capable of effecting the transmissions. Italians, Russians, Jews, Poles, in short "Americans of all nationalities," took them at their

[1] The legislature of New York has not been blind or unresponsive to this need. In 1925 the Civil Practice Act was so amended as to simplify greatly the appointment of committees for persons depending on government compensation.

word and paid huge freight, brokerage, and interest charges. Extremely little money or food seemed ever to reach the designated recipients. Excuses and evasions put off anxious remitting parties. Even where a so-called banker had to confess flat failure to deliver, and could not beg off on the ground of unavoidable casualty, the acrobatics of foreign exchange often enabled him to "refund" at an 80 per cent or 90 per cent discount. All in all, while many of these mishaps may have been due to genuine disasters or honest lack of business skill, there must also have been an enormous amount of fraud. The great pity was that general confusion and obscurity prevented its detection and punishment.

This chapter is not a cheerful one. War, both immediately and in its after effects, brought to the Society's notice much suffering which it was never able to counteract. Yet in the narrower scope of possible accomplishment, war brought also the stern joy of being tried and not found wanting. Perhaps it may be a trifle indecorous to compare the Society's highly respected officers and attorneys with the crew of Kipling's *Bolivar*. Certainly the comparison must not be pressed too far. But, like that swaggering, roisterous, hard-bitten crew, they took their overloaded, undermanned ship "out across the bay," and then sailed on with stout confidence into the none-too-placid early days of peace.

X

LEGAL AID GROWTH

PRECEDING pages have contained many intimations of the spread of legal aid work. This narrative is now at a point where specifications may profitably be given. These specifications will show how the central idea has spread and been applied not alone to an increasing territorial area, but also with growing efficiency and intensity.

At the very outset any attempt to attribute to The Legal Aid Society anything like sole credit for the expansion of this good work must be vigorously and cheerfully disclaimed. In America, for instance, the large Chicago institution now known as the Legal Aid Bureau of the United Charities is the outgrowth of an entirely independent movement. More than that, the tap root of this western body, originally named the Bureau of Justice, was the first unrestricted legal aid organization. Founded in 1888, it began forthwith to supply legal service regardless of the applicants' nationality, race, or sex. The New York Society seemingly did not do this in substance until 1889, or avow openly its purpose of aiding all until Mr. v. Briesen became president in 1890. Honor should be rendered where honor is due. Nor can it well be possible that the example of the New York Legal Aid Society gave formative impulse to the admirable German development along similar lines, although this development largely or entirely post-dates 1890. Even nearby Jersey City in 1894 initiated legal work for the poor without knowing at all about the kindred effort across the bay. But, on the other hand, the force of New York's example is too often overlooked. So Mr. v. Briesen in 1901 was able to poke a bit of fun at the Boston *Transcript*, which thus applauded the incorporation of the local legal aid society: "Another charity has been organized in Boston, the first of its kind here, and in our natural pride at all the good we undertake to accomplish we would perhaps be pardoned if we doubted the existence of a similar one elsewhere. We do so like to feel we are setting an example!" After all, even Back Bay should recognize that *some* good things come out of Gotham!

Indeed, one of the very first legal aid extensions was so extremely remote from New York that the connection would never be suspected but for direct evidence. John P. Coldstream, writing in 1905 of the Legal Dispensary at Edinburgh, Scotland, said: "It is worthy of remark that the idea of founding the institution was first obtained from a notice of the work of the Legal Aid Society, of New York, appearing in an Edinburgh newspaper about twenty years ago." That chronology throws us back into the dubious days of the Deutscher Rechts-Schutz Verein. How amazingly far the flickering little candle threw his beams! Nor is distance the only striking element of Mr. Coldstream's tribute. For, almost from time out of mind, Scotland had operated a plan of legal poor relief considered far and away the best in the British Isles. But this plan was drawn on the inadequate combative theory — ample assistance for the poor man in his lawsuits, nothing by way of general pacific advice or conciliation. And the Scots, despite all their long experience, found that the American idea of a complete poor man's law office filled a vital need, hitherto unsatisfied.

Through most of the American legal aid bodies New York's contribution is easily traceable. The purpose clause of The Legal Aid Society's constitution has usually been adopted word for word. The Society's reports show in summary form how many applications from other communities for advice and assistance reached its office. The report covering 1898 says that requests for information were arriving, but does not name the inquirers. In 1900 Boston, Philadelphia, and Baltimore are mentioned; next year the new names are Edinburgh (Scotland), Alleghany (Pennsylvania), Cincinnati, and Southampton (England), as well as Newark (New Jersey) where a society "has existed for a number of years on the model of ours." In 1904 are added Portland (Oregon), San Francisco, Los Angeles, Sioux City, Minneapolis, Atlanta, Louisville, Richmond, Baltimore, Cleveland, Pittsburgh, and Buffalo. The next year adds Washington, D. C. In 1907 far-off Sydney, Australia, was heard from. The snowball, not satisfied with rolling downhill, was rolling overseas. Of course, these inquiries sometimes led to nothing. But by 1910 there were thirty active societies in the United States alone, of which eight had been formed during that single year. During 1913 forty American societies actually existed and eleven more were in process of formation. To round out the story, it may be added that by the date of The Legal Aid Society's fiftieth birthday the kindred organizations in the United States and Canada numbered just three or four short of an even hundred.

Now these bodies, spread from coast to coast, must not be thought of as mere points on the map or separated oases in a legal desert. Each serves a considerable area. More than that, they are reticulated. The United States has become a network of legal aid. Existence of the Society in New York and of the Bureau in Chicago does not mean merely that the poor New Yorker and the poor Chicagoan can get justice in their respective cities. It means also that so far as the Easterner needs the help of the courts in the western metropolis, he may have it; and vice versa. Add the other ninety-odd centres of relief for poor suitors, and the multiplied capabilities of modern legal aid become manifest. These capabilities, however, were bound to remain theoretical only until vitalized by an adequate coöperative system. To evolve such a system became the immediate task of Mr. v. Briesen and other leaders as soon as the numerical development of their agencies reached an advanced stage.

A considerable amount of coöperation grew naturally from the pursuit of common aims. This might be expressed by joint handling of cases which called for activity in two or several jurisdictions. It might be expressed by such action as the attendance of Mr. v. Briesen and the president of the Boston Legal Aid Society at the 1905 annual meeting of the Philadelphia Legal Aid Society. But when Mr. v. Briesen discovered, during his vacation in 1907, that the German legal aid organizations were holding annual conventions attended by delegates from dozens of different cities, he saw at once the possibility of unifying the American work, and bringing into it system and uniformity, through similar periodical conferences. No doubt the American visit of Ida Kirch, a legal aid representative from Frankfort-on-Main, spread and clarified the idea. At the invitation of the Pittsburgh Society, the first American convention of legal aid workers assembled in the Pennsylvania city on November 10, 1911.

Messrs. v. Briesen and McGee represented the New York Society. Both made important speeches. Twelve other societies sent delegates. Reginald Heber Smith, the leading American authority on legal poor relief, thus summarizes the convention and its consequences: "The discussion disclosed that there were many practical reasons for the formation of an alliance. A central office could lead in propaganda work in new fields and could provide a clearing house through which cases could be transferred for action from one city to another. Legal aid work was developing in Europe and the movement had assumed an international character, so that there was need of some official to whom foreign legal aid societies could send cases for reference to the proper local society. It was further pointed out that, by combining, the legal aid societies might take a part in national problems and in remedial legislation. Such beneficial results were so obvious — indeed they had earlier been presented by New York — that it is remarkable that the union was not effected sooner than it was. As a result of this first conference in Pittsburgh a committee was appointed to draw up a plan for a permanent central organization."

". . . At a second convention, held in New York in 1912 and attended by representatives from 12 societies and bureaus, the committee's report was accepted and there was formed the National Alliance of Legal Aid Societies.[1] The purpose of this alliance, as stated in section 2 of its constitution, was:

> Its object and purpose shall be to give publicity to the work of the legal aid societies of the United States, to bring about coöperation

[1] This convention was the occasion of Joseph H. Choate's inspiring address based upon the verse beginning:

"He comes with succor speedy to those who suffer wrong."

and increase efficiency in their work, and encourage the formation of new societies.

"Mr. Arthur v. Briesen, president of the New York Legal Aid Society, was unanimously elected president of the alliance and its valuable, though limited, accomplishments were almost entirely due to his personal enthusiasm and zeal. The organization had no real power vested in it and it was fatally handicapped by lack of funds. The constituent societies paid no dues, the central committee, which had power to fix dues not in excess of $25 per annum, never authorized the collection of any dues; indeed, the constitution itself made no provision for the office of treasurer. The expenses which necessarily were incurred were paid by the president out of his own pocket.

"The national alliance did little more than serve as the vehicle through which two subsequent conventions were called, the first at Chicago in 1914 and the second at Cincinnati in 1916. These gatherings of legal aid workers served to build up an *esprit de corps*, they facilitated the exchange of cases between offices in different parts of the country, and through papers read and discussion they afforded a much needed forum and clearing house for the presentation and exchange of ideas about the work, its technique, and its true function. The influence of a man like Mr. v. Briesen must have been very great in encouraging and inspiring the legal aid attorneys, many of whom were poorly paid and inadequately supported in their own communities. The whole weight of his forceful personality was thrown in the direction of making legal aid a more useful servant of the community, for his genius enabled him to see more clearly than anyone else the ultimate goal toward which all legal aid work was developing. His vision is revealed by a paragraph in an informal letter that he sent to the Cincinnati convention to regret and explain his absence on account of his advancing years:

'That legal aid societies, since the national alliance was born at Pittsburgh, have increased in number and efficiency is apparent. That credit is due to those who brought about these gratifying results need not be stated. Hundreds of thousands of poor and helpless men and women, to say nothing of poor and helpless children, have reason to bless these institutions. I believe that very few, however, will now think of their work as a blessing, for they take it to be one of the institutions of the country, one of the things that makes this country great and glorious. By this time they accept this gift as a natural right which, indeed, it is, marking an important step forward in civilization.'

"After 1916 the national alliance became quiescent. It had never been a controlling factor in guiding the development of the work, it had neither funds nor power; so far as providing the leadership which the legal aid movement needed, this loose type of association was impotent."

Even had it not suffered from inherent weakness, the National Alliance could hardly have gained any headway in the years immediately succeeding 1916. The war blocked its projected meeting at Philadelphia in 1918. Both war and legal aid were young men's work, and for the time being the former made imperative and well-nigh comprehensive demands. Legal aid offices struggled with diminishing personnel to keep their heads barely above water. Ties between them snapped. The whole movement might have been dashed back into primitive conditions of uncoördinated effort. But another and a saving power manifested itself with dramatic timeliness. Mr. Root's warm praise of Mr. v. Briesen at the Conference of Delegates from Bar Associations on September 3, 1917, has already been noted. That was a red letter day for legal poor relief, when after weary striving and waiting one of its dearest hopes began to come true. The resolution proposed to and adopted by the meeting read:

It is the sense of this conference that bar associations, State and local, should be urged to foster the formation and efficient administration of legal aid societies for legal relief work for the worthy poor, with the active and sympathetic cöoperation of such associations.

At last the Bar of the country as a whole espoused legal aid. The New York Society took a prominent part in the proceedings. Its vice-president and former Attorney-in-Chief, Carl L. Schurz, made the opening statement and answered questions put by Bar representatives from Virginia and Maryland. Moorfield Storey, Richard W. Hale, and Reginald Heber Smith of Boston spoke for legal aid. Gentlemen from Georgia, Indiana, and Missouri contributed to the discussion. Charles A. Boston of New York offered the resolution. The whole tone and scope of the session were encouraging to hard-driven legal aid workers the country over.

Further steps had to await clearing up of war activities, but they came without undue delay. On May 13, 1919, a special committee appointed by the Association of the Bar of the City of New York to investigate the need for organized legal aid, the Society's efforts to meet this need, and the possible contribution which the Association might make, issued a highly significant report. The committee concluded that the Society was doing as broad and efficient work as its limited resources permitted; that adequate maintenance of legal aid was imperatively necessary; that previous support by the community in general and the Bar in particular had been very far from adequate; and that the Bar, which greatly benefited from the Society's activity, should give full coöperation and aid. Further time was asked to weigh certain practical suggestions. An advance draft of Reginald Heber Smith's report to the Carnegie Corporation on the whole legal aid movement had been furnished the committee. Publication, later in 1919, of this report under the title "Justice and the Poor" gave great impetus to the coöperative activities already under way.

In 1920 the New York State Bar Association passed a strong resolution recommending assumption by the Bar of responsibility for legal aid. During the same year the American Bar Association gave a morning session to discussion of, and created a special committee on, the topic. This committee's report led in 1921 to an amendment of the Association's constitution, providing the standing committee on legal aid work which has ever since operated vigorously and effectively. On January 20, 1922, a special committee of the New York State Bar Association described the broadening activities of The Legal Aid Society, pointedly called attention to the fact that of the Society's contributions in 1921 only about one quarter had come from lawyers, and urged practical performance of the 1920 resolution. This report the Bar Association approved and circulated among all local bar associations in the State. Contemporaneously the New York County Lawyers' Association had examined legal aid work and was urging lawyers to support it. We left the Association of the Bar of the City of New York considering practical ways and means. Within a few years came very helpful action which will be referred to in a future chapter. And it should be remarked here that shortly before the Society's fiftieth anniversary this powerful local Bar Association also established a standing committee on legal aid. That action guaranteed firm backing to the Society, since under New York City conditions legal aid can be much better furnished by separate organizations devoted exclusively or largely to it than by bar associations or their members.

Meanwhile The Legal Aid Society, emerging from its war activities weary yet full of fight, had turned again to plans for national coöperation with its sister societies. The executive committee of the old National Alliance met at Mr. McGee's office early in 1921, aware that the Alliance was moribund, but hopeful of handing on the torch to some stronger organization. A special committee of men nationally prominent in the legal profession was formed to bridge the gap,[1] and to this committee the Carnegie Corporation made a grant for carrying forward the proposals of "Justice and the Poor." There followed a National Conference of Legal Aid Bureaus and Societies at Philadelphia on March 24 and 25, 1922.

About this meeting hung an atmosphere of mingled hope and sadness, determination for the future and sorrow for the lost past. Even that stout optimist and resolute fighter Mr. McGee expressed his belief that "the period prior to the War was a golden age in legal aid work." Of the four older ante-bellum leaders only Albert F. Bigelow of Boston and Mark Acheson, Jr., of Pittsburgh remained. Mr. v. Briesen and Rudolph Matz of Chicago were dead. The strong group of younger men had been scattered and shattered in the war. Reading Mr. McGee's address, one almost expects to find him echoing Franklin and expressing doubt as to whether he is gazing on a rising or a setting sun!

[1] Their names speak for themselves: Albert F. Bigelow, William Draper Lewis (then Dean of the University of Pennsylvania Law School), George Wharton Pepper (then Senator from Pennsylvania), Dean Roscoe Pound, Elihu Root, Moorfield Storey, Professor William R. Vance, and Dean John H. Wigmore.

But the sun was rising, although not without difficulty. To quote again from Mr. Smith: "In the course of the debates it was said 'the national alliance is like a federal government without power of taxation.' 'There is an imperative demand for such elementary things as standardized records of work, conventionalized classifications of the nature, source, and disposition of cases and for uniformity of financial accounting.' 'There is great need for a central clearing house to provide for the proper reference of cases.' 'There is no definite head, no leadership in the legal aid movement.' The upshot of this discussion was a unanimous resolution appointing a special committee to bring about a new national organization. The report of the Philadelphia convention summarized the feelings of the delegates of the local societies by saying 'they are determined to integrate themselves into a national federation. They are no longer contented with the loose and impotent association which the national alliance, by virtue of its ineffective structure, has necessarily been. They propose to recast the form of their national organization so that as a representative legislative and executive body, it may provide a genuine leadership in extending and improving the work.'

"The special committee, after a series of meetings, decided that it was impracticable to make over the national alliance into a satisfactory central body, because what was needed was a real delegation of power by the individual local societies and bureaus to a central organization. This could be accomplished only with the consent of the local societies. After the draft plan for the new national association had been formulated, printed, and distributed, a constitutional convention was held at Cleveland on June 7 and 8, 1923. Duly accredited delegates were present representing 23 legal aid societies and bureaus and including all the larger and stronger organizations in the United States. The special committee submitted its plan and stated:

> 'We have considered that, in effect, we had been given a mandate by those competent to speak, to draft a form of framework for a national structure.
>
> 'In this report we do not debate or argue the need for a strong national organization. The lack of it in the past has retarded legal aid development. That is a fact known to everyone. The need of it, if legal aid work is to develop in the future, is also a fact known to everyone.
>
> 'We have bent our energies to devising a plan of federation which, while still leaving the local societies and bureaus free and independent, would also vest in the central or national body enough power to be able to carry on its particular work.'

"After general debate and some perfecting amendments, the constitution was unanimously adopted and the constituent organizations became members by signing the constitution. . . . The Hon. William Howard Taft, Chief Justice of the United States, was elected honorary president of the new organization, the other officers chosen being a president, secretary, treasurer, and an executive committee of seven persons intentionally selected to represent different types of legal aid offices operating in various sections of the country. The following letter, written by Hon. Elihu Root to the special committee, was read at the convention:

> 'I have received your letter of May 1, telling me of the proposed June meeting of delegates from legal aid organizations and the plan to form a national association.
>
> 'Will you please count me as being heartily in favor of that plan? It becomes every year more evident that something is wanted to establish a contact between the system of administering justice, of which we are so proud, and the very people who need it most. The people who know how can easily get a very good brand of justice, but

the people who don't know how have little reason to suppose that there is any justice here. I am afraid they are getting a very bad idea of our institutions. It is becoming evident also that this subject must be dealt with, in the first instance at least, by private enterprise. Methods may be evolved which can ultimately be applied by government, but those methods cannot be evolved out of anybody's inner conscience, or out of any legislative committee. They must be worked out experimentally and that must be done by organized private enterprise. The present organization in the form of a national alliance of legal aid societies is plainly inadequate. We need a national body which can act itself in accordance with the authority derived from the local societies. I think that is plainly the next step toward promoting genuine legal aid, and especially toward preventing the plunder of the poor under the false pretense of legal aid.'

"The purposes of the new national association as formally set forth in section 2 of Article I of the constitution are:

'The objects and purposes of this association shall be to promote and develop legal aid work, to encourage the formation of new legal aid organizations wherever they may be needed, to provide a central body with defined duties and powers for the guidance of legal aid work, and to coöperate with the judiciary, the bar, and all organizations interested in the administration of justice.'

"The last clause of this section represents a thought that was entirely lacking in the purpose clause of the old national alliance, and which, as time goes on, is likely to be the most important function of the present national body. The legal aid organizations have a direct contribution to make to the better administration of justice in the United States. They realized that if they were to be heard they must speak with a single voice and therefore they ceded to their national body 'supervision over legal aid work in its national aspects, over the relationship between legal aid organizations and all other national organizations.'"

A local history cannot properly follow the National Association much beyond this point. In the State of New York, however, further articulation of legal aid bodies has been accomplished. The fact is worthy of record, even though it forces us slightly to overstep the bounds of the semi-centennial period 1876–1926. For the call leading to formation of the New York State Federation of Legal Aid Societies went out about the beginning of 1927 from the New York State Bar Association. Thus in the Empire State the two lines of affiliation forming the topic of this chapter have interacted. So thoroughly has the Bar adopted the legal aid principle that it projected and engineered a union of legal aid bodies.

Two other events, one falling within, the other without this history's strict time limits, may well be noted here, although they do not directly touch the New York Society. These events vividly illustrate the spread of the work which so largely found its beginnings in New York City. First, after due advance preparation under the auspices of the League of Nations there met at Geneva from July 30 to August 2, 1924, an international committee of legal aid experts. The Carnegie Corporation financed the meeting. France, England, Norway, Italy, Poland, Spain, the United States, and Japan sent representatives, and helpful communications came through the Austrian and German governments. This was not the first international legal aid meeting. In October, 1913, delegates from Denmark, Holland, Belgium, Austria, Switzerland, and the United States (needless to say, the American delegate was Mr. v. Briesen) attended the convention of German Legal Aid Societies at Nuremberg. But the League of Nations meeting holds out splendid promise of increasingly efficient world-wide justice for the poor.[1]

Second, actually during the drafting of this chapter, the first case ever handled before the United States Supreme Court by a legal aid lawyer has been argued and won for the poor client. On June 17, 1925, Nephi Giles, an employé of the Bountiful Brick Company of Utah, while crossing the tracks of the Bamberger Electric Railroad Company on his way to work, was struck by a train and killed. His widow claimed an award of workman's compensation, and won before the Industrial Commission and the courts of Utah. But there was a question whether Giles' fatal injury arose, in the words of the applicable statute, "out of and in the course of his employment." To settle this question the case was carried to Washington. The widow lacked means to follow up the appeal. Her plight came to the notice of the Boston Legal Aid Society, which deputed Samuel B. Horowitz to argue the case for the claimant, with the happy result above indicated. So at the end, if not at the beginning, of this chapter Boston may properly claim a pioneer honor. And once more we may quote the Boston *Transcript*: "By this action the Boston Legal Aid Society has importantly helped to maintain the cardinal element in the structure of effective democracy — namely, that all citizens are entitled to the equal protection of the laws, and to their day in court for the determination what that protection rightly should be, even if the battle has to be carried up to the highest court of the nation."

[1] As these words are written, the Legal Secretariat of the League of Nations is preparing for publication an official list of all legal aid organizations in the world and a compilation of laws in the various countries relating to legal aid for the poor.

XI

FINANCES AND THE VOLUNTARY DEFENDERS

THE tale of the Society's finances down to 1901 has been fully laid before the reader. But financial problems arising after that date are given only passing mention in the previous chapters. This seems an appropriate place for more detailed discussion.

During the first twenty-five years there were four principal sources of revenue. First, fees and commissions paid by clients. Sums thus realized have tended to become more dependable in later years. Recently they have been meeting from 12 per cent to 16 per cent of the total annual expenditures. Second, membership dues. Very inadequate when Mr. v. Briesen came into office, these dues gained in amount and reliability while he was at the helm. Third, donations of various sorts, including testamentary gifts. Mr. v. Briesen's distaste for perennial mendicancy will be recollected, as well as the impossibility of accurately estimating in advance the receipts from this source. Fourth, proceeds of charity concerts, theatrical performances, lectures, and the like. The first of the four items having been summarily appraised, it remains to follow the other three through the second quarter-century of the Society's existence. In doing this, it will be convenient to reverse the order of enumeration, considering charity performances first, donations next, and dues last.

The heyday of the Society's "benefits" ran from 1906 to 1913. Seven of the eight annual performances were operas, six being given at the Metropolitan Opera House by stellar casts, while one was brilliantly and successfully staged at the Manhattan Opera House; the remaining performance was a concert at Carnegie Hall with Marcella Sembrich, Ignace Paderewski, and Timothée Adamowski as the performing artists. The aggregate net receipts, in round figures, were $25,850. For each production the Society's treasurer, Louis Windmüller, published an elaborate souvenir programme with pictures and descriptions of the players, as well as explanations and illustrations of legal aid work. The 1906 programme contained tributes to the Society from Mark Twain and Andrew Carnegie. In the former, Mr. Clemens appears at his serious best. Mr. Carnegie's statement is brief enough to quote verbatim: "The champion of the wronged poor is one of the highest types of Civilized Heroes. What a career for a millionaire's son." How Messrs. v. Briesen and Windmüller must have yearned to catch an appropriately gilded youth and impress him into their service!

In 1909 the opera to be sung was Smetana's "Bartered Bride," and it occurred to the kindly Mr. Windmüller that the occasion might be an apt one to heal, for local New York purposes at least, the breach between Austrians and Czechs. He therefore arranged to have Mme. Gadski sing between acts the Austrian national hymn "Gott erhalte Franz den Kaiser." But the Czechs would none of it. They held a mass meeting on the upper East Side which voted to boycott the performance if the Teutonic anthem were introduced. Some even hinted darkly at riots and civil commotions. The Society's astute treasurer decided to take no chances. He reprinted his programme with an English parody of the contentious hymn, wherein "Franz der Kaiser" became

"Legal Aid Society," and the verses humorously explained why the change was made. Mme. Gadski also moved to the safe side. She sang "America." But the weather man must have been a Bohemian, and uninformed of the new plan. On the night of the performance it snowed and hailed, rained and thundered; so that despite all pains the Society realized only $900 from the opera.

In 1914 Ellen Terry gave "Scenes from Shakespeare" as a Legal Aid benefit at Aeolian Hall. The proceeds were small, and from that time on the special theatrical or musical performance has never reappeared as an item contributing to the Society's expenses.

Next among the revenues now being discussed come donations. Here one possibility, so far entirely ignored, takes a prominent place. Legal aid is work beneficial to the general public. In some American cities it is being carried on by public bureaus. Could the New York Society properly ask and wisely receive contributions from the municipal treasury? Mr. v. Briesen gave this question a negative answer in early 1899: "[Our Society] has refrained from seeking public financial support, largely because it would not expose itself to partisan control. We all know that his Honor the Mayor of New York has criticized the practice under which charitable institutions receive money from the city on the ground that those institutions appoint officers and servants without showing the proper consideration to the party in power in the matter of such appointments. Our Society cannot afford to select its officers on political grounds. Their selection must necessarily depend wholly on the question of fitness. Hence, public support which necessarily would be tainted by politics is excluded." At the twenty-fifth birthday dinner a variant of the same point was publicly and rather dramatically emphasized. Theodore Roosevelt, who knew the uglier side of New York politics, paused in his speech to ask Mr. v. Briesen point-blank whether he thought "there could be a change in the law which would make it the duty of the State to try to carry the burden that your Society has carried."

Mr. v. Briesen: "No."

Mr. Roosevelt: "I do not see how it could be done. The State can do a great deal, but it is an error to believe that the State can do anything like all."

Oddly enough, M. Bruwaert, French Consul-General, who spoke later on the programme, was unwilling to take his practical politics even from the Vice-President of the United States: "We have no such organization as this in France. We do not need it, because in France it is thought to be a national duty to give to the poor the right and the means to secure justice. . . . [Poor Frenchmen can] obtain justice . . . by going to the district attorney, with his assistance and the assistance of an *avoué* and *avocat*, appointed by the district attorney, they can secure justice without paying for it, and they can be assured of getting it within a short time." Perhaps the Consul-General's confidently superior tone was justified. They may arrange these things better on the Continent. But more than one of his auditors must have thought of our own bitter experience with unpaid assigned counsel, and have heard the echo of Shakespeare's mocking tag anent "the breath of an unfee'd lawyer."

Certainly, though, the idea of help from the City did not die easily. In 1907, when the Society had for some time been sailing close to the wind and seemed unlikely to make up much financial leeway, a bill was introduced in the Legislature for enabling New York City to allow the Society an annual sum not to exceed $25,000. Mr.

v. Briesen still stood out against municipal aid, and it is significant that the Educational Alliance refused to apply for a similar grant, saying "that to do so would establish an unwise and dangerous precedent [of applying] public money . . . to the use of a private association." Proceedings at Albany were not particularly edifying. Apparently all was plain sailing in the Assembly, but in the upper house Senator Grady caused the defeat of the measure when it first came up. A wrathful cry arose from the New York City press, the vote was reconsidered, and the bill passed 28 to 7, although Senator Cassidy declared that "charity which was supported by taxpayers under compulsion lost all the sweetness of charity" and Senator Grady objected because the bill "would compel persons who paid their own legal expenses to help pay those of others in whom they had no interest." *Laissez-faire* did not expire with the nineteenth century. It is needless to say that these political contortions only increased Mr. v. Briesen's disquietude, and he openly expressed relief when the City authorities declined an appropriation because of depressed financial conditions.

In fact, five years later the president said while speaking of the City's power to appropriate: "Every one of the directors of The Legal Aid Society has assured me, and I them, that we would immediately resign if public money were to be used for the purpose of furthering the cause of our Society." This was put very distinctly on the ground of particular political conditions, and not on the ground that governmentally sustained legal aid must be everywhere and at all times impracticable. Even in New York for Mr. v. Briesen himself there did come an occasion when his position altered. During February, 1915, while the depression of the early war had its deadening grip on the country's business, and while the Society was still bearing the prodigious burden of the "furniture club" case, he wrote: "It is a pity that when the Society is thus induced to give its aid in straightening out the claims of so many thousand people, the Board of Estimate and Apportionment should have refused a corresponding support. One should think that the great city of New York would be unwilling to accept charitable work at our hands without making at least an effort to help cover our expense; especially in a year in which it was most difficult to raise money from private contributors." But no help came from the City — none ever has come in direct financial form, although a later passage in this chapter will show a helpful public contribution to the recently developed criminal court work. Perhaps a sound conclusion on the whole matter is that when the Society falls into such desperate need as to take the risk of seeking public money, the municipal treasury will be too cramped to respond. The same economic forces affect both.

Donations from non-political sources have increased slowly with the passage of time, and now aggregate from $30,000 to $35,000 per year. Recent annual reports show a steadily lengthening list of legacies and other large capital gifts, both restricted and unrestricted. The disturbing feature, which will be examined again at a later page, is that in every year of the last nine or ten a current deficit of between $1,000 and $12,500 has compelled the financial officers to dip into unrestricted capital. One very definite attempt to offset this condition gives opportunity to trace the succession to the presidency:

Mr. Hughes resigned in 1921 to become Secretary of State in the Harding cabinet. On February 24, 1921,

Egerton L. Winthrop, Jr., was elected the fourth president of the Society. Mr. Winthrop was an eminent lawyer, with high and clear ideals of public service. He had extraordinary ability to bring about worthy results in quiet, unruffled fashion. This ability had been displayed throughout his presidency of the previously unruly New York City Board of Education from 1905 to 1913. It was again displayed during his leadership of The Legal Aid Society, to which he gave unstinted thought and attention. Mr. Winthrop died on January 12, 1926. As a significant tribute his friends almost at once raised a memorial fund for the special purpose of meeting the Society's outstanding deficit and thus enabling Allen Wardwell, who took office as the fifth president just before the fiftieth anniversary, to enter upon his work with temporary freedom from acute financial problems. So liberal were the subscriptions that a portion of the fund is still on hand for future needs.

Another very large gift, not made directly to the Society but having emphatic bearing upon its future, deserves special mention. In 1925 Edward S. Harkness gave the Association of the Bar of the City of New York, as a memorial to his father-in-law Thomas Edgar Stillman, a fund of $150,000, the income "to be applied to rendering, furthering and procuring legal aid to deserving persons who cannot afford to pay for the services of an attorney." The letter of gift permits the Association to furnish such assistance through an independent organization which in the judgment of its Executive Committee "is satisfactorily and efficiently rendering the kind of service for which this fund is hereby created." Ever since the establishment of this memorial trust the Executive Committee has appointed its income to The Legal Aid Society.

Finally, the financial survey comes to membership dues. Here a steady evolution and adaptation of the constitution can be traced. Beginning with the simple twenty-dollar annual membership fee, we have seen successfully added the cheaper associate membership and also the more highly priced life membership and "patron's" participation. When Mr. Wardwell became treasurer, — an office he held from the time of Mr. Windmüller's death in October, 1913, until 1925, — a very carefully considered and effective elaboration of the membership clause began. In the 1927 redraft of the constitution which George S. Hornblower completed shortly before his death, this single clause covers well over a page and a half of type. It seems fair to say that there is now a form of membership appealing to the inclination and the pocket book of every man or woman who approves justice and fair dealing. Particularly Mr. Wardwell and his associates have striven to enroll members of the Bar as regular supporters of an enterprise in which they are primarily concerned, and to obtain from them contributions fairly proportionate to their pecuniary abilities. This attempt to take advantage of the Bar's increasing interest in legal aid work has had marked success. No longer can it be said, as it could in 1921, that the Society is running three quarters on laymen's money and only one quarter on lawyers' money. Nowadays lawyers, both as members and as donors, contribute the lion's share.

The facts just covered stand out prominently in the Society's history from 1919 to 1926. Without too violent a break of continuity we may trace the other impressive features of that period. Once the organization returned to standard working trim after the war, a quiet campaign of internal smoothing and polishing began.

The routine of the offices was carefully considered. Improvements in method were applied. Rules for the conduct of attorneys received thoughtful supervision. As already mentioned, Mr. Hornblower did a thorough job on the constitution and by-laws. One insertion which he made in the purpose clause of the constitution gives a clue to the great external development of the time. If the reader will consult this clause as reprinted in its latest form on a preliminary page of the book, he will see that the Society's purposes now include rendition of "*gratuitous legal aid to any poor person accused of crime.*" From those new words hangs the tale of a very important social experiment.

To pick up the loose threads we must return to the beginning of legal aid history. The Society's founders have left an absolutely unmistakable record of their intention to assist indigent criminal defendants. There is explicit talk about aiding "those impecunious Germans who had fallen into the hands of the police through ignorance of the laws here, through recklessness or misguidance," and also "poor innocent Germans . . . kept for weeks and months in prison." Then much later came a time when for absolute lack of money and personnel the Society had to refuse most criminal business, despite a dark suspicion that the interests of the poor were not adequately safeguarded before police magistrates and in other criminal tribunals. Now a suspicion of this kind preyed bitterly on Mr. v. Briesen's mind. Others also were worried. In 1897 Mr. Goeller wrote about the assignment by the Court of General Sessions of counsel — who were entitled to no fee, except in murder cases — for indigent prisoners: "As a rule these [assigned] attorneys try to get from the prisoner or his friends a fee. If unsuccessful in this attempt they pay little attention to the case, make little, if any, preparation, often not appearing in Court at the trial. If this Society had counsel who could look after these assigned cases, justice would be done, prisoners properly defended, and there would be no necessity for such an officer as Public Defender, a bill for the establishment of which office has been introduced in the Legislature." To attain this apparently simple result took nearly twenty-five years.

The disquietude of the president and his successive Attorneys-in-Chief was no purely theoretical matter. Occasional excursions by the Society into the criminal field disclosed errors and abuses dolefully suggesting further undiscovered wrongs. A specific case or two will give point to this assertion. One day a middle-aged German woman entered the East Side office desperately distressed, and pleaded with the attorneys to save a poor innocent boy then languishing in the Tombs. A day or so before she had separated two boys who were at fisticuffs in front of her house. They ran away, but one of them, resenting petticoat interference, paused long enough to cast an epithet at the peacemaker. Soon after, the woman happened to see this same youngster standing on a street corner. Slipping up unseen, she seized him by the collar, shook him, and on sudden impulse cried to a policeman: "Here, take him — he insulted me!" To her surprise the officer did so, and led the boy off to the police station, followed by the interested crowd which always gathers on such occasions.

Now full of contrition, the German woman also followed, intending to plead for the prisoner's discharge. But at the station a wildly excited Austrian woman pressed forward, swearing over and over again that the boy had stolen five dollars from her. The truth seemed to be that two youths actually had picked the Austrian's pocket, and made a clean getaway. Their victim, seeing a boy in the law's clutches, jumped to the conclusion that this must be one of her Artful Dodgers. In the noisy, crowded police court next morning the youngster's bail was set at $1,000 on the larceny charge, and for lack of it he went to prison. The whole proceeding was swift and perfunctory; the German woman tried to tell her story, but a big policeman pushed her away. She did not even catch the boy's name.

From the East Side Branch an attorney went to the jail, obtained a permit to enter, and moved from cell to cell, questioning the prisoners. He came at length upon a tall, flaxen-haired lad whose story tallied exactly with that of the German woman. The young fellow was a Connecticut farmer boy, but lately come to the city and living with his brother, at an address which had been scared out of his mind. He did remember the name of his brother's employer. The Society hunted up the brother, and through him got in touch with the prisoner's father. Down to New York came the old man, an immigrant speaking scarcely any English. Day after day he sat in the office, following the lawyers with pleading eyes and hoping for good news of his son's case. Meanwhile the Society carefully worked up its evidence for the grand jury, the District Attorney doing likewise. The case was heard after the boy had been two weeks in the Tombs, and the grand jury discharged him. The boy, crying for joy at his release, covered the attorney's hands with kisses. Then he and his father went back to the Connecticut farm. A happy ending, one is tempted to say. But how much better if proper legal representation had enabled the defendant to clear himself at the beginning in the police court. All subsequent expense, humiliation, and agony of mind might have been saved.

Erratic applications of criminal law were by no means confined to the police courts. Only a few months after the remarkable case just described, the East Side Branch learned that a boy of seventeen had been arrested and was being held for the Federal grand jury on the charge of mailing an indecent letter. It was June, bail had been set at the imposing figure of $1,000, and the grand jury would not meet until October. A shyster lawyer promised to get the young man out for $20, took the money from the parents, and then said he "could n't do it so cheap." At least he managed to get bail reduced to $500, but even that was more than could be squeezed out of the family. The Society found the charge to be an outright fabrication. The boy had incurred the enmity of an uncle by testifying against him in a family legal squabble. This uncle procured the writing of the indecent letter, and caused it to be mailed to a woman of bad repute and worse veracity. She carried the missive to Anthony Comstock, swearing before him and later before the United States Commissioner that the handwriting was the boy's. By hook and by crook the prisoner's family scraped together $250, the Society succeeded in having this cash bail accepted, and the young fellow was set free for the summer. When the grand jury convened, it refused to indict. In another case arising subsequently, the Legal Aid lawyers found that there was grave doubt as to the sanity of a certain convicted forger at the time of his alleged offence. Although the man had already served three years of his sentence, they obtained a new trial for him in a distinctly spectacular proceeding. Later still — in fact after some effort had been made to establish a criminal branch — a poor Russian laborer named Barbshish was held on the serious charge of assaulting a sixteen-year-old typewriter girl. Since both the victim and her employer positively and persistently identified the Russian as the assailant, his case looked black. But the Society traced the whereabouts of Barbshish before, at, and after the time of the crime, piecing together a perfect alibi through the testimony of a street-car conductor, a factory superintendent with his time book, and two of the defendant's fellow workmen. The jury acquitted.

From 1896 on Mr. v. Briesen frequently urged the assignment of legal aid men for duty in the Police Magistrates' Courts both to prevent miscarriage of justice by reason of the summary methods necessarily employed there, and to forestall outrageous swindles which shysters were known to perpetrate on frightened, ignorant defendants. After the establishment of the East Side Branch indications were observed that legal swindlers regularly fattened their pocketbooks in the police courts of that locality. Also it appeared that frequent injustice resulted from the fining or imprisonment of immigrants who knew no English and could not even apprehend the charges against them. Ultimately Mr. McCook put his influence behind the idea of raising special funds to place an assistant attorney definitely on police court work, particularly at the Essex Market court. The Society's directors voted favorably, and the plan was announced by the newspapers, April 20, 1906. Frank E. Bollman attended the court long enough as a volunteer observer to convince himself that regular assignment of lawyers to this work would be most desirable. Some of the magistrates agreed with him, although others were sceptical. This, however, was the very year of the opening struggle to establish a Brooklyn branch. The task of financing two simultaneous extensions proved too great.

In 1909 legal aid leaders returned to the charge, spurred forward by the Rev. John A. Wade, formerly chaplain of the Tombs and at the moment chaplain of the New York Police Department. During the Society's annual meeting this clergyman bluntly asserted that half the lawyers then practising at the Criminal Courts Building could be sent to jail themselves without substantial injustice. He went on: "I want to tell you that I am so dead in earnest about this matter that if you will not take it up I won't rest until I have carried it to some organization that will. . . . This is not a thing for the church to take up. There is a stigma on the profession of lawyers as a result of the state of things which obtains in our criminal courts which it is for the profession to remove."

Needless to say, these charges aroused much attention. Nor were alleged specifications lacking. Here are a few of the stories told. One of the most notorious criminal practitioners — criminal in more senses than one: he served a term for subornation of perjury — had affixed to his office wall a dummy telephone instrument through which he conducted sham discourse with judges, to the wonderment and awe of his clients and their friends. Anybody in the shadow of a criminal charge would pay the price demanded by a lawyer who arranged acquittals over the wire! Another shyster who had received $150 for defending a young man on a felony charge went to his client's mother after the jury brought in a verdict of conviction and assured the anguished woman that if she would give him $1,000 he could win her son's freedom. All the money the mother had in the world was $544. This the lawyer took, without even appearing in court when sentence was imposed. The defendant went to Sing Sing. One lawyer deliberately postponed the trial of an innocent client, meanwhile bullying the latter into drumming up trade for him at the prison. It was finally noticed that on the average about half the prisoners in the forty cells of the client's tier retained his lawyer. This significant observation precipitated the trial and after nearly a year of the Tombs the client was acquitted. From professional criminals the shysters reaped perennial harvests by keeping the crooks always in their debt and therefore on a vicious circle of recurrent crime to pay lawyer's bills. Nothing which could be called an asset eluded the grasp of these attorneys and their runners. Jewelry of course was quickly snapped up. One lawyer was said to have taken a set of false teeth for a retainer; another, three subway tickets — but surely this latter must have caught a wigging for debasing the financial standing of the criminal Bar!

The Wade plan of campaign against the iniquitous system involved a considerable amount of clerical service for poor criminal defendants from employés of the Society. But the actual conduct of trials and indeed practically all true legal services were to be voluntarily contributed by public spirited practitioners. Several prominent lawyers expressed their willingness to help. A well-chosen committee attacked the details and funds were publicly solicited. Before the end of May, 1909, the newspapers announced that offices either had been or were to be opened on Lafayette Street, near the Tombs, and that the "first criminal case assigned to the Legal Aid Society by Judge Foster was that of an ignorant Russian, accused of assault." This sounds like the Barbshish matter, but the dates do not coincide.

Bearing in mind that 1909 was a year of financial ebb-tide wherein Mr. v. Briesen strove unsuccessfully to re-open the discontinued Brooklyn Branch, the reader will not be surprised to learn that the Criminal Branch failed to start during this twelvemonth. The Society sought at least $10,000 for the expenses of the new venture and obtained only about $1,000 in pledges. But on May 11, 1910, a modest tentative start was made. Edwin T. Gibson, whom Mr. v. Briesen described as "a most competent young attorney," went on duty for the Society at the Essex Market Police Court. The papers warmly cheered his advent. They willingly assumed his legal ability. What struck them was the fact that he had been fullback of the Cornell football team. Indeed, a bit of brawn hardly seemed out of place in that rough district. The "Essex Market Bar Association" or "Essex Immortals," as the New York *Sun* slyly dubbed them, appear to have greeted Mr. Gibson wryly enough. They regarded his presence as a hint that the good old days were passing. With approval and help from the magistrates, the new lawyer for criminal defendants went effectively to work. He continued to be good copy, soon figuring humorously in an assault case. His client, a woman, asserted that the complainant had beaten *her*, and carried a bottle of arnica to lend the defence verisimilitude. On the stand she dramatically reënacted the battle, words and blows complete. One of the latter thwacked against Mr. Gibson's jaw and broke the bottle, to the great delight of observers.

Before the end of the year, the District Attorney assigned to each police court, including that at Essex Market, a deputy to discharge substantially the same functions as those undertaken by the Legal Aid's man. So Mr. Gibson was withdrawn to the main office, from which he could attend any criminal court in the city where his services were desired. He handled hundreds of cases with good success. But this entering wedge ought to have been forced further. No single lawyer could possibly meet the demands of the situation. Even in 1910, when the District Attorney so substantially bettered police court conditions, several judges of the Court of General Sessions declared, according to Mr. v. Briesen, "that conditions are *worse now than ever before* and that something should be done to 'clean out these vultures.'" Lack of money prevented the Society from extending its service. So, naturally enough, the wedge gradually slipped out and the crack closed. We first hear of Mr. Gibson as moved from the main office to the cramped quarters of the Seamen's Branch. Then in 1913 all definiteness of location for criminal work disappears. The report says merely that 25 cases were referred to and handled by the Society. The year 1914 by coincidence shows the identical figure, and Mr. McGee writes a belated epitaph for the Wade plan: "The Society was compelled some years ago to give up the idea of having a separate and distinct Criminal Branch." Thus matters slumped back substantially into the state existing from 1900 or thereabouts to 1910.

Yet hope had not all evaporated even after these successive failures. Indeed, a more powerful movement was already shaping itself, and was destined actually to succeed. In 1912, another bill to establish the office of Public Defender had been introduced at Albany. It failed of passage, but a discussion opened which refused to die out. On October 25, 1914, the Sunday *World* printed a leading article by Judge Edward Swann, arguing against the public-defender notion and urging that The Legal Aid Society, if properly subsidized, could better attain the desired end at a fraction of the cost. A letter from Walton J. Wood, Public Defender of Los Angeles County, California, published by the *Globe* on December 4, 1914, took issue with Judge Swann at practically every point except the possibility of using The Legal Aid Society. Even as to this suggestion Mr. Wood insisted that "the superintendent of the Legal Aid Society" should for these purposes "be an officer of the state with duties imposed upon him by law. . . ." Committees of the New York County Lawyers' Association in 1914 and 1915 investigated the desirability of a public defender and reported adversely, though not without dissent. The Association of the Bar of the City of New York also set a committee on the matter. The consequent report was, in substance, that so far as civil matters were concerned The Legal Aid Society could discharge the public defender function; that the City should not assume this work unless prepared for a general policy of free administration of justice; and that as to criminal matters there was only assertion, and neither proof nor good reason to believe, that wrongs requiring remedy existed.

This did not quiet the discussion, however. The report last described called forth denials, and the controversy continued through 1915 and 1916. In 1917 words became deeds. Under the leadership of James Bronson Reynolds a group of men and women definitely convinced that something was wrong in the administration of criminal law, but not advocates of the public defender as a panacea, announced themselves as the Voluntary Defenders Committee. Their plan related particularly to the New York County Court of General Sessions, which tried felony cases — that is, those involving the more serious offenses. The judges of this court had power to assign counsel to indigent defendants; but except in first degree murder cases such assigned counsel were entitled to no recompense from the public treasury, and in all cases were supposed to receive nothing from private sources.[1] It was the old losing game of trying to make bricks without straw. Speaking in behalf of the Committee, William Dean Embree later said that a small group of about a dozen lawyers had "made a profession of handling assigned cases. . . . Usually . . . only some member of this volunteer band . . . was available [in the court room] to a perplexed judge when he assigned counsel. . . . As a rule [the assigned lawyer] has no facilities to do the work. He has no assistants or investigators, sometimes not even an office. He haunts the criminal courts by day, and at night plods around in the weary task of seeking witnesses. He has no easy time picking up enough pay cases to eke out a living. The temptation to try to get some money for his supposedly gratuitous services out of the defendant or his family or friends is enormous." There was your typical assigned counsel: often shifty and shady by nature; even when inclined to square dealing, forced into crookedness by the conditions of his life; and, honest or dishonest, practically never able to give his clients first-class service.

But the remedy was far from being clear or easy. The average reputable lawyer might be willing to lend time and skill for the betterment of criminal procedure. What, though, did he know of its particular quirks and difficulties? Very likely he did not normally enter a criminal court once in five years. And what facilities in the way of "underworld" acquaintance did he or his office force have which would enable them to grub around the mucky roots of criminal charges and find the obscure

[1] There seems to be some doubt whether it is technically unethical for an assigned lawyer to receive private pay. But the statement in the text is probably fair.

actual facts? The answers to these questions are manifest. The Voluntary Defenders Committee wisely began by establishing an office with a staff chosen for aptitude bearing upon the particular task at hand. Mr. Embree, who has just been quoted, resigned the post of Assistant District Attorney to become the Committee's first chief counsel. He had worked as a prosecutor for no fewer than four District Attorneys, Messrs. Jerome, Whitman, Perkins, and Swann. His associate counsel, Timothy N. Pfeiffer, had been Deputy Assistant under District Attorneys Whitman and Perkins. To aid these capable and thoroughly experienced lawyers, the Committee provided not merely ordinary office help but a small corps of trained investigators, who were capable linguists and "knew their way about town." This group could give the accused poor man legal and fact-finding service of a type almost unavailable previously to anybody. They could carry ably from beginning to end any conventional criminal case.

So far, matters were on a strictly businesslike basis. Lawyers and investigators received moderate salaries for full-time work. It may be added that the Committee launched its undertaking with reasonably adequate financial backing from people of means, including John D. Rockefeller, Jr.; also that the City gave, rent-free, the entire second floor of its building at 57 Centre Street, near the Criminal Courts Building and the Tombs. Before many years passed, the City donated an even better office in the Criminal Courts Building itself. But the word "Voluntary" in the Committee's title had real significance. Practically every lawyer in private practice who had served with distinction for the District Attorney's office during the last ten or fifteen years was persuaded to put his name on a list of counsel willing to volunteer for more complex and difficult cases than Messrs. Embree and Pfeiffer could find time to defend unaided. Such voluntary "senior counsel" were promised that the regular office staff would do every stroke of the tedious pick-and-shovel work prior to trial, an assurance impossible under the earlier Wade plan.

The new organization swung into action on April 1, 1917. Three months later Mr. Embree published a most encouraging report. Judges had coöperated cordially, assigning some two hundred cases to the Committee's lawyers. Results were satisfactory. This did not mean that the Voluntary Defenders got most of their clients off. They were out for the truth, not for a record of acquittals at any price. Three fourths of the clients not merely were guilty but pleaded guilty without trial, although often the admissions of guilt came only after thorough investigation of the defendants' stories and the evidence against them. Far from deserting these men, the Defenders carefully laid before the sentencing judge all facts and considerations which might properly influence his determination of the penalty. Not a single client coupled his confession with insistence upon a trial; those who tended at first to take this attitude ultimately agreed to deal honestly and frankly with the court. Twelve prisoners, steadfastly asserting innocence, went to trial. Two of their cases were tried by volunteer "senior counsel," ten by Messrs. Embree and Pfeiffer. All these defendants were willing to waive their privilege against self-incrimination and take the stand. There resulted eight acquittals and four convictions, the decisions practically without exception seeming just to the Committee's counsel. This leaves to be accounted for thirty or forty cases of the two hundred. In a number of these, proper investigation showed innocence and led the District Attorney to drop the prosecutions. In several others, observation by alienists established insanity and the defendants became patients instead of convicts.

The last statement is significant. Invariably the defendants' real character and condition received attention hitherto absolutely unknown in criminal court routine. Strong emphasis was laid on the social side of the work. Once again to quote Mr. Embree's first report: "Every case is thoroughly investigated . . . for facts of family and other environment which may lead up to the defendant's anti-social conduct and consequent arrest. The result of this investigation is of great assistance to the Court in imposing sentence, and when the defendant is discharged or paroled, it is indispensable to the work of the Committee in obtaining proper employment and otherwise assisting the client to regain his place in society." This comprehensive service has broadened and gained efficiency with every year. Contacts with the numerous beneficent organizations of New York and other localities have multiplied. A single specific instance from a recent report will tell the story more convincingly than any abstract statement:

"Several months ago a woman, who was physically ill and whose husband was in jail, asked counsel to represent him. She was obsessed with the idea that he would be sent to prison for ten years as a second offender under the Baumes laws and, although counsel spent much time in trying to convince her that he would receive little or no punishment, she was almost hysterical and would not be convinced. Finally counsel told her that when the case should be disposed of she would probably go out of the office happy and smiling. She frequently came into the office in connection with the case and also relative to obtaining aid in securing employment for herself. From time to time small sums of money were given her to help in time of acute need. About the time she was becoming encouraged about the outcome of her husband's case, her baby became desperately ill and was taken to Bellevue Hospital. It became necessary for counsel to obtain a court order to allow her husband to go to Bellevue Hospital to give blood transfusions to the child. Finally it died and Miss Arculeo [the Social Service member of the staff] arranged with the Catholic Charities to give it a burial.

"After the mother had recovered from the strain of the child's death and had recuperated from her illness, she was overjoyed at being informed that counsel had succeeded, upon the sentencing judge's recommendation, in having her husband's sentence in the Penitentiary so shortened as to result in his being released within a few weeks. Miss Arculeo succeeded in arranging with the Probation Officers in New Jersey (where he had been convicted of a petty crime) that they would not, at the end of the Penitentiary sentence, imprison him for a violation of probation. About three weeks after the defendant's release, his wife telephoned counsel:

> 'Both my husband and I are working and he is making a good salary. We'll soon be millionaries. We already have a small apartment and I have never been so happy in all my life.'"

Out of such single instances, too, a large bulk of reliable organized information is being steadily built up. From this growing aggregate it becomes increasingly practicable to draw sound general conclusions respecting social tendencies, the actual effects of criminal legislation, and the consequences of various practices in dealing with criminals and those accused of crime. For instance, the Committee itself has been able to point out positively defects in the substance and administration of the bail laws causing needlessly prolonged imprisonment of accused men pending trial. The public expense thus incurred, while serious enough, is overshadowed by the unjustifiable suffering inflicted. In 1924 the Committee also called attention to the importance of empowering police magistrates to grant new trials where newly discovered evidence indicates that convictions before them have been miscarriages of justice. Recently Louis Fabricant, while chief counsel for the Committee, published in *The Legal Aid Review* an article recommending other, and perhaps more fundamental, legal changes.

The foregoing brief account sufficiently indicates methods of operation and results accomplished. One should add, perhaps, that the voluntary senior counsel were less and less used until they dropped out of the scheme entirely. But several large offices now lend their younger men occasionally to assist the Defenders. As time went on, it became clear that the services rendered by the Voluntary Defenders Committee on the criminal side of the courts so aptly rounded out those rendered on the civil side by The Legal Aid Society that an amalgamation of the two was highly appropriate. On April 16, 1920, the Committee proposed to join forces with the older organization and continue its own work as the Voluntary Defenders Committee of The Legal Aid Society. The proposal was accepted. This union has been distinctly beneficial in many ways. For example, persons consulting the Committee have always used its office as a source for miscellaneous legal information. By 1921 the Defenders found these inquiries running annually into the hundreds. Many poor people — and for that matter many opulent ones — cannot draw the distinction between civil and criminal remedies. So the Defenders were asked about property rights, marital rights, and domestic rights; about methods of getting back security given for bail; about petitions for restoration to citizenship; and about diverse other problems covering pretty much the whole field of general practice. District Attorney Joab H. Banton discovered that about one complaint in three made to his office was of civil rather than criminal character. He therefore, in 1923, suggested assignment to the Voluntary Defenders staff of a legal aid lawyer to handle civil problems exclusively. This precise scheme was not put into effect, but because of their articulation with the Society the Defenders could and did make a working arrangement with the prosecutor under which he referred all purely civil complaints to them. They personally furnished legal advice to the complainants, and passed along to the Society's civil branches such matters as called for further action. To take the figures of a recent year, in 1926 we find Mr. Banton thus referring 68 cases, the Committee's staff disposing of 44, and the remaining 24 moving on to the appropriate offices of the Society.

The arrangement just described suggests very harmonious relations between the Committee and the prosecutor. Such relations indeed exist. Mr. Banton has publicly appealed for funds to keep the Defenders going. Complete confidence prevails between the two. Frank discussions of evidence pro and con on pending cases are not uncommon, leading sometimes to prompt pleas of guilty, sometimes to the dropping of prosecutions. Discharges on the recommendation of the District Attorney after conference have been running between 45 and 90 per year. Even where such an interchange does not dispose of the controversy, it draws the issues more tightly, making trial simpler, swifter, and cheaper. One striking instance will illuminate these generalizations. In 1925 a man was tried for a crime involving swindling. He had been frequently arrested for similar swindles and had admitted his guilt. In the present case he sturdily maintained innocence. But the complainant positively identified the defendant as the offender. Now the defendant had a letter tending to establish his presence at Detroit, Michigan, on the day when the swindle was perpetrated in New York City. This was hearsay and inadmissible as evidence, but it roused the judge's curiosity. The prisoner had been in jail over sixty days awaiting trial, and this confinement would count on any sentence given him. Yet he refused to accept the court's offer of a sixty-day sentence if he would plead guilty, although that meant immediate release. Deciding that there must be some virtue in the alibi, the judge declared a mistrial, discharged the jury, and turned the case over to the Voluntary Defenders for investigation.

They found by routine search that their client not only had a substantial criminal record, but also was a drug addict. On going beyond this bad start the defence strengthened. The Detroit Legal Aid Bureau obtained and sent to the Defenders affidavits from local witnesses which bore out the prisoner's claims. Although the District-Attorney might at the new trial have objected successfully to the use of these documents as evidence, he liberally waived technicalities and let them be put in. But the jury convicted. Still the Defenders were not satisfied. At their request, the sentencing of the defendant was postponed until photostatic copies of a Detroit hotel register purporting to bear his signature could be obtained. Meanwhile, entirely without the knowledge of the prisoner or his counsel, the court and District-Attorney started an investigation of their own. They sent to Detroit a representative who reported back in full confirmation of the alibi. When the defendant came up (as he supposed) for sentence, the judge surprised him by setting aside the conviction and ordering his release. This result could never have been reached unless all parties had worked earnestly for a really just disposition of the case.

From other sources besides the prosecutor's office has come praise in various forms. One client, although convicted, said: "I thank you, counsellor. You could n't have given me a better defense if I paid you $1,000." Many criminal defendants apply on their own initiative to be represented by the Defenders. Men serving sentences seek help from this office in obtaining commutations or pardons. Parenthetically, it may be remarked that much of this work has to be turned away because it is very time consuming and the small office staff is hard pushed in carrying out the Defenders' primary function. Also parenthetically, one remarkable application for this sort of assistance justifies quotation: "From every standpoint of reason or from every premise of syllogism you are in my estimation amply justified in writing the Governor again. *I bet a man with money or political pull or feministic magnatization would get a commutation.*"

The judges warmly approve the Committee's effort. In 1921 six of them answered in writing requests for their opinions as to the merits of the work. These letters vary widely in phraseology, but substantially unite in saying that the Defenders have proved themselves a great aid to the proper administration of criminal justice. During 1925 the Committee received this letter:

"I served as a juror in General Sessions this last December, and was much impressed by the care and sincerity of the work done in court by the Voluntary Defenders. There was nothing perfunctory or mechanical about it, and it made one feel that all that the law touched was not necessarily legalistic. I am enclosing part of my juror money as a slight testimony of appreciation for public work done public spiritedly."

The Baumes Laws, compelling imposition of very severe penalties upon repeaters or habitual criminals, have much increased the Defenders' labors and responsibilities. More accused men feel practically forced to fight their cases, and every new felony case tried for a previous offender is fraught with very serious possibilities. Hence has arisen a necessity for still more intensive preparation, which makes less immediate the possibility of extending Voluntary Defender service to other courts than that of New York County. Even in this limited field the Committee finds the man power of its small staff inadequate. The report for 1924 advocated an expansion to four lawyers, six investigators, and two clerical assistants — approximately a doubling of personnel and expense. No increase has yet been made in the number of workers, and from the report for 1927 we draw an intimation that at least such a degree of expansion is still needed. For this report shows that during 1927 the Defenders represented 558 defendants, and its foreword states: "In the Court of General Sessions of the County of New York . . . approximately 1500 defendants each year are without means to retain counsel."

So at the end of a chapter beginning with financial problems, our discussion reverts to the original topic. In 1927 it cost the Voluntary Defenders Committee roughly $18,000 to handle 558 cases. This makes the cost per criminal case rather over $32. Simultaneously the Society's other offices dealt with 30,853 civil matters at an aggregate expense of about $79,300. Hence the cost per civil case is under $2.60 — more, to be sure, than the good old "dollar-per-case" standard of the nineteenth century, but fairly comparable with that figure by reason of money's decreased buying power. Any expansion, then, of the criminal work means a heavy drain on the Society's resources. Indeed, a cold-blooded statistician might assert that this work even at its present figure is an extravagant luxury and should be dropped.

That, however, is an entirely unsound view. Not alone are the Voluntary Defenders helping out at one of the weakest spots in all the legal firing line. Inside their restricted ambit they are giving a demonstration of legal aid performed under most trying conditions and yet with a closer approximation to perfect handling of each individual client's problem than the Society's other divisions, cramped as they are for funds and men, have yet been able to attain. The Defenders can dig deeper into the facts, and for that reason are better able to see the social implications of their clients' predicaments. At the moment their organization is the flower and crown of New York legal aid achievement. Its methods point the way toward an ultimate comprehensive appreciation of the legal problem of the poor, not as an isolated phenomenon but as one aspect of the whole integrated obstacle which human poverty offers for organized society to overcome. To abandon the Defenders' work, to curtail it, indeed not to expand it and simultaneously to increase the capability of the other offices to perform service of an equally high quality, would be a desertion of the legal aid ideal.

XII

1926 AND AFTER

ON April 6, 1926, The Legal Aid Society's first half-century of service was duly celebrated by a dinner at the Hotel Roosevelt. The word "duly" is advisedly used. For this celebration vividly indicated the scope and strength to which the legal aid movement had attained. Other kindred New York City bodies, such as the Educational Alliance, joined in the ceremonies. The fourth annual convention of the National Association of Legal Aid Organizations, held at New York on April 7 and 8, 1926, synchronized with the semi-centennial celebration. Delegates to the convention, attending the dinner as the Society's guests, represented legal aid throughout the nation. More than that, the auspices under which the dinner was held had special significance. Arrangements were in the hands of the Association of the Bar of the City of New York, the New York County Lawyers' Association, the Brooklyn Bar Association, the Bronx County Bar Association, the Chamber of Commerce of the State of New York, and the Merchants' Association of the City of New York. Thus hard-headed business openly declared itself as standing behind legal aid. The Bar, too, renewed its declaration of adherence in no uncertain terms. William D. Guthrie, President of the Association of the Bar, presided and prefaced the remarks of the other speakers by a striking address. Concerning the Bar's attitude he said: "I deem it my duty . . . to emphasize its desire to dedicate itself to this cause and to serve the poor to the fullest measure of its ability and resources. We recognize this as one of the most important and essential duties of the profession to society. . . .

"I should add that we of the Bar regard legal aid to the poor as a patriotic and social service of the highest order. Our systems of government will not endure if the poor in our populous cities are denied redress or protection because they are unable to pay for the service of lawyers, and are thus placed at a great and unjust disadvantage in securing their legal rights. Such a condition would inevitably cause oppression, suffering and tragedy, and it would generate a bitter feeling of disloyalty, a sense of which in our masses would involve a terrible danger. . . . As has been very truly said, 'the first duty of society to the poor is not to give them charity but to secure them justice.' And this in our judgment cannot be more effectively realized than through legal aid organizations."

He expressed the hope that these organizations soon "will be enabled to continue their activities and not have them curtailed by lack of necessary funds. . . ." As an earnest of the realization of this hope, he announced the initiation of a Fiftieth Anniversary Endowment Fund for the Society by a gift of $25,000 from William Nelson Cromwell and also a further contribution of $1,000 to this fund from the Society's faithful friend William G. Low. Mr. Guthrie might have added that he himself was contributing $1,000.

The other speakers were Charles Evans Hughes, Louis Marshall, and District-Attorney Banton. Of these, the last named naturally focussed his attention upon the Society's rather newly begun activities in the criminal courts. He coined a telling phrase by speaking of "the rich-poor defendant in a criminal case" — poor because he had no money to recompense ordinary private counsel, rich because, so far as the capacity of the Voluntary Defenders to take cases extended, he was assured "service that a millionaire cannot buy," service that no law office in New York was equipped to furnish. Mr. Banton took issue with a proposal just made by Mr. Marshall that the Defenders be made public officers: "I would not do that. I am saying that out of the heart of experience. Do not deprive the people of New York of the privilege of supporting out of their generosity an organization such as this. We have enough money in New York to underwrite this. . . . If you could come [to the criminal courts], if you could know what I know, could feel what I have felt, could see what I have seen, the coffers of New York could not hold the money. It would pour into The Legal Aid Society to strengthen its operation in the Criminal Court Building." A significant tribute, indeed, coming as it did from the public prosecutor of one of the world's busiest criminal tribunals, the very man whose duty it was to oppose the Defenders in every case of theirs which went to trial.

Mr. Hughes and Mr. Marshall differed somewhat on points of phraseology, but in substance were not far apart. They both perceived the democratic duty of the man of talent well-trained to lend his less gifted or less fortunate fellow man brotherly help which would start him fairly on the right road. Mr. Hughes drew this to a point on the Society's prime functions: "A lawyer who maintains a large office with the necessary outlays for rent and clerk hire [must] charge enough to make both ends meet. The poor man cannot engage such a lawyer. When he has a claim that he desires to enforce, what can he do? Where shall he go? He sees the courthouse, but how shall he get in? . . . He needs expert assistance."

That assistance must come from men of talent well-trained, and through legal aid it does come. "We are trying to make firm the foundations of the Republic through confidence in the administration of justice; through love of country; not of the flag in a sentimental way — that is well enough — but through love of the institutions of the country; in respect for the judicial institutions of the country and by the determination that when we say we will regard neither rich nor poor we mean not simply impartiality and integrity of courts; we mean actual advice, representation, the power of the expert bar, the strong man of democracy at the service of the weak."

With this the book might stop, for Mr. Hughes framed in his concluding sentence the end which legal aid has sought and to a great extent attained during its first fifty years. But without more this history would seem to mirror a dangerous complacency. Indeed, the whole volume down to this point has been a tincture of optimism, somewhat diluted by statements of unavoidable shortcomings but certainly containing few adverse criticisms of the Society or its work. All legal aid geese have appeared as swans. For that manner of presentation, excuse is not lacking. A little hero worship does no harm, and may well be bestowed upon a group of men and women who have labored hard, persistently, and quite unselfishly for the betterment of society. Again, what legal aid has done, and done well, is practically clear gain. The community is so much better off. Shortcomings of legal poor relief on individual cases have not in any respect made conditions worse than or even as bad as they would have been if the movement had never existed. Thus a mere narrative is reasonably enough colored by emphasizing successes, and letting many failures, now harmless because they are over and done with, sink into oblivion.

But another aspect must be considered. Legal aid has moved from the class of timid experiments into that of established institutions. It is right to applaud any slight measure of success attained by a tentative venture. The permanent organization, however, must respond to a more harshly critical test. It may not rest content with accomplishing *some* good in *some* way. What is now demanded is the greatest possible benefit attained in the best possible manner. There is little doubt that this idea lay in the minds of many who went homeward through the April night from the semi-centennial dinner. Dealing with the Society's work, the report for 1926 says: "That there are some obvious omissions no one would deny. This is plain in connection with the criminal side of the work, which is now confined to the defence of poor persons accused of crime in one court of the Borough of Manhattan only. The importance of a careful survey of legal aid work in the city has been brought to the attention of the Sage Foundation, which has recently made a grant of $7,500.00, or as much thereof as may be necessary, to make such a survey. It is to be carried on under the auspices of a committee of six, consisting of three members of the Legal Aid Committee of the Association of the Bar and of three members appointed by the Welfare Counsel of the City of New York. Ex-Judge W. Bruce Cobb has been selected to make the survey with such other assistants as may be required. His report will be submitted to the Committee of Six with suggested recommendations for their consideration and action. It is hoped that this report may be completed and the action of the Committee taken by October or November of this year. Such a well-considered report should give those interested in legal aid work a clear conception of what has been accomplished, what the present deficiencies are, and should mark the lines for future effort. The four societies now engaged in legal aid work in New York, including this Society, have signified their readiness to coöperate in every way in the effort to make this report as comprehensive and as helpful as possible."

Judge Cobb's investigation, although diligently pushed, took longer than was expected. Unrealized complexities developed in New York's legal aid situation. These were carefully unfolded and with final publication of the survey report on March 5, 1928, those interested in the present condition and future needs and possibilities of New York legal poor relief now have before them a statement which could hardly be excelled in comprehensiveness or clarity. No mere summary can serve as an adequate substitute for the original, and none will here be attempted. But a few general observations are ventured to suggest what may be ahead of The Legal Aid Society.

Three topics invite comment: equipment (including personnel), methods, and policies. The first topic raises a monetary problem. With sufficient funds, the Society can certainly obtain adequate physical accommodations and go far toward obtaining an adequate staff of workers. Confidence is not lacking that material resources will increase. While this history was being written, the main office moved to larger and thoroughly modern quarters, and the staff of at least one branch was augmented. But the fact remains that this beneficent institution does not yet receive financial support at all comparable with that accorded other organizations working for human welfare in aspects no whit more important. One can only hope that the increasing body of literature about, and growing familiarity with, legal aid will bring wider and more intense appreciation of its significance to our civilization, which is, as Dean Pound has said, essentially a legal civilization. Already, perhaps, there is a fair consensus of opinion that to shut down The Legal Aid Society would be to bring a municipal calamity upon New York. From this point it may be no seven-league stride to realization that material conditions restricting the Society's usefulness are forcing the community to suffer a constant series of calamities none the less real because taken for granted and let pass unnoted. When opinion reaches that stage, District Attorney Banton's remark about the inadequacy of New York's coffers to hold the money will sound a great deal less fanciful.

Turn for a moment from the question of getting means to the manner of utilizing them when obtained. Once upon a time there was talk of a legal aid building. Joseph H. Choate said in 1912 that the Society was entitled to a house of its own. But no single house or building could suffice. The far-spread branches are creations of sound policy. Nor should the branches at least be geographically tied down. As tides of population and business sweep hither and yon across the map of New York, the poor man's lawyer must move with them. A goodly rent endowment fund will serve actual working needs better than any fixed structure. Salary endowment of course needs no recommendation. It would solve a problem that has existed ever since Mr. Lexow first found his compensation too small and finally had to resign. Legal aid needs veterans who will hold their positions year after year. Too many poor men's lawyers have of necessity been young, with all the enthusiasm but also all the inexperience and immature judgment of youth. The task confronting legal aid is worthy of the best and ripest intellectual effort. In New York one of Mr. McGee's notable achievements has been holding his veterans and greatly retarding the "labor turnover" at all his offices. He could do this better if his men were assured pay which, while not equal to the high financial rewards won by successful commercial lawyers, would suffice for the real needs of the legal aid workers and their dependents. Why should not such assurance, or at least part of it, come from endowment by generous citizens? A single American law school has recently obtained five endowments of $200,000 each for research professorships. In all likelihood the Attorney-in-Chief of The Legal Aid Society has for the past ten or fifteen years been, and emphatically hereafter will be, able to contribute as much to practical advancement and application of law as any of those research men. Who will endow *his* chair?

Comment on the first topic of equipment here merges with comment on the second topic of methods. One cannot discuss man-power without considering how it is to be applied. This brings us pretty well to the heart of the survey report by Judge Cobb. One of his leading points, made with great dexterity and courtesy, but unmistakably driven home, is that at the present time New York legal aid as a whole does not satisfy other New York welfare agencies, which are its most obvious allies and perhaps its most intelligent critics. Some of the complaints against legal aid by the welfare organizations carry very deep indeed. It is even asserted that the poor men's lawyers, who have always known well enough the necessity of speed and pertinacity, perform too slowly and lack determination. To which, of course, the lawyers reply that their social service friends are trying to live in a dreamland of perfect legal organization, where right unfailingly triumphs over might in jig time when a learned counsellor presses the button. The lawyer knows — those who have read this book know — that the actual legal organization is sadly different, and that all too often delay or apparent loss of interest is due to professional impossibilities of moving a worthy claim ahead fast, or ever moving it at all. But into the matters of charge, reply, and countercharge we need not carry this chapter, since Judge Cobb has covered the entire ground of controversy with admirable dispassionateness.

What significantly strikes the reader in this part of the survey report is that the social workers' criticism does not extend to every arm of The Legal Aid Society. The trend of their comment is toward expression of satisfaction with work done by the Seamen's Branch and the Voluntary Defenders. What have these two offices in common that they should be picked out for commendation? Quite obviously, a plain perception of the social implications of those problems which they respectively face. These offices meet the other welfare workers halfway, comprehending clearly a common task demanding united effort. For concrete suggestions to spread this attitude further through the Society's structure — and likewise to make the social service people see better the lawyer's side of the shield — we may refer again to the Cobb report. Also there really is some prospect that with the increasing emphasis in our better law schools upon sociological aspects of legal practice, legislation, and court decisions, a crop of young men may soon be available who will view the law not at all as an isolated end unto itself. As to the Voluntary Defenders another specific fact should be remarked. The Defenders have investigators and use them to the full. So likewise does the National Desertion Bureau, a remarkably effective agency of limited scope already gratefully referred to in connection with the old East Side Branch. Very significantly, this Bureau also is praised by the general welfare agencies. Reasons need be no more than outlined. Honest, expert investigators can build up a just case to its maximum strength and thoroughly demolish an undeserving case. They can be the eyes and ears of a legal aid office. Running such an office without an ample investigating corps is worse than running a submarine without a periscope. This, save for rare and partial exceptions, is what sheer lack of means has forced the Society to do from the beginning, absolutely against its managers' best judgment. Let the community produce money for a reasonable staff of investigators, and one ground of complaint will vanish.

The third topic for comment is that of policies. Again the social service agencies' criticisms are valuably suggestive. They incline to charge The Legal Aid Society with rendering unsatisfactory service in domestic relations cases and cases involving complicated social situations. To a large extent this reflects the consequence of straitened resources. Plainly, though, it forces out for reëxamination the legal side of a perturbing problem. Nowadays the Society much more freely represents husbands as well as wives in divorce proceedings. How can its lawyers best serve the community with respect to unhappy marriages? Probably the answer can never be reached without prolonged study, or ever compressed into a single brief pronouncement. But it must be sought, and there is a growing mass of case material in the Society's records to be drawn upon for sound generalizations. The welfare critics are also troubled because of the customary rejection of personal injury cases. The reasons for this policy have been stated. They too must come up to be revalued. It is perhaps true that under the old dispensation most personal injury claimants forced to fight for damages could get lawyers of some kind. But there is substantial doubt whether, even with such guidance as the Society felt free to give, they could always get lawyers who would prove honest, faithful, and competent. Nor is it altogether unlikely that the present judicial investigations of "ambulance chasing" may lead to difficulty in obtaining for a commonplace accident case *any* lawyer, even though he boast not one of the desirable qualities eumerated above. If a chasm in legal administration is thus created either by the literal lack of ordinary practitioners or by lack of character in those who offer themselves, the Society must consider ways and means of filling this gap. It is at the moment filling a very similar gap in the criminal courts, and has never turned away from the general task of making all the poor man's legal rights matters of hard, substantial fact rather than of vaporous, unsatisfying theory.

For a fitting conclusion we must hark back to the first paragraph of the first chapter. There it was said that this book would deal with the greatest movement of all English and American legal history for bringing justice to the poor. Can that bold assertion be sustained? Appraising the institutions of one's own time is an effort perilously verging upon guesswork. A foothill near at hand blocks out the real mountain beyond. Only in the long perspective of years can their true proportions surely become manifest. And it must be admitted that legal aid is still very young. Mr. Lexow, the Society's first Attorney, has helped in preparing this history. So the movement's whole life span, thus far, is covered by the professional career of a single lawyer. It must also be admitted that as yet philosophic writers on modern society have seen little of the towering mountain in legal aid. The index to a recent brilliant and scholarly history tracing the whole rise of American civilization does not contain the term, and the text seemingly can yield no slightest passing reference to the topic. Books of reference likewise fail us. Our greatest encyclopaedia is a blank on this method of legal poor relief.

But there are signs and portents of no mean order that posterity will see matters otherwise. By way of negative evidence, take the disheartening story of older institutions for equalizing justice. Nothing could be much less effective than these capricious, fleeting, often sheerly delusive devices in England and the United States down to the last quarter of the nineteenth century. Probably not one of them could boast that it had operated with consistent vigor and growing success for fifty years. Yet, to follow momentarily an allied line of thought which soon leads back to the original topic, these futilities had a clear significance, although perhaps a bitter one. Mere obstinate recurrence of effort, however vain, in the teeth of more than five centuries of failure showed that the problem must be important. If important under old-fashioned monarchy, it has become a life-and-death matter under modern democracy. We have no individual despot, benevolent or otherwise, to whip us into line; we rely rather upon voluntary habits of law observance. Such habits are inevitably undermined unless law is made popularly acceptable. By 1876 the United States was drifting fast into an era of industrialism and concentrated populations, with the added problem of prodigious immigration. Making the country's law generally acceptable and keeping it so had become a task more difficult and more imperative than most men dreamed. Failure meant national disaster. The situation contained elements of terrible menace.

Then began legal aid, and almost at once began its affirmative justification. The handful of men who labored for the Society in New York from 1876 to 1890 perhaps lacked ambitious breadth of imagination. But within a narrow chosen field they did their work so well as to awaken in Mr. v. Briesen's mind a conception of sweeping splendor. Holding that vision steadfastly before him, he shaped a masterly pioneering experiment. At every forward step he found the ground still firm under foot. Before his death powerful allies were joining the advance. Business men fell into line; men of the law shifted their attitude from distrust or indifference to warm enthusiasm; the organized Bar, an aggregate of careful conservatism, began to take over as its own the legal aid cause; experience in other countries was justifying Mr. v. Briesen's faith. His successors, bearing the ideal nearer fulfilment, see opening before them a straight and broadening path to the distant goal. The cry is not now — indeed, at no time in the fifty years has it ever been — for retreating, stopping, or changing direction; it is all for more and better legal aid work of the kind already begun. Never talking or thinking in pretentious words about his efforts, Mr. v. Briesen made himself one of mankind's great benefactors. Through him countless individual lives have been brightened, the integrity of our institutions has been upheld, and the lot of all humanity has been definitely ameliorated. The future history, the future encyclopaedia, will not overlook Arthur v. Briesen or that growing force for righteousness which he fashioned, launched, and directed — the strong lance of justice, pledged always to the winning of a better day.

INDEX

INDEX

www.ingramcontent.com/pod-product-compliance
Lightning Source LLC
LaVergne TN
LVHW020618110826
845149LV00002B/516

* 9 7 8 1 4 1 8 1 8 7 9 2 7 *